THE SUFFERING SERVANT OF THE LORD:
A PROPHECY OF JESUS CHRIST

AN EXPOSITION OF ISAIAH 52:13–53:12

Second Edition

DAVID J. MACLEOD
PROFESSOR OF BIBLE AND THEOLOGY
EMMAUS BIBLE COLLEGE

WIPF & STOCK · Eugene, Oregon

Wipf and Stock Publishers
199 W 8th Ave, Suite 3
Eugene, OR 97401

The Suffering Servant of the Lord
A Prophecy of Jesus Christ
By MacLeod, David J.
Copyright©2016 by MacLeod, David J.
ISBN 13: 978-1-5326-5164-9
Publication date 11/1/2019
Previously published by Emmaus Bible College, 2016

The Suffering Servant of the Lord

Contents

INDICES

DEDICATION

FOR TWO WONDERFUL EDITORS AND FRIENDS

†DR. ROY B. ZUCK, EDITOR OF *BIBLIOTHECA SACRA* (1986–2013)

DR. JOHN H. ("JACK") FISH III, EDITOR OF *THE EMMAUS JOURNAL* (1991–2012)

AND FOR

THOSE WHO ATTENDED
THE 55TH ANNUAL CONFERENCE FOR BRETHREN
AT GUELPH BIBLE CONFERENCE CENTRE, ONTARIO, CANADA
(JUNE 3–5, 2011)

EDITOR'S PREFACE

BY
JOHN H. FISH III

After twenty-five years of *The Emmaus Journal,* I am delighted to present the first *Emmaus Journal Monograph*, a series of expositions on the fifty-third chapter of Isaiah, written by my good friend and colleague, Dr. David MacLeod. Dave has served as my associate editor since *The Emmaus Journal* began publication. Since that time he has contributed an article to every issue of the journal, with only one exception.

I have had the privilege of serving the Lord alongside Dr. MacLeod for over fifty years—since our student days at Dallas Theological Seminary. Over the years I have greatly appreciated a particular characteristic that is evident in all of his writings—he is both a preacher-scholar and a scholar-preacher. His expositions of Scripture are a preacher's delight, because he not only presents clear explanations of a passage with penetrating applications and illustrations, he also (mainly in the footnotes) gives alternate interpretations along with the arguments for and against them. For those who just want a clear presentation of this great chapter on the Servant of the Lord in Isaiah 52:13–53:12, I recommend that you just read the text of these chapters without getting lost in the footnotes. For those who want to see the supporting exegesis and arguments, the footnotes are a rich mine of material.

Isaiah was the gospel writer in the OT. His presentation of the person and work of the coming Messiah reaches a height found in no other writer before the apostles themselves. Indeed, many reading Isaiah 53 for the first time think they are reading a passage from one of the NT evangelists. I commend to you this fine work by Dr. David MacLeod. The literature on this portion of Scripture is immense. I think you will find that this study by David MacLeod ranks among the finest.

INTRODUCTION

BY

DAVID J. MACLEOD

The following chapters had their beginning as expository sermons delivered at the annual men's conference at the Guelph Bible Conference Centre in Ontario, Canada in June, 2011. I wish to thank Judge Ralph Carr and the conference committee for inviting me to this very special event. Subsequently I have given the lectures/sermons at three other conferences. During a memorable visit to Ireland, I expounded Isaiah 53 at a two-day conference at Kilkenny Christian Assembly (Oct. 1–2, 2011). The second occasion was the European Workers' Conference in Lyon, France (Aug. 17–21, 2014). I especially want to thank Dr. and Mrs. Thomas Marinello (Tom and Patti) of Tyndale Theological Seminary in the Netherlands for hosting me in their lovely home and for providing taxi service between Amsterdam and Lyon. Finally, the messages were delivered at the Lake Geneva Summer Conference at historic Conference Point in Williams' Bay, Wisconsin. Along the way, I should mention that this series of expositions was delivered at Arbor Oaks Bible Chapel in Dubuque, Iowa. Subsequently the sermons have been delivered to a number of congregations in the Greater Chicago area.

I mention this history because I continued to work on the lectures/sermons every time I delivered them. As I did so, the sermons morphed into journal articles and then monograph chapters. The materials available to me were mountainous, and I have read only a miniscule amount of them. I have come to appreciate the words of Augustine who, with the ocean before his eyes, said, "I see the depths, but I cannot get to the bottom."[1] "This saying can easily be applied to Isaiah. The bottomless depth of this text is reflected in the vicarious event: an innocent one bears the guilt of others, perishes by it, and will nevertheless have 'success.'"[2]

[1] Augustine, Sermo 28:7, PL 38:182.

[2] Bernd Janowski, "He Bore Our Sins: Isaiah 53 and the Drama of Taking Another's Place," in *The Suffering Servant: Isaiah 53 in Jewish and Christian Sources*, eds. Bernd Janowski and Peter Stuhlmacher, trans. Daniel P. Bailey (Grand Rapids: Eerdmans,

I am thankful to the Lord for enabling me to complete this project, and I am thankful to a number of fellow students who helped get me started in my study. I should mention a sermon on the passage by Dr. Bruce Waltke, my first Hebrew teacher, delivered at Believers' Chapel in Dallas in the early 1970s. I was so taken with it that I typed it up and put it in my files for future use. I have read a number of Christological expositions, including the classic volume of David Baron, the devotional study by Dr. Robert Culver, the superb exegetical work of Dr. Duane Lindsey, and a series of sermons by Dr. S. Lewis Johnson, Jr. I have also read the comments of that giant of 19th century German scholarship, Franz Delitzsch. Along the way, I have also been helped by the works of Christopher R. North, Edward J. Young, J. Alec Motyer, Gary V. Smith, John N. Oswalt, John Goldingay, and David Payne. My footnotes will give a fuller account of my indebtedness to others.

I should also thank those who encouraged me as a writer. First, I want to thank the late Dr. Roy B. Zuck (1932–2013), editor of *Bibliotheca Sacra*, the quarterly journal published by Dallas Theological Seminary. Many years ago Roy befriended me and encouraged me in the writing of journal articles. He shepherded twenty-eight of my essays/expositions into the pages of *BibSac*. Back in 2011 he encouraged me with a steady stream of e-mails to write my expositions of Isaiah 53 as articles. Sadly, he died in 2013 before he read a word of my work. Second, I want to thank my colleague and friend, Dr. Jack Fish, editor of *The Emmaus Journal*, who has edited the chapters of this monograph as well as forty other articles of mine for our journal. Jack's knowledge of the original biblical languages and theology has made him an excellent editor of biblical and theological essays. Finally, I want to thank Mrs. Susan Tyler, our meticulous proofreader, who has protected us from countless misplaced punctuation marks, grammatical errors, and infelicitous phrases.

One final note is in order. I have finished this work more convinced than ever that the passage is a straightforward prophecy of Jesus Christ written by the prophet Isaiah some seven hundred years before the birth of the Savior. The parallels between Isaiah 52:13–53:12 and the life of Christ are striking. In fact, the plethora of alternative interpretations indicates that apart from the life and death of Jesus Christ, Isaiah 53 is

---

2004), 48–74 (esp. 70–71). I am indebted to Janowski for the above quotation from Augustine.

an insoluble riddle. Years ago Charles H. H. Wright concurred, "Our view of Isaiah 52–53 is that the prophecy was an enigma, which could not be fully understood in the days before Christ, but which has been solved by the sufferings, death, resurrection, and exaltation of Him who was both Son of Man and the Son of God."[3] Furthermore Jesus quoted Isaiah 53:12 and referred it to himself. **"For I tell you that this which is written must be fulfilled in Me, 'And He was numbered with transgressors'; for that which refers to Me has its fulfillment"** (Luke 22:37). In fact, Matthew, Mark, Luke, John, Acts, Romans, and 1 Peter all quote Isaiah 53 as messianic.[4] I happily concur with the Lord Jesus Christ and the writers of the inspired text of the New Testament that in Isaiah 53, as well as in Moses, the Psalms, and "all the prophets," we are told **"things concerning Himself"** (Luke 24:27).

---

[3] Charles H. H. Wright, *The Suffering Servant of Jehovah* (London: Francis Griffiths, 1905), 7.

[4] In response to evangelical scholars who deny the messianic interpretation of Isaiah 53, Todd S. Beall wrote, "Admittedly, the use of the OT in the NT is a complex topic, since the NT writers use the OT in a variety of ways. Each passage needs to be studied carefully: first the OT context, then the NT, to see how the writer is using the text. But for the evangelical scholar, if a NT writer cites an OT passage and interprets it in a certain way, we need to appropriate the NT data into our understanding of the original OT passage. Since the Bible ultimately has one author, the NT understanding of an OT passage is an important part of the picture—not simply how 'Matthew' took it, or 'Paul' took it, but how God intended it to be understood. I am not saying here that the NT understanding should trample on the original OT context; rather, it should be seen as in harmony with it. If we believe that the entire Bible is the Word of God, then it is not only permissible but essential to allow the NT writers to shed some light on an OT passage. There is ultimately one author for the whole Bible" ("Evangelicalism, Inerrancy, and Current OT Scholarship," *Bible and Spade* 28:1 [2015], 18–24 [esp. 19]).

ABBREVIATIONS

AncB	The Anchor Bible
AncBRL	The Anchor Bible Reference Library
ANF	*The Ante-Nicene Fathers*, edited by Alexander Roberts and James Donaldson
BASOR	*Bulletin of the American Schools of Oriental Research*
BBB	*Believers Bible Bulletin* (Believers Chapel, Dallas, Texas)
BDAG	*A Greek-English Lexicon of the New Testament and other Early Christian Literature* by Walter Bauer, English translation by W. F. Arndt, F. W. Gingrich, and F. W. Danker, revised by Frederick William Danker
BDB	*A Hebrew and English Lexicon of the Old Testament* by Francis Brown, S. R. Driver, and Charles Briggs
Bib	*Biblica*
BibSac	*Bibliotheca Sacra*
BSC	Bible Student's Commentary
BST	The Bible Speaks Today Commentary
BT	*The Bible Translator*
CBSC	Cambridge Bible for Schools and Colleges
CHS (L)	*Commentary on the Holy Scriptures* by John Peter Lange, trans. Philip Schaff
Darby	*New Translation* by J. N. Darby
EmJ	*The Emmaus Journal*
EncJud	*Encyclopaedia Judaica* (1972)
ESV	*The Holy Bible: English Standard Version*
ETL	*Ephemerides theologicae lovanienses*, Louvain
EvQ	*The Evangelical Quarterly*
Exp	*The Expositor*

ExpB	The Expositor's Bible (1903)
FC	*The Fathers of the Church*, edited by Joseph Deferrari
GKC	*Gesenius' Hebrew Grammar*, edited by E. Kautzsch, second English edition revised by A. E. Cowley
HALOT	*The Hebrew and Aramaic Lexicon of the Old Testament*, by Ludwig Koehler and Walter Baumgartner, English translation edited by M. E. J. Richardson
HCSB	*Holman Christian Standard Bible*
HCOT	Historical Commentary on the Old Testament, Leuven, Belgium
Herm	Hermeneia
HTR	*Harvard Theological Review*
IBHS	*An Introduction to Biblical Hebrew Syntax*, by Bruce K. Waltke and M. O'Connor
ICC	International Critical Commentary
IntB	*The Interpreter's Bible*, ed. George Arthur Buttrick
ISBE	*The International Standard Bible Encyclopedia*, edited by James Orr (1939)
ISBErev.	*The International Standard Bible Encyclopedia*, revised edition, edited by Geoffrey W. Bromiley (1979–88)
JBL	*Journal of Biblical Literature*
JE	*The Jewish Encyclopedia*
JMGBH	*A Grammar of Biblical Hebrew* by P. Joüon and T. Muraoka
JSOT	*Journal for the Study of the Old Testament*
JSOTSS	*Journal for the Study of the Old Testament Supplement Series*
KJV	King James Version (Authorized Version)
LCL	The Loeb Classical Library
LHBOTS	Library of Hebrew Bible/Old Testament Studies

LXX	The Septuagint
MT	Masoretic text (the authoritative Hebrew text of the Old Testament for Rabbinic Judaism)
NAC	New American Commentary
NASB	*New American Standard Bible*
NCBC	New Century Bible Commentary
NET	*The New English Translation* (NET Bible)
NICOT	New International Commentary on the Old Testament
NIDNTT	*New International Dictionary of New Testament Theology*, edited by Colin Brown
NIDOTTE	*New International Dictionary of Old Testament Theology and Exegesis*, edited by Willem A. Van Gemeren
NIV	*New International Version*
NKJV	*New King James Version*
NPNF	A Select Library of the Nicene and Post-Nicene Fathers, edited by Philip Schaff
NRSV	*New Revised Standard Version*
NT	New Testament
NTL	New Testament Library
ODCC	*Oxford Dictionary of the Christian Church*, edited by F. L. Cross
ODJR	*The Oxford Dictionary of the Jewish Religion*, 2d ed. (2011)
OT	Old Testament
OTL	Old Testament Library
OTS	*Oudtestamentische Studiën*, Leiden
PC	*The Pulpit Commentary*, edited by H. D. M. Spence and Joseph S. Exell

PL	Patrologia latina [Patrologiae cursus completus: Series latina], ed. J.-P. Migne, 162 vols. (Paris, 1844–1864).
PNTC	Pillar New Testament Commentaries
PTR	*Princeton Theological Review*
PTS	Patristische Texte und Studien
REB	*Revised English Bible*
RRJ	*Reformation and Revival Journal*
RSV	Revised Standard Version
PTR	*Princeton Theological Review*
SBB	Soncino Books of the Bible
SBJT	*The Southern Baptist Journal of Theology*
SOAS Bulletin	*Bulletin of the School of Oriental and African Studies*
Str.-B.	Herman L. Strack und Paul Billerbeck, *Kommentar zum Neuen Testament aus Talmud und Midrasch*
TDNT	*Theological Dictionary of the New Testament*, edited by Gerhard Kittel and Gerhard Friedrich, English translation edited by Geoffrey W. Bromiley
TDOT	*Theological Dictionary of the Old Testament*, edited by G. Johannes Botterweck, Helmer Ringgren, and Heinz-Josef Fabry, English translation by David E. Green
TEV	*Today's English Version*
TLOT	*Theological Lexicon of the Old Testament*, edited by Ernst Jenni and Claus Westermann
TNTC	Tyndale New Testament Commentaries
TWOT	*Theological Wordbook of the Old Testament*, edited by R. Laird Harris, Gleason L. Archer, Jr., and Bruce K. Waltke
TynB	*Tyndale Bulletin*
VT	*Vetus Testamentum*
WBC	Word Biblical Commentary

WC	Westminster Commentaries
WHSB	*Williams' Hebrew Syntax*, 3d ed., by Ronald J. Williams, revised by John C. Beckman
WSA	*The Works of St. Augustine: A Translation for the 21st Century*, edited by John E. Rotelle
YJS	Yale Judaica Series
ZPEB	*Zondervan Pictorial Encyclopedia of the Bible*

"Without the New Testament, the Old Testament would be a labyrinth without a clue, a syllogism without a conclusion, a torso without a heart, a moon without a sun, since Christ is the proper interpreter of the Old Testament." (Franz Delitzsch)[1]

✱✱✱✱✱✱✱✱✱✱✱✱✱✱✱✱✱✱✱✱✱✱✱

"As to this salvation, the prophets who prophesied of the grace that would come to you made careful searches and inquiries, seeking to know what person or time the Spirit of Christ within them was indicating as He predicted the sufferings of Christ and the glories to follow. It was revealed to them that they were not serving themselves, but you, in these things which now have been announced to you through those who preached the gospel to you by the Holy Spirit sent from heaven — things into which angels long to look." (1 Peter 1:10–12, NASB)

---

[1] Franz Delitzsch, "Must We Follow the New Testament Interpretation of Old Testament Texts," in *The Old Testament Student* 6 (Nov., 1886): 77–78 (esp. 77).

CHAPTER 1

FROM GOLGOTHA

TO GOD'S RIGHT HAND:

ISAIAH 52:13-15

PART I: INTRODUCTION TO ISAIAH 52:13–53:12

THE IMPORTANCE OF THE PASSAGE

Through the centuries students of the Bible have almost unanimously celebrated the importance of Isaiah 52:13–53:12. Isaiah has been known in the church from early times as the "Fifth Evangelist," and his prophecy as the "Fifth Gospel." It is from those texts which speak of the suffering Christ, most notably chapter 53, that Isaiah especially derives these designations.[1] Ivan Engnell, Professor of OT at the University of Upsala, Sweden, has said that it "may without any exaggeration be called the most important text of the Old Testament."[2] Polycarp, a disciple of the apostle John and an early martyr (c. 69–c. 155), called it the "golden *passional* of the Old Testament evangelist."[3] It may have been remarks like this that led Augustine (AD 354–430) to write, "Some say he should be called an evangelist rather than a prophet."[4]

---

[1] John F. A. Sawyer, *The Fifth Gospel: Isaiah in the History of Christianity* (Cambridge: Cambridge University Press, 1996), 1, 86-87 and passim.

[2] Ivan Engnell, "The 'Ebed Yahweh Songs and the Suffering Messiah in 'Deutero-Isaiah,'" *Bulletin of the John Rylands Library* 31 (1948): 54-93 (esp. 73).

[3] Quoted by Franz Delitzsch, *Biblical Commentary on the Prophecies of Isaiah*, trans. James Martin, (Edinburgh: T. & T. Clark, 1877; reprint ed., Grand Rapids: Eerdmans, 1965), 2:303. Delitzsch called him, "Polycarp the Lysian," possibly in reference to the Elysian Fields of Greek mythology, which were the final resting place of the souls of heroic and virtuous men.

[4] Augustine, *The City of God*, 18.29, in *NPNF*, 1ˢᵗ Series, 2:376. Cf. Sawyer, *The Fifth Gospel*, 1.

Martin Luther, the great reformer, said it was of such importance that "we must [all] memorize it."[5] A Puritan minister, during the time of Oliver Cromwell's "protectorate" (1653–58), called it "Honey from heaven, the marrow of the Gospel, the Prophet Isaiah's Crucifix…giving out the hot and bright beams of God's great love, setting Christ apart to a cursed and bitter Passion, for man's blessed and sweet Redemption."[6]

John Albert Bengel (1687–1752), the noted commentator, spoke of its great power, "By that 53rd chapter of Isaiah, not only many Jews, but even Atheists, have been converted: history records some; God knows them all."[7] Franz Delitzsch, thought by many to be the greatest commentator on Isaiah, called this prophecy "the most central, the deepest, and the loftiest thing that the Old Testament prophecy, outstripping itself, has ever achieved. It looks as if it had been written beneath the cross upon Golgotha, and was illuminated by the heavenly brightness of the [Lord's command], שֵׁב לִימִינִי (šēḇ lîmînî, "Sit at my right hand")."[8]

William Urwick, a 19th century British Hebrew scholar, wrote, "Here we seem to enter the holy of holies of Old Testament prophecy— that sacred chamber wherein are pictured and foretold the sufferings of Christ and the glory which should follow."[9] Charles Haddon Spurgeon, the great pastor-evangelist of London, exclaimed, "What a chapter! The Bible in miniature. The Gospel in its essence."[10]

---

[5] Martin Luther, *Lectures on Isaiah, Chapters 40–66*, trans. Herbert J. A. Bouman, Luther's Works, vol. 17 (St. Louis: Concordia, 1972), 215.

[6] Thomas Calvert, *Mel Cæli, Medulla Evangelii; or, The Prophet Isaiah's Crucifix, Being An Exposition of the Fifty third Chapter of the Prophecie of Isaiah* (London: Tho. Pierrepont, 1657). The above quote is actually part of the extended title of Calvert's work and is found, accordingly, on the title page.

[7] John Albert Bengel, *New Testament Word Studies*, trans. Charlton T. Lewis and Marvin R. Vincent (Philadelphia: Perkinpine and Higgins, 1864; reprint ed., Grand Rapids: Kregel, 1971), 1:805-806. Mitch Glaser, president of Chosen People Ministries, has also argued for the apologetic value of the chapter. "Isaiah 53 is unquestionably our most powerful biblical tool for Jewish evangelism, as it answers many of the fundamental issues Jewish people might have regarding the possibility that Jesus might be the promised Messiah" ("Introduction" to *The Gospel According to Isaiah 53*, eds., Darrell L. Bock and Mitch Glaser [Grand Rapids: Kregel, 2012], 27).

[8] Delitzsch, *Biblical Commentary on the Prophecies of Isaiah*, 2:303.

[9] William Urwick, עֶבֶד יְהֹוָה: *The Servant of Jehovah. A Commentary, Grammatical and Critical, upon Isaiah LII.13–LIII.12* (Edinburgh: T. & T. Clark, 1877), 65.

[10] Charles H. Spurgeon, "Isaiah 53:5—'With His Stripes We are Healed,'" in *My Sermon Notes* (1884; reprint ed., Grand Rapids: Baker, 1981), 2:249-52 (esp. 249).

Another well-known preacher called it "the Mount Everest of Messianic Prophecy."[11] Union Seminary (New York) president, Henry Sloane Coffin, called it "the most influential poem in any literature."[12] NT scholar Joachim Jeremias observed, "No other passage from the Old Testament was as important to the Church as Isa. 53."[13] Barry Webb, Old Testament professor at Moore Theological College in Sydney, Australia, called it "the jewel in the crown of Isaiah's theology, the focal point of his vision."[14]

The authors of the NT certainly thought highly of it. Southern Baptist scholar, Page Kelley, explained, "If for some reason the entire song were to disappear from the book of Isaiah, it could be almost completely reconstructed from the quotations borrowed from it by New Testament writers."[15] OT scholar and theologian, Robert Culver, added, "Perhaps the most distinguished thing about it is the fact that this very portion stands in the background of almost every New Testament treatment of the great events connected with our Lord's passion, death, burial, resurrection, ascension, exaltation, and second coming."[16] Gleason Archer, Professor of OT at Trinity Evangelical Divinity School, wrote, "The profoundest remarks upon the meaning of Calvary are not to be found in the New Testament. It is an impressive evidence of divine inspiration of the Scriptures that an Old Testament passage, composed more than [seven] hundred years before the event, presents the fullest and tenderest interpretation of the Crucifixion to be discovered in the entire Bible."[17] This observation of Archer lends weight to the assertion

---

[11] Kyle M. Yates, *Preaching From the Prophets* (Nashville: Broadman, 1942), 102.

[12] Henry Sloane Coffin, "The Book of Isaiah, Chapters 40–66: Exposition," in *The Interpreter's Bible*, ed. George Arthur Buttrick (Nashville: Abingdon, 1956), 5:614.

[13] Joachim Jeremias, *The Eucharistic Words of Jesus*, trans. Norman Perrin, NTL (London: SCM, 1966), 228.

[14] Barry G. Webb, *The Message of Isaiah*, BST (Downers Grove, IL: Inter-Varsity Press, 1996), 209.

[15] Page H. Kelley, "Isaiah," in *The Broadman Bible Commentary*, ed. Clifton J. Allen (Nashville: Broadman, 1971), 5:340.

[16] Robert D. Culver, *The Sufferings and the Glory of the Lord's Righteous Servant* (Moline, IL: Christian Service Foundation, 1958), 20.

[17] Gleason L. Archer, *In the Shadow of the Cross* (Grand Rapids: Zondervan, 1957), 3.

of Blaise Pascal (1623–1662), who said in his Pensées, "the most weighty proofs of Jesus are the prophecies."[18]

One further example of the importance to which Bible students and scholars attach to the text is the number of people who have written about it and continue to write about it. Robert Pfeiffer, at one time Professor of Hebrew at Harvard University, wrote, "The extant literature on the monumental fifty-third chapter of Isaiah is so vast that, perhaps, no person could read it in a single lifetime."[19] Professor Pfeiffer was speaking, of course, of commentaries, books, and articles in at least a dozen languages.[20]

The Setting of the Passage

Isaiah the prophet served the Lord during the reigns of Uzziah (Azariah) (792–740 BC), Jotham (750–735 BC), Ahaz (735–715 BC), and Hezekiah (715–686 BC), kings of Judah.[21] It was the era of the divided kingdom (Israel, the northern kingdom, and Judah, the southern kingdom). His visions were concerned primarily with Judah and the city of Jerusalem (Isa. 1:1). His active ministry extended over a period of about forty years—from the year that King Uzziah died (740 BC, 6:1) until after the invasion of Sennacherib, (701 BC, 36:1). He lived until at least 681 BC, when he recorded the death of Sennacherib (37:38). He

---

[18] Blaise Pascal, Pensées, trans. A. J. Krailsheimer, rev. ed. (New York: Penguin, 1995), § 335, p. 102.

[19] Robert H. Pfeiffer, "Preface" to Frederick Alfred Aston, *The Challenge of the Ages*, rev. ed. (Scarsdale, NY: Research Press, 1970), 3. Not all students of Isaiah have written on the chapter. It was the intention of S. R. Driver, one of the original editors of the International Critical Commentary, to write a commentary on the whole of Isaiah, but he abandoned the project because he was overwhelmed by the problem of the identity of the suffering servant. See John Goldingay and David Payne, *A Critical and Exegetical Commentary on Isaiah 40–55*, ICC (London: T. & T. Clark, 2006), 1:ix; cf. Christopher R. North, *The Suffering Servant in Deutero-Isaiah*, 2d ed. (London: Oxford University Press, 1956), 1.

[20] Cf. North, *The Suffering Servant in Deutero-Isaiah*, 1.

[21] Scholars differ on the precise dates of the kings. Those given here are based on the calculations of Edwin R. Thiele, *The Mysterious Numbers of the Hebrew Kings*, rev. ed. (Grand Rapids: Zondervan, 1983), 118, 131, 133, 174, 176. John Bright (*A History of Israel* [Philadelphia: Westminster, 1959], 468) offers the following dates: Uzziah (783–742), Jotham (742–735), Ahaz (735–715), Hezekiah (715–687/86), Manasseh (687/86–642).

died, according to tradition, at the hands of Manasseh (reigned 696–642 BC), who had him sawn in half with a wood saw.[22]

Isaiah began his ministry when both Judah and Israel were enjoying political, military, and economic prosperity (cf. 2 Kings 14:25, 28; 2 Chron. 26). "The prosperity produced a spirit of self-confidence and self-indulgence that resulted in oppression, injustice, foreign alliances, and religious hypocrisy."[23] These sins were denounced by Isaiah, who predicted the overthrow of the northern kingdom (Israel) at the hands of Assyria (e.g., Isa. 28:1-13) and of the southern kingdom (Judah) by Babylon (e.g., 39:1-8). The first captivity (Israel by the Assyrians) began during his lifetime in 723/22 BC, and the second (Judah by Babylon) began in 586 BC about a hundred years after his death.

The book may be divided into two parts. The first part (chs. 1–39) deals primarily with judgment upon Judah for her sins; the second part (chs. 40–66) contains prophecies of comfort, salvation and future glory.[24] The second part may be subdivided into three sections:[25]

1. The deliverance from captivity in the near future by Cyrus, chs. 40–48 (cf. 45:1-4).
2. The deliverer, viz., the Servant of the LORD who will bring a greater spiritual deliverance in the distant future, chs. 49–55 (or 57).
3. The delivered, i.e., the future glory of the people of God in the millennium and in the eternal state, chs. 56 (or 58)–66.

These three subdivisions deal respectively with

1. The purpose of peace (comfort)
2. The Prince of peace (with an emphasis on the cross)
3. The program of peace (with an emphasis on the crown, i.e., the servant's reign over his kingdom)[26]

---

[22] The Martyrdom of Isaiah 5.1, in R. H. Charles, ed., *The Apocrypha and Pseudepigrapha of the Old Testament*, vol. 2: *Pseudepigrapha* (Oxford: Oxford University Press, 1913), 162. According to Charles (155), the Martyrdom of Isaiah has survived as one of three parts of the Ascension of Isaiah. This account of Isaiah's death is also given by Justin Martyr (AD 110–165). Cf. Dialogue with Trypho 120, in *ANF*, 1:259. Also see: Josephus, *Jewish Antiquities* 10.38, trans. Ralph Marcus, in *Josephus*, LCL (Cambridge: Harvard, 1951), 6:178-79.

[23] F. Duane Lindsey, *The Servant Songs: A Study in Isaiah* (Chicago: Moody, 1985), 35.

[24] Lindsey, *The Servant Songs*, 19-20.

[25] Lindsey, *The Servant Songs*, 35.

[26] Lindsey, *The Servant Songs*, 35.

In the immediate context (52:1–2; cf. 49:1–26) Isaiah foresaw Israel's restoration from captivity. He was looking ahead to the sufferings of the people under the Babylonians (cf. 39:1–8) and to their eventual deliverance from captivity. He saw the temporal deliverance that Cyrus would provide, but he also saw the glorious restoration of Israel in the Servant of the Lord in the last day. He saw the Servant passing through death into glory and Israel entering that glory with him.

His range of vision saw the end of the Babylonian captivity and the Servant working among the captives for their deliverance. Yet there was a gap of 535 years between the end of the Babylonian captivity and the arrival of Christ, and there has been a huge gap of time between the death of Christ and the yet future restoration of Israel. These gaps of time were hidden from Isaiah's eyes.

The OT prophet's perspective of the future has often been illustrated by a man looking at two mountain peaks in the distance. The two peaks look as if they are side by side. As he hikes toward them he comes to the first peak only to discover that the second peak is still many miles in the distance.

So it is with OT prophecy. The prophet may see Israel's return from the Babylonian captivity and the Servant of the LORD as contemporaneous events. However, the return from Babylon took place two hundred years after Isaiah, and the Servant of the LORD did not appear on the scene for another five hundred years.

Isaiah was not wrong, however; the restoration from Babylon prefigured a much greater restoration of Israel to the land in the end time when the Servant of the LORD returns to this earth in great glory, and when Israel will share that glory (cf. Zech. 14:1-21).[27]

In the present context (52:1-10) the prophecy looks on to a future time when Zion will be a holy city. She will be holy because all her sins will be washed away (cf. 4:3-4). In chapter 53 "the good news is reported that this forgiveness and cleansing is attained through the death of the Servant" (vv. 4-6, 8, 11-12).[28] The setting is undoubtedly millennial,[29]

---

[27] Merrill F. Unger, *Unger's Commentary on the Old Testament* (Chicago: Moody, 1981; reprint ed., Chattanooga, TN: AMG Publishers, 2002), 1292.

[28] Gary V. Smith, *Isaiah 40–66*, NAC (Nashville: Broadman and Holman, 2009), 434. "After describing, in his own majestic and beautiful style, the future glory and salvation of Israel...the prophet proceeds to introduce the person by whom so great a salvation would be effected" (Moses Margoliouth, *The Penitential Hymn of Judah and Israel after*

as "all the ends of the earth [will] see the salvation of our God" (v. 10).[30]

Delitzsch wrote, "[This] glorious restoration of Israel...is still in the future; and this gap [of time] was hidden from the prophet's view. It is only the coming of Christ in glory which will fully realize what was not yet realized when he entered into glory after the sufferings of death, on account of Israel's unbelief."[31]

THE LITERARY GENRE OF THE PASSAGE

Isaiah 52:13–53:12 is generally called "a servant song." The term "servant song" is "a scholarly convention," in that other than telling us the chapter is poetic it does not really identify the literary genre of the passage.[32] In any case there is a collection of four of these "servant songs" in Isaiah, and Isaiah 52:13–53:12 is the fourth.[33] Although the four

---

the Spirit: An Exposition of the Fifty-Third Chapter of Isaiah, 2d ed. [London: Longman, Brown, Green, and Longmans, 1856], 5).

[29] Unger, Unger's Commentary on the Old Testament, 1292.

[30] Melugin speaks of "the eschatological hymn (52:9-10) which precedes the fourth 'servant song'" (Roy F. Melugin, The Formation of Isaiah 40–55 [Berlin: Walter de Gruyter, 1976], 168).

[31] Delitzsch, Biblical Commentary on the Prophecies of Isaiah, 2:304, n.1; cf. Lindsey, The Servant Songs, 55-56, 74-75.

[32] Melugin, The Formation of Isaiah 40–55, 64.

[33] The four were specified by Bernard Duhm, Das Buch Jesaia übersetzt und erklärt (1892; 4th ed., Göttingen, Vandenhoeck & Ruprecht, 1922), 19, 311 (42:1–4; 49:1–6; 50:4–9; 52:13–53:12). For a summary of his view, see Joseph Blenkinsopp, Isaiah 40–55, AncB (New York: Doubleday, 2002), 76–81. Later scholars have disputed the extent of the "songs." Duane Lindsey, for example, accepted the following units: 42:1–9; 49:1–13; 50:4–11; 52:13–53:12 (The Servant Songs, 35–36, n. 2, 59, 79, 97). Others have rejected Duhm's thesis altogether. For example, see Tryggve N. D. Mettinger, A Farewell to the Servant Songs: A Critical Examination of an Exegetical Axiom , trans. Frederick H. Cryer (Lund, Sweden: GWK Gleerup, 1983), 45–46 and passim.

Some scholars have argued that Isaiah 61:1–3 constitutes a fifth "servant song." See: Oswald T. Allis, The Unity of Isaiah: A Study of Prophecy (Philadelphia: Presbyterian and Reformed, 1950), 82, n.3; Robert B. Chisholm, Jr., "The Christological Fulfillment of Isaiah's Servant Songs," BibSac 163 (Oct., 2006): 387–404 (esp. 401–404); Webb, The Message of Isaiah, 234; John N. Oswalt, The Book of Isaiah, Chapters 40–66, NICOT (Grand Rapids: Eerdmans, 1998), 562–65; Smith, Isaiah 40–66, 631. Cf. also: Delitzsch, Biblical Commentary on the Prophecies of Isaiah, 2:424–25; Randall Heskett, Messianism Within the Scriptural Scrolls of Isaiah, LHBOTS 456 (New York: T. & . Clark, 2007), 260–61; Brevard S. Childs, Isaiah, OTL (Louisville: Westminster/John Knox, 2001), 504–5. Childs' discussion initially seems sympathetic to the view, but in the end he

passages are more accurately called "servant poems,"[34] the scholarly convention will be followed in this chapter.

In the first of these ("the call of the Servant," 42:1-9) "Yahweh (the LORD) gives a distant, or long-range prophecy of his servant who will bring salvation and establish a proper order on the whole earth."[35] The second servant song ("the commission of the Servant," 49:1-13) places a "greater emphasis…on the physical and spiritual restoration of the nation Israel."[36] The third "song" ("the commitment of the Servant," 50:4-11) "amplifies the sufferings and patient endurance of the Servant, which were only hinted at in the previous songs."[37] In the "magnum opus" of the servant songs, viz., the fourth ("the career of the Servant," 52:13–53:12), "the Servant-Messiah's suffering and his consequent exaltation are revealed with equal emphasis."[38]

Some have argued that while both the sufferings and the exaltation are fully treated, it is the exaltation of the Servant that is the predominant theme—"*victorious and triumphant* through his vicarious suffering."[39] One commentator seeks to stress this point by entitling the section "The Song of the Servant's Victory."[40]

---

rejects it. Webb, on the other hand says, "He is both the Servant of chapters 40–55 and the Messiah of chapters 1–35, for—this is what we must notice—these are one and the same person."

[34] John L. McKenzie, *Second Isaiah*, AncB (Garden City, NY: Doubleday, 1968), xxxi-xxxii, 36, 103, 115, 129.

[35] Lindsey, *The Servant Songs,* 36.

[36] Lindsey, *The Servant Songs,* 59.

[37] Lindsey, *The Servant Songs,* 79.

[38] Lindsey, *The Servant Songs,* 79-80.

[39] Engnell, "The 'Ebed Yahweh Songs and the Suffering Messiah," 74. See also: Lindsey, *The Servant Songs,* 98. August Pieper, a professor at Wisconsin Lutheran Seminary, wrote, "The theme of the 53rd chapter is not the suffering of the Servant as such, but rather His triumph over suffering and His exaltation out of this humiliation" (*Isaiah II: An Exposition of Isaiah 40–66*, trans. Erwin E. Kowalke (Milwaukee, WI: Northwestern Publishing House, 1979), 430-31). Lindsey adds "that only a premillennial understanding of Christ's second advent recognizes the fullest significance of the Servant's exaltation." As an illustration of that approach he cites Unger, *Unger's Commentary on the Old Testament*, 1293-1301.

[40] Kelley, "Isaiah," 341. Kelley points out that all references to the Servant's suffering are translated in the past tense ("He *was* despised and rejected," 53:3; "He *was* wounded for our transgressions," 53:5; "He *was* cut off out of the land of the living," 53:8). On the other hand, the verbs that speak of the Servant's triumph and glory are in the future tense ("My servant *shall* prosper," 52:13; He *shall* see his offspring, he *shall* prolong his days," 53:10; "He *shall* divide the spoil with the strong," 53:12).

This title goes too far, however, in minimizing the Servant's sufferings. It is true that the song's emphasis on exaltation is often obscured by the titles given to the passage in sermons and popular commentaries, e.g. "The Suffering Servant," and "The Man of Sorrows." A title which gives proper emphasis to the Servant's victory without minimizing his sufferings is Page Kelley's suggestive "The Travail and Triumph of the Servant."[41]

As to the genre of the "Servant Song," commentators have offered a variety of suggestions:[42] (1) It is "a prophetic liturgy...[in] the form of a dirge" that is sung by a chorus;[43] (2) it is a prophetic allegory or parable of Israel's humiliation and triumph;[44] (3) it is a thanksgiving psalm;[45]

---

[41] Kelley, "Isaiah," 340-41. As noted above, Kelley emphasizes victory over suffering in one of his proposed titles ("The Song of the Servant's Victory") but adopts a more balanced title in his exposition ("The Travail and Triumph of the Servant").

[42] See the summaries in James Muilenburg, "Isaiah 40–66: Introduction and Exegesis," in *The Interpreter's Bible*, ed. George Arthur Buttrick (Nashville: Abingdon, 1956), 614; Smith, *Isaiah 40–66*, 432; and Lindsey, *The Servant Songs*, 111.

[43] Gerhard von Rad, *The Message of the Prophets*, trans. D. M. G. Stalker (New York: Harper and Row, 1965), 222-223; idem., *Old Testament Theology*, trans. D. M. G. Stalker (New York: Harper and Row, 1965), 2:256. Muilenburg ("Isaiah 40–66," 614) argued that the nearest parallel to the fourth Servant Song in the Old Testament was lamentation: that of Jeremiah, the individual laments in the Psalms (e.g., Pss. 6, 22, 31, 33, 69, 88, 102) and the laments of Job (3:3-26; 6:2-7, 21; 9:25–10:22; 29:1–31:37). See also: Sigmund Mowinckel, "The Servant of the LORD," in *He That Cometh*, trans. G. W. Anderson (Nashville: Abingdon, 1954), 187-257 (esp. 200). However in other laments the narrator speaks in the first person lamenting his own suffering. In Isaiah 53:1-10, however, the "we" narrators speak of the salvation they have received through the sufferings of another. Nevertheless, as Melugin conceded, "Without doubt the poem is influenced by the language of the lament psalm and its related forms" (Roy F. Melugin, *The Formation of Isaiah 40–55* [Berlin: Walter de Gruyter, 1976], 74). The narrators in verses 1-9 do lament the sinfulness of their countrymen in their oppression of the Servant.

[44] Johannes Lindblom, *The Servant Songs in Deutero-Isaiah: A New Attempt to Solve an Old Problem* (Lund: G. W. K. Gleerup, 1951), 37-51 (esp. 46-47). Lindblom errs in two ways: (1) in identifying the Servant as a "fictitious person...conjured up in the prophet's imagination" instead of as an actual historical person, and (2) in identifying the Servant as Israel and not as Christ.

[45] Whybray wrote, "The poem which has been preserved in ch. 53 is a third person psalm of thanksgiving composed for and sung at a religious assembly of the Jewish exiles." Whybray erred in identifying the Servant as Deutero-Isaiah and not Messiah, and he missed the eschatological note in the song. See R. N. Whybray, *Thanksgiving for a Liberated Prophet*, JSOTSS 4 (Sheffield: JSOT, 1978), 134. Westermann says that the two main parts of the poem (vv. 2-9, 10-11a) "point to an individual psalm of thanksgiving" but notes that the genre is here altered in two ways: (1) The narrator is not

(4) it is a "confession on the part of those who experienced salvation;"[46] and (5) it is a new literary creation ["a speech of salvation"] in which there are two speeches of salvation [52:13–53:11-12] and between which (53:1-10) there is a report by the nations concerning the suffering and triumph of the Servant.[47]

Selecting one of the above options need not detain us here.[48] It will be enough to say that a number of the elements mentioned in these and other theories have some merit. The song certainly contains elements of lament, confession on the part of Israel for her rejection of the Servant, thanksgiving for the salvation provided for Israel and the world by the Servant, and a report of all the Servant suffered as well as the exalted position he now enjoys—and will yet enjoy.

THE DIVISIONS OF THE PASSAGE (AN OUTLINE OF THE CAREER OF THE SERVANT)

The poem is carefully constructed, containing five stanzas of three verses each. The first and last stanzas are commendations of the Servant by God. The middle three speak of the Servant's degradation and suffering.[49] The poem centers on two great contrasts: (1) The contrast

---

the man who experienced deliverance, but is told by others in the third person, and (2) those who tell of the Servant's deliverance "have themselves been given salvation by what happened" to and through him (Claus Westermann, *Isaiah 40–66*, OTL, trans. David M. G. Stalker, Old Testament Library [Philadelphia: Westminster, 1969], 256-57).

[46] Westermann, *Isaiah 40–66*, 257. Smith (*Isaiah 40–66*, 432-33) wrote, "The basic purpose of this message is to announce to Israel and the world that the Servant has provided salvation for 'us' and 'the many.'"

[47] Melugin, *The Formation of Isaiah 40–55*, 74, 167. Cf. also Brevard S. Childs, *Isaiah*, OTL (Louisville: Westminster John Knox, 2001), 411. Childs refers to the genre of the passage as " a new literary creation." There is much to commend Melugin's view, chiefly its simplicity, but one must object to his view that those reporting in vv. 1-9 are the nations. What is said here could only be spoken by Israel.

[48] The above list does not exhaust the theories advanced. Muilenburg ("Isaiah 40–66," 614) also mentions the following: (1) The poem is a sacrificial hymn after the manner of the Mystery religions. (2) It is a prophetic remodeling of a liturgical composition belonging to the annual festival of the enthronement of Yahweh. (3) It is a liturgy modeled on those from the Akkadians and the god Tammuz.

[49] Oswalt, *The Book of Isaiah*, Chapters 40–66, 376; Cf. Bruce K. Waltke, "The Real Value of Jesus Christ: An Exposition of Isaiah 52:13–53:12" (Dallas: Believers Chapel Tape Ministry, n.d.), 2-3. This sermon, by the writer's former professor, has been of real help in his understanding of Isaiah 53. The pagination is that of a manuscript transcribed by the writer from the taped message.

between the Servant's humiliation and suffering and his exaltation and (2) the contrast between the opinion of the people about the Servant and what was actually true about him.[50]

    a.   *A Divine Oracle: God Evaluates and Appraises His Servant, 52:13-15*

    b.   *A Nation's Lament: Israel Confesses Their Failure to Recognize and Value God's Servant, 53:1-9*

    c.   *A Divine Oracle: God Promises to Exalt His Servant For Doing His Will, 53:10-12*

    d.   *Summary:*   God speaks, 52:13-15

                              Israel speaks, 53:1-9

                              God speaks, 53:10-12 (except for verse 10, where Isaiah interjects his own commentary).

THE SUBJECT OF THE PASSAGE (I.E., THE IDENTITY OF THE SERVANT)

The subject of the poem is identified as "**My servant.**"[51] The speaker is the LORD, i.e., Yahweh (יהוה), cf. verse 12. The servant is not named,

---

[50] See Paul R. Raabe, "The Effect of Repetition in the Suffering Servant Song," *JBL* 103 (1984): 77-81. As Raabe has demonstrated these two contrasts are highlighted by nineteen key-words. He nicely lays out the contrasts in two helpful charts.

[51] Walther Zimmerli's summary is still definitive: The term עֶבֶד comes from the verb עָבַד, which means "to work, to serve." In OT usage the root meaning ("worker") has been replaced by an emphasis on a specific personal relationship of the עֶבֶד. In other words the implied counterpart to the עֶבֶד is not one who is idle ("non-worker"), but אָדוֹן, "the master." The עֶבֶד is the "worker who belongs to a master." In common or secular usage has the following meanings: (1) The עֶבֶד as slave, "the man whose chief characteristic is that he belongs to another." In Israel the slave was not treated as mere chattel but as a man with human rights. This was because he was part of the cultic fellowship and because Israel remembered that it had once been a slave in Egypt [Exod. 20:2; Deut. 5:6; 6:12]. (2) The עֶבֶד "in royal service," i.e., the man who left his natural tribal organization to become part of Saul's paid army became עֶבֶד הַמֶּלֶךְ ["servant of the king"], cf. 1 Sam. 18:5; 22:9; 2 Sam. 2:12, 13, 15. As the monarchy grew in power other groups of officials were also given the designation עֶבֶד [1 Sam. 21:7; 2 Kings 15:34; 22:12]. (3) עֶבֶד "as a description of political submission," [e.g., the Gibeonites, Josh. 9:11]. Here the term has the connotation of abasement. (4) עֶבֶד "as a humble self-designation," i.e., on the basis of court usage "עֶבֶד became a formal expression of humility in everyday politeness" [2 Sam. 9:8; 2 Kings 8:13]. (5) עֶבֶד as "servants of the sanctuary," e.g., Josh. 9:23 where the Gibeonites are condemned to be עֶבֶד לְבֵית אֱלֹהָי

("slaves in the house of my God"). This usage is not typical of the OT, however, because עֶבֶד is personal. Unlike Carthaginian inscriptions, one does not find the expression "עֶבֶד of the house of God" used of Israelites. Instead, when speaking of temple servants, one finds the term עֶבֶד used in connection with a person, not the sanctuary (e.g., "Solomon's servants," Ezra 2:55, 58; Neh. 7:57, 60; 11:3). When speaking of "temple servants" the OT uses another term altogether (נְתִינִים, i.e., those given to the service of the sanctuary). In religious usage עֶבֶד has the following meanings: (1) עֶבֶד as a humble self-designation of the righteous individual before his God. It may be a confession of the lowliness of the speaker [Exod. 4:10; Deut. 3:24], the demand by God for total obedience [Exod. 20:5; Deut. 5:9], and the servant's obedience to Yahweh the God of Israel [Ps. 119:176]. (2) עֶבֶד in the plural as a term for the righteous, i.e., for those who "seek refuge in him" [Ps. 34:22] and who "love his name" [Ps. 69:36]. (3) עֶבֶד יהוה in the singular as a term for Israel [Isa. 41:8]. As עֶבֶד יהוה Israel has been created by Yahweh [Isa. 44:2, 21], elected by him [Isa. 41:8-9; 44:1; 45:4], and brought from the ends of the earth [41:9]. (4) יהוה עֶבֶד "as a term to denote especially distinguished figures," e.g., the patriarchs [Gen. 24:14; 26:24; Ps. 105:6], Moses [Ex. 14:31; Num. 12:7-8], David [1 Kings 11:34; Ps. 89:3, 20], the prophet, the messenger of the word of Yahweh [1 Kings 14:18; 18:36; 2 Kings 14:25], and Job [Job 1:8; 2:3; 42:7, 8]. See W. Zimmerli and J. Jeremias, *The Servant of God* (Naperville, IL: Allenson, 1957), 9-34; idem., "παῖς θεοῦ," in *TDNT*, trans. and ed., Geoffrey W. Bromiley (Grand Rapids: Eerdmans, 1967), 5:654-677. Cf. U. Rüterswörden, H. Simian-Yofre; H. Ringgren, "עֶבֶד," *TDOT*, 10:376-405.

Of particular importance for the present chapter is the use of עֶבֶד יהוה for "the suffering servant of God" in Isaiah. In the immediate context of the "Servant Songs" (Isaiah 40–55) the term עֶבֶד appears twenty-one times, twenty times in the singular and once (54:17) in the plural. Delitzsch uses the figure of a three-story pyramid to illustrate Isaiah's idea of "the servant of Yahweh." The base or first level of the pyramid is the elect nation of Israel as a whole (41:8, 9; 42:19 [twice], 43:10; 44:1, 2, 44:21 [twice]; 45:4; 48:20). The central section or second level is "that Israel which was not merely Israel according to the flesh, but according to the spirit," i.e., the believing remnant within the nation, especially the prophets (44:26; 54:17; cf. 65:8-9, 13, 14, 15; 66:14). At the apex or third level is "the person of the Mediator of salvation springing out of Israel," viz., the servant who suffers vicariously for his people (42:1, 3; 49:5, 6, 7; 50:10; 52:13; 53:11). See Delitzsch, *Biblical Commentary on the Prophecies of Isaiah*, 2:174. In Isaiah 49:3 the servant is called "Israel." This in no way undermines the fact that Isaiah is here speaking of an individual person. Delitzsch (2:160) wrote, "But Israel was from the very first the God-given name of an individual. Just as the name Israel was first of all given to a man, and then after that to a nation, so the name which sprang from a personal root has also a personal crown. The servant of Jehovah is Israel in person, inasmuch as the purpose of mercy, upon the basis of which and for the accomplishment of which Jehovah made Jacob the father of the twelve-tribed nation, is brought by him into full and final realization." Earlier, Delitzsch (2:174) wrote, "The coming Servant...appears as the embodied idea of Israel, i.e., as its truth and reality embodied in one person." For a helpful discussion and brief refutation of other views, see Lindsey, *The Servant Songs*, 64-66.

but modern scholars have made numerous proposals.[52] In this chapter the passage is expounded with the deep conviction that the servant is the Lord Jesus Christ.[53] There are two lines of evidence supporting this interpretation.[54]

The External Evidence Pointing to Jesus Christ

The external evidence is evidence outside of the book of Isaiah itself. There is the testimony of the NT and the later New Testament community. In the Gospels, the book of Acts, and the Epistles there are many quotations of Isaiah 53 and allusions to it, and they identify the Servant as Jesus Christ.[55] Isaiah 53 is quoted more often in the NT than any other OT passage.[56]

---

[52] Heskett groups the non-Messianic views under eight headings: (1) Views that interpret the Servant as Israel, (2) views that interpret the Servant as an individual distinct from Israel, (3) views that interpret the Servant in light of the Tammuz myth, (4) views that compare the Servant with Moses, (5) views that interpret the Servant in relation to Cyrus, (6) views that interpret the Servant as an Israelite king, (7) views that interpret the Servant as the author of Second Isaiah, and (8) views that appeal to figurative usages or spiritual senses. See Heskett, *Messianism within the Scriptural Scroll of Isaiah*, 134-49. For an even more complete list of opinions, which sets forth the various options within Heskett's categories, cf. North, *The Suffering Servant in Deutero-Isaiah*, 6-116. Among individuals other than Jesus identified as the Servant in the history of exegesis, North lists Jeremiah, Josiah, Hezekiah, Job, Isaiah, Uzziah, Deutero-Isaiah, Zerubbabel, an anonymous saint or prophet, an unknown teacher of the Law, Eleazar, Jehoiachin, Moses, a messianic-political figure contemporary with Deutero-Isaiah, Ezekiel, Cyrus, Meshullam [the elder son of Zerubbabel], and the rising and dying god of Babylonian mythology [Tammuz]. Colin Kruse offered a careful study of eighteen scholars who wrote between North's day (1955) and his own (1978). See "The Servant Songs: Interpretive Trends Since C. R. North," *Studia Biblica et Evangelica* (1978): 3-27. For a helpful, albeit brief, summary, see Lindsey, *The Servant Songs*, 11-19.

[53] On the history of the Messianic interpretation of Isaiah 52:13–53:12, see Joachim Jeremias, "παῖς θεοῦ," in *TDNT*, 5:686-700.

[54] The critical fraternity is completely dismissive of the Christological interpretation defended here. John L. McKenzie summarized the unbelief that pervades modern Isaiah scholarship: "The venerable belief in the Christian church that the Servant poems, in particular the fourth, are predictions of Jesus Christ…is defended by no one today except in a few fundamentalist circles. This type of predictive prophecy does not appear in the Old Testament" (*Second Isaiah*, xlix).

[55] Cf. Lindsey, *The Servant Songs*, 4-9.

[56] See *The Greek New Testament*, 4th ed., eds. Barbara Aland, Kurt Aland, Johannes Karavidopoulos, Carlo M. Martini and Bruce Metzger (Stuttgart: United Bible Societies, 1993). The "Index of Quotations" (888) cites the following quotations (Old Testament order): Isa 52:15 LXX (Rom. 15:21); 53:1 LXX (John 12:38; Rom. 10:16); 53:4 (Matt. 8:17); 53:7-8 LXX (Acts 8:32-33); 53:9 (1 Pet. 2:22); 53:12 (Luke 22:37). The "Index of

It is difficult to pick just one example, but the one that comes most readily to mind is the account of Philip and the Ethiopian eunuch in Acts 8:26-39. Philip was directed by an angel to a desert road, where he came upon a carriage in which there rode a court official from Ethiopia. Luke reports that Philip ran to catch up to the carriage. Dr. S. Lewis Johnson, one of the writer's revered professors, once humorously observed that he was glad that Philip ran. "If he had not run," said Johnson, "the eunuch would have been out of Isaiah 53 into Isaiah 54" by the time he got to the carriage![57] Philip *did* get there in time; he heard the man reading Isaiah 53 (verses 7 and 8) and asked him if he understood what he was reading. The eunuch answered, **"Well, how could I, unless someone guides me?"** He invited Philip up into his carriage, and Philip, using Isaiah 53 as his starting point, **"preached Jesus to him."** The account goes on to tell us that the man believed and was baptized. Philip's understanding of Isaiah 53 agrees with the uniform testimony of the NT.[58]

Not only does the NT identify Jesus as the Servant, but this has been the unanimous interpretation of Christian writers until late in the eighteenth century.[59]

Allusions and Verbal Parallels" (897) cites the following allusions and parallels: Isa. 52:13 (Acts 3:13); 52:15 (1 Cor. 2:9); 53 (Luke 24:27, 46; 1 Pet. 1:11); 53:2 (Matt. 2:23); 53:3 (Mark 9:12); 53:4 (1 Pet. 2:24); 53:4-5 (Rom. 4:25); 53:5 (Matt. 26:67; 1 Pet. 2:24); 53:5-6 (Acts 10:43); 53:6 (1 Pet. 2:25); 53:6-7 (John 1:29); 53:7 (Matt. 26:63; 27:12, 14; Mark 14:60-61; 15:4-5; 1 Cor. 5:7; 1 Pet. 2:23; Rev. 5:6, 12; 13:8); 53:8-9 (1 Cor. 15:3); 53:9 (Matt. 26:24; 1 John 3:5; Rev. 14:5); 53:11 (Rom. 5:19); 53:12 (Matt. 27:38; Luke 23:33, 34; Heb. 9:28; 1 Pet. 2:24). Also see the essays in *Isaiah in the New Testament*, eds., Steve Moyise and Maarten J. J. Menken (London: T. & T. Clark, 2005).

[57] S. Lewis Johnson, "Preaching the Lord Jesus and the Faith that Does Save: Acts 8:26-40" (PDF file, Dallas: SLJInstitute.net [BelieversChapel.org]), 15. Johnson attributes this comment to Bishop John Taylor Smith (1860–1938), Anglican Bishop of Sierra Leone and Chaplain-General of the British Armed Forces.

[58] Commenting on Philips's encounter with the eunuch, Bock wrote, "Our text is significant because it highlights a point Luke loves to make about Jesus. Not only is Jesus a figure described and predicted centuries in advance, but even the seeming incongruity of his death is a part of that description. Juxtaposing Jesus' humiliation in an unjust crucifixion with God's vindication of Jesus in resurrection shows where God's vote lies in disputes about who Jesus is" (Darrell Bock, "Isaiah 53 in Acts 8," in *The Gospel According to Isaiah 53*, 133-44 [esp. 143]).

[59] The one exception was Dutch theologian, Hugo Grotius (1583–1645). See North, *The Suffering Servant in Deutero-Isaiah*, 26-27. The reason for the rise of alternate interpretations was the introduction of the idea that the prophecy had a second author ("Deutero-Isaiah") in addition to Isaiah, an idea that followed upon the denial of

Early in the Christian era the Servant was sometimes identified by the Jews as the righteous man, but gradually it came to be universally accepted in the synagogue and in Jewish writings that the Servant was to be identified as the Messiah. This Messianic interpretation was universal until the twelfth century. Some Jews believed there would be two Messiahs,[60] "Messiah ben David," who would restore the Davidic dynasty, and "Messiah ben Joseph," who would suffer[61] (like the Servant of Isaiah 53).[62]

---

predictive prophecy in the Servant Songs and other portions of the book (North, 28-46 and *passim*). North's book is still the best on the history of the interpretation of the Servant Songs. There have been articles updating the discussion, but North sets forth the essential questions and interpretations.

[60] North, *The Suffering Servant in Deutero-Isaiah*, 15; cf. George Foot Moore, *Judaism* (Cambridge: Harvard, 1927), 2:370, n. 3. See *Sukkah* 52a in *The Babylonian Talmud*, 18 vol. ed., Seder Mo'ed, vol. 3, ed. I. Epstein (London: Soncino, 1978), 246-247.

[61] There is a tendency in some scholarship to downplay the vicarious nature of Messiah's sufferings in Jewish writings on Isaiah 53 (cf. Moore, *Judaism*, 1:546-52; Emil Schürer, *The History of the Jewish People in the Age of Jesus Christ*, rev. ed., eds. Geza Vermes, Fergus Millar and Matthew Black [Edinburgh: T. & T. Clark, 1979], 2:547-49). That not all saw Messiah suffering vicariously for the nation is true, although some did. The only point being made here is that from the 2d to the 12th centuries the Messianic interpretation of the Servant in Isaiah 53 was almost universally held by the Jews. For documentation of the idea that some ancient Jewish authorities not only held Isaiah 53 to be Messianic but also understood his sufferings to be vicarious, cf. A. McCaul, *The Doctrine and Interpretation of the Fifty-Third Chapter of Isaiah* (London: London Society's House, 1888), 18-23; David Baron, *The Servant of Jehovah: The Sufferings of the Messiah and the Glory that Should Follow* (New York: Doran, 1921), 143-58. Also see: Ad. Neubauer, ed., *The Fifty-Third Chapter of Isaiah According to the Jewish Interpreters*, 2 vols., vol. 2: *Translations*, by S. R. Driver and Ad. Neubauer (1877; reprint ed., New York: KTAV, 1969). The following examples and pagination are from Driver and Neubauer: Book of Zohar (14-15); Yalqut Shimoni [a later Midrash or rabbinical commentary] (9-10); Babylonian Talmud, Sanhedrin 98b (7); Midrash Rabbah [on Ruth 2:14] (9); Raymund Martini's edition of Sifre (10-11, but cf. Schürer, 2:549); Rabbi Mosheh El-Sheikh [mid 16th cent. Palestine] (258-59); Midrash P'siqtha (11). See also Appendix I of this monograph.

[62] North, *The Suffering Servant in Deutero-Isaiah*, 15-17. For documentation of the Jewish Messianic interpretation, see North and Neubauer, ed., *The Fifty-Third Chapter of Isaiah According to the Jewish Interpreters*, vol. 2: *Translations*. Also see E. W. Hengstenberg, *Christology of the Old Testament*, trans. Theodore Meyer and James Martin (Edinburgh: T. & T. Clark, 1854–58; reprint ed., Grand Rapids: Kregel, 1956), 2:311-19. As North observes (18), it is often thought that the Jews abandoned the Messianic interpretation of Isaiah 53 because Christians had used it so effectively in evangelizing the Jews. Since the twelfth century the most common view among Jewish writers and in the synagogue is the collective one, i.e., the Servant is the nation of Israel in dispersion.

The Internal Evidence Pointing to Jesus Christ

The internal evidence is the evidence provided by Isaiah himself in his predictions and descriptions of the Servant. No man other than Jesus Christ has done the things attributed to the Servant in Isaiah 53. Frederick Aston lists the following items for consideration:

- He is portrayed in the features of a human personality, 52:13–53:3.
- He is an innocent sufferer, 53:4, 5, 8, 9, 12.
- He is a voluntary sufferer, v. 7.
- He is a silent sufferer, v. 7.
- His suffering is vicarious, i.e., substitutionary, vv. 4, 5, 6, 8, 10, 11, 12.
- His suffering is redemptive, v. 5.
- His suffering ends in death, vv. 8, 10, 12.
- His death gives way to resurrection, v. 11.
- His atoning work leads the straying people to confession and repentance, vv. 1, 4-6.
- His suffering is ordained by God and fulfills the divine will and purpose, v. 10.
- His redemptive work inaugurates a life of exaltation and [ultimately] kingly glory.[63]

In response to these prophecies and descriptions, F. B. Meyer remarked, "There is only one brow which this crown of thorns will fit."[64] Charles Spurgeon agreed, "If the Man of Nazareth, the Son of God, be not right visible in these...verses, they are dark as midnight itself."[65] Like Cinderella's slipper, the description fits only one person, namely, Jesus Christ.[66]

---

[63] Frederick Alfred Aston, "The Servant of the LORD in Isaiah LIII," *EvQ* 11 (July, 1939), 193-206 (esp. 199); idem., *The Challenge of the Ages*, 21st ed. (New York: Research Press, 1970), 8.

[64] F. B. Meyer, *Christ in Isaiah* (London: Marshall, Morgan, and Scott, 1950), 125.

[65] Charles Haddon Spurgeon, "The Sure Triumph of the Crucified One," *The Metropolitan Tabernacle Pulpit* (Pasadena: Pilgrim Publications, 1971), 21:241. In context Spurgeon was speaking of Isaiah 52:13-15.

[66] Old Testament scholar, Charles H. H. Wright, wrote, "Our view of Isaiah lii-liii is that the prophecy was an enigma, which could not be fully understood in the days before

Dr. Jack Fish of the Emmaus Bible College faculty tells an interesting story from his teen years. While a senior in high school (1958–59), it was his responsibility, along with his friend, the late Peter Fosberg, to open the school day by reading the Scriptures. In those days many American high schools began the day in each home room with the pledge of allegiance to the flag, a reading from the Bible, and the recitation of the Lord's prayer.

Jack and his friend wanted to evangelize their fellow students at Westfield High School (New Jersey), so they read salvation texts from the New Testament every day. Several weeks into the school year, one of the students complained and pointed out that according to state law, only Old Testament texts could be read. The law was worded in such a way that it included both Jews and Christians in the exercise. There were no Jewish students in this class, so no one had complained until this student raised an objection.

The teacher ordered Jack and Pete to read from the Old Testament from that point on. The next day, Pete read from the Old Testament; specifically, he read from Isaiah 53. After he had read about half of the chapter, the boy who had complained about their New Testament readings called out loudly, "You are not allowed to read from the New Testament."

Pete responded, "I *am* reading from the Old Testament." The complaining boy rejoined, "No, you are not. That is the New Testament." Several other members of the class joined in the attack on Pete. Even the teacher joined in. She came over to him and took the Bible away, saying, "Here, let me see that!" She looked at the passage Pete was reading and exclaimed in surprise, "Why, it *is* in the Old Testament!"

In this chapter we now turn to the first stanza of the great "Servant Song." The "big idea" or "primary focus" of the paragraph is to assure the reader that in spite of appearances to the contrary, the Lord will exalt his Servant.[67] As von Rad observed, "The unusual aspect of this great poem is that it begins with what is really the end of the whole story, the

---

Christ, but which has been solved by the sufferings, death, resurrection, and exaltation of Him who was both Son of Man and the Son of God" (*The Suffering Servant of Jehovah Depicted in Isaiah LII and LIII* [London: Francis Griffiths, 1905], 7).

[67] Smith, *Isaiah 40–66*, 434.

Servant's glorification and the recognition of his significance for the world."[68]

In verse 13 Yahweh announces his Servant's exaltation. This announcement is developed along two lines: First, many of his own Jewish people were appalled at his humiliation, which left him looking less than human; second, in the future, kings and nations who experience his work of purifying their sins will be amazed as they see his exaltation and understand his saving work.[69]

PART II: EXPOSITION OF ISAIAH 52:13-15

YAHWEH ANNOUNCES THE EXALTATION OF HIS SERVANT, VERSE 13[70]

> **Behold, My servant will prosper,**
> **He will be high and lifted up and greatly exalted.**

The Servant will Achieve Success Through Wise Action

"**Behold, My servant will prosper.**" With the word "behold," or "see," (הִנֵּה, *hinnēh*) the LORD calls attention to his Servant.[71] It is like the words of Pontius Pilate, "**Behold, the Man!**" (John 19:5). The Latin Vulgate has the familiar translation, "Ecce Homo." Here, however, it is not Pilate speaking. David Baron wrote that this "may be described as God's *Ecce Homo*."[72] This declaration "is intended to introduce something startlingly new and wonderfully important"—important to Israel, who first heard it, and important to readers today.[73]

---

[68] von Rad, *The Message of the Prophets*, 223; idem. *Old Testament Theology*, 2:256.

[69] Cf. Lindsey, *The Servant Songs*, 101.

[70] The outline used here is a slight modification of that of Lindsey, *The Servant Songs*, 100-110.

[71] The particle הִנֵּה, says Baron, is the word "by which in Scripture God seeks to call the attention of men to matters which are of the utmost importance" (David Baron, *The Servant of Jehovah: The Sufferings of the Messiah and the Glory that Should Follow* [New York: Doran, 1921], 52). Here it calls attention to the following noun ("my servant"). Cf. *HALOT*, s.v. "הִנֵּה," 1:252.

[72] Baron, *The Servant of Jehovah*, 51.

[73] Robert D. Culver, *The Sufferings and the Glory of the Lord's Righteous Servant* (Moline, IL: Christian Service Foundation, 1958), 23.

Yahweh points to the Servant as if he were present (confirmed by his direct address to the Servant, ["you"], in v. 14)," and he "calls attention to the person and theme now to be introduced."[74] The Servant is mentioned only here and in chapter 53, verse 11. He never speaks in the poem, and except for verse 14 ("you") he is always spoken of in the third person.

"**My servant will prosper**" (NASB).[75] The verb translated "prosper" (שָׂכַל, *śāḵal*)[76] is sometimes translated "deal prudently" (KJV, Darby), i.e., act intelligently or wisely.[77] Since intelligent or wise action is usually effective, the word here is generally understood as synonymous with "to act with result," i.e., to be successful.[78] This is how a number of English versions translate it.[79] The TEV's "My servant will succeed in his task" captures the idea.

How does one evaluate a servant? The only way to do so is to ask, did he do what he was commissioned to do? Did he complete the task? If he did not, then he is a worthless servant. If he did complete the task, he is successful and is approved by his master.[80] The nature of the Servant's successful task will be spelled out later in the Servant song (esp. 53:4-6) where his vicarious death on behalf of his people is described.

The Servant will be Rewarded for His Successful Mission

In the next line, God makes it clear that the Servant accomplished his work and fulfilled his mission. As a consequence of his success, God will reward him. That the reward is so great indicates that in the eyes of God he performed his task wonderfully. "**He will be high and lifted up and**

---

[74] Lindsey, *The Servant Songs*, 101; cf. Urwick, *The Servant of* Jehovah, 98.

[75] The NASB has, "My servant will prosper" (cf. also: NRSV).

[76] The form in the Hebrew text is יַשְׂכִּיל (3rd pers. msc. sg. hiphil imperfect).

[77] The NIV has, "My servant will act wisely" (cf. also: ESV, HCSB).

[78] Delitzsch, *Biblical Commentary on the Prophecies of Isaiah*, 304-5.

[79] The REB has, "My servant will achieve success" (cf. NET). This translation is preferred by BDB, s.v. "שָׂכַל," 968 and *HALOT*, s.v. "שָׂכַל," 2:1329. Westermann wrote, "It is one of the Hebrew verbs which denote both an action and its results. This wider meaning enshrines the lesson taught by experience, that prudence in action leads to success. However, the way in which the song develops shows that in this case the verb only refers to the result—my Servant will succeed, achieve what he proposes (as in Josh. 1:8)" (Isaiah 40–66, 258; also: R. N. Whybray, *Isaiah 40–66*, NCB [Grand Rapids: Eerdmans, 1981], 169); Oswalt, *The Book of Isaiah, Chapters 40–66*, 378; Smith, *Isaiah 40–66*, 435.

[80] Cf. Waltke, "The Real Value of Jesus Christ," 3.

greatly exalted." Each of the three words ("high," "lifted up," and
"greatly exalted") is significant and should be considered closely. "He
will be high" (רוּם, *rûm*).[81] The translation "high" is possible, but in this
verse it would be better translated, "He will rise." This is the normal
Hebrew word for "to rise up."[82] A number of versions translate, "He will
be raised" (NIV, REB, HCSB).[83] "[He will] be lifted up" (נָשָׂא,
nāśā).[84] The versions generally agree with this translation (cf. NASB,
NIV, ESV, HCSB, NRSV, NET). "[He will] be greatly exalted" (גָּבַהּ,
gābah).[85] Again, there is general agreement on this translation (NASB,
NIV, ESV, HCSB, REB, NET).

Oswalt noted that the first two verbs (רוּם and נָשָׂא, "high and lifted
up") are used in three places in Isaiah to describe God (6:1; 33:10;
57:15). Furthermore, in Isaiah 2 (vv. 6-22) the prophet forcefully speaks
against all prideful exaltation of human beings. He said, "**The pride of
man will be humbled and the loftiness of men will be abased; and the
LORD alone will be exalted** (שָׂגַב, *śāgab*) **in that day**" (v. 17). Oswalt
asks, "Whom do [these verbs] describe here?" Is Israel to be "exalted to
the place of God? Is it a prophet of Israel?" He answers, "In each case the
answer must be no. This is the Messiah or no one." He adds that Paul's
great hymn in Philippians 2:5-11 is a reflection on this text. The one
who took "the form of a bond-servant" God has "highly exalted."[86]

Delitzsch wrote, "The three verbs...consequently denote the
commencement, the continuation, and the result or climax of the
exaltation." He adds that the verbs speak of "the three principle steps" of
Christ's exaltation in the historical fulfillment, "viz., the resurrection, the
ascension, and the sitting down at the right hand of God."[87]

---

[81] The form in the Hebrew text is יָרוּם (3rd pers. msc. sg. qal imperf.).

[82] Waltke, "The Real Value of Jesus Christ," 3. On the possible renderings of the verb,
see BDB, s.v. "רוּם," 926-927; *HALOT*, s.v. "רוּם," 2:1202-05.

[83] Goldingay and Payne argue that the verb must be repointed (יְרוֹם) to get this passive
sense (*A Critical and Exegetical Commentary on Isaiah 40–55*, 2:289). But see BDB, s.v.
"רוּם," 926.

[84] The form in the Hebrew text is נִשָּׂא (3rd pers. msc. sg. niphal perf.).

[85] The form in the Hebrew text is גָּבַהּ (3rd pers. msc. sg. qal perf.).

[86] Oswalt, *The Book of Isaiah, Chapters 40–66*, 378-79.

[87] Delitzsch, *Biblical Commentary on the Prophecies of Isaiah*, 2:305.

YAHWEH COMPARES INITIAL JEWISH ASTONISHMENT AT THE SERVANT WITH ULTIMATE GENTILE COMPREHENSION, VERSES 14-15

> Just as many were astonished at you, My people,
> So His appearance was marred more than any man
> And His form more than the sons of men.
> Thus He will sprinkle many nations,
> Kings will shut their mouths on account of Him;
> For what had not been told them they will see,
> And what they had not heard they will understand.

In verses 14-15 there is a partial description of the task the Servant was sent to do. In chapter 53 a fuller description is given. In verse 14 the horrible physical cost to the Servant is described. In verse 15 the tremendous spiritual benefit of his work is alluded to.

Israel was Appalled at the Servant's Inhuman Disfigurement, verse 14

The Astonishment of the People

A comparison or comparative contrast is introduced by "just as" (כַּאֲשֶׁר, ka'ăšer) at the beginning of verse 14.[88] The contrast is between the

---

[88] The sequence of three particles in vv. 14-15 (כַּאֲשֶׁר ["just as," v. 14a]; כֵּן ["so," v. 14b, "so his appearance"]; כֵּן ["so," v. 15a, "so he will sprinkle") is complicated. The comparative conjunction כַּאֲשֶׁר serves as the protasis or beginning of the comparison or comparative contrast. The apodosis or completion of the comparison is often introduced by the particle כֵּן (cf. BDB, s.v. "כַּאֲשֶׁר," 455). The problem in the present context is that there are two clauses introduced by כֵּן. Is the apodosis introduced by one or both of these particles—or neither? There are at least four solutions to the problem: (1) The text is defective. There should be only one כֵּן in the passage [v. 15]. The כֵּן in verse 14b is a mistake due to scribal error and should be emended to כִּי, "because" [Charles Cutler Torrey, *The Second Isaiah* (New York: Scribner's, 1928), 415]. There is no textual evidence for this emendation, and it can therefore be dismissed. The sense yielded by this emendation would fit somewhere in solution # 4. (2) There is a double apodosis: "just as many were shocked at you, *so* was his countenance marred...*so* shall he sprinkle ..." J. A. Alexander explains the sense as follows: "Their abhorrence of him was not without reason, and it shall not be without requital." The comparison, then, is between two shocks: shock at his disfigurement and shock at the requital or reward, i.e., his exaltation [*Commentary on the Prophecies of Isaiah*, rev. ed. (Edinburgh: T. & T. Clark, 1875; reprint ed., Grand Rapids: Zondervan, 1974), 2:287]. (3) Both כֵּן clauses are

"many," most likely Israelites (the "we" of 53:1-6)[89] who were appalled at the Servant's sufferings and the "kings" of the many nations who are sprinkled (i.e., cleansed) by him and who will be in reverent awe of him because of the effects (purification or cleansing) of the Servant's suffering.

Two things merit careful consideration in verse 14: first, the astonishment of the people at the Servant, and second, the terrible disfigurement of the Servant. **"Just as many were astonished at you."** The NASB has, **"many were astonished at you, My people."**[90] The words, "my people" are not in the original text. The "you" spoken to by God is the Servant himself. It is a bit awkward in that he is spoken of in

---

parenthetical, and the apodosis comes in the second line of verse 15, "Kings will shut their mouths on account of Him." The contrast is between the many who despised the Servant—Jews, "members of the covenant"—and the kings (Gentiles) who stand in silent awe before him. "The many are astonished, the kings close their mouths" [Edward J. Young, *The Book of Isaiah*, NICOT (Grand Rapids: Eerdmans, 1972), 3:336-37, 339]. (4) The כֵּן in verse 14b is part of an explanatory parenthesis, and the apodosis is introduced by the כֵּן in verse 15. Here commentators are in essential agreement, but they differ in exactly what is being compared. [a] Some see the comparison as between *the Servant's degradation and His exaltation*. Delitzsch wrote, "Just as His degradation was the deepest degradation possible, so His glorification would be of the loftiest kind" [*Biblical Commentary on the Prophecies of Isaiah*, 2:306]. [b] Others see the comparison between *the two responses of astonishment*. "The astonishment with which men later greeted the Servant's exaltation was exactly as great as had been their previous horror at the way in which he suffered and was treated with scorn" [Westermann, *Isaiah 40–66*, 258; Gleason L. Archer, "Isaiah," in *The Wycliffe Bible Commentary*, eds. Charles F. Pfeiffer and Everett F. Harrison (Chicago: Moody, 1962), 646]. [c] Still others see the comparison between *the two groups of people* in the text, that is, "between the 'many' individuals [mainly Israelites] who are appalled at the fact of the Servant's suffering, and the 'kings' [representatives of 'many' nations] who will be awed at the effects [expiatory purification or cleansing] that will result from the Servant's suffering." Thus, "*Just as* many were appalled at his inhuman treatment and disfigurement and death, *so* kings will be astonished when they comprehend the meaning of his debasement and the universal application of that death". [Lindsey, *The Servant Songs*, 105, citing personal correspondence from Kenneth L. Barker]. Lindsey and Barker argue that while the apodosis does begin with the first colon of verse 15, the structural points of the comparison are found in the second colon. Barker noted the following structural correspondence in the comparison: עָלָיו ("on account of him") in v. 15 answers to עָלֶיךָ ("at you") in v. 14; יִקְפְּצוּ ("will shut") in v. 15 answers to שָׁמְמוּ ("were astonished/appalled") in v. 14; מְלָכִים ("kings") in v. 15 answers to רַבִּים ("many") in v. 14.

[89] There is a contrast in verses 14-15 between the "many" and the "many nations," i.e., Gentiles. The narrower group in verse 14 are evidently Israelites ("members of the covenant"). See Young, *The Book of Isaiah*, 3:339.

[90] That "you" refers to "my people" is also the interpretation reflected in the REB.

the third person ("him") elsewhere in the passage.[91] It appears that the Servant himself is present as God speaks, and he is addressed in a parenthetical aside before the Lord again begins to speak of him in the third person.[92] The "many" of verse 14 despised and rejected the Servant, as chapter 53 will make clear.

Here we read they were "astonished" at what they witnessed at the time of the Servant's death. The Hebrew word (שָׁמֵם, šāmam)[93] in various contexts can mean "to be devastated, be desolated, to tremble, to be astonished, to stare at." Here it means "to be appalled," i.e., "to be filled or overcome with horror, consternation, fear, or dismay."[94] It describes the negative response of people to acts of destruction, desolation, and total obliteration. For example, it is used in Ezekiel (27:35; 28:19) of the reaction of the people as they see the destruction and ruins of the city of Tyre.

One can feel the meaning of this when one sees photos and films of the destruction caused by tornadoes. In the late spring of 2011 nearly 1,000 tornadoes ripped across the heartland of the United States. One particularly violent storm caused massive destruction in Joplin, Missouri.

---

[91] The Syriac version and possibly the Aramaic Targum (this is debated) as well as two Hebrew manuscripts support the reading עָלָיו ("concerning him"). Some scholars have therefore emended the text to read, "concerning him" (James Muilenburg, "Isaiah 40–66: Introduction and Exegesis," in *The Interpreter's Bible*, ed. George Arthur Buttrick [Nashville: Abingdon, 1956], 5:616; Blenkinsopp, *Isaiah 40–55*, 346; cf. also: NIV, NRSV, TEV). However, the MT reads עָלֶיךָ ("concerning you"), and this reading is supported by the two major Qumran Scrolls of Isaiah (1QIsaᵃ and 1QIsaᵇ) as well as the LXX and the Vulgate. Furthermore, this is the harder reading in light of the uniform use of the 3ʳᵈ person for the Servant elsewhere in the Servant Song. Also, it is not uncommon in poetic or prophetic language for there to occur "a more or less abrupt transition from one person to another" (GKC § 144p, p. 462). In light of these considerations, the reading of the MT ("concerning you") should stand. See: Christopher R. North, *The Second Isaiah* (London: Oxford University Press, 1964), 227; Oswalt, *The Book of Isaiah, Chapters 40–66*, 373, n. 53; Smith, Isaiah 40–66, 436, n. 325. On the Isaiah scrolls at Qumran, see *Discoveries in the Judaean Desert*, vol. 32: Qumran Cave 1, II. *The Isaiah Scrolls*, Part 1: *Plates and Transcriptions*, eds., Eugene Ulrich and Peter W. Flint (Oxford and New York: Oxford University Press, 2010), Column 44 (pp. 88-89, 1QIsaᵃ) and Column 33, Plate 69 (pp. 140-41, 1QIsaᵇ). Cf. also: Darby, KJV, NASB, ESV, HCSB, REB, NET.

[92] In the NET Bible the first colon or line of verse 14 is treated as a parenthesis: "(just as many were horrified by the sight of you)."

[93] The form that appears in the Hebrew text is שָׁמְמוּ, 3d pers. pl. qal perf. of שָׁמֵם.

[94] Cf. *HALOT*, s.v. "שָׁמֵם," 2:1564. Cf. *The Random House Dictionary of the English Language*, s.v. "appall," 71.

TV viewers and magazine readers could only get a faint idea of the desolation. The people of Joplin knew the reality of what it is to be appalled. They told reporters that they couldn't find their streets or neighborhoods because they had been obliterated.[95] One woman said to a TV cameraman that it was one thing to see a twister from a distance; it was another to be inside a house that the twister was smashing to pieces. She was visibly traumatized. That is the force of the Hebrew word used here. If one looked at the wreckage of Jesus on the cross, one would be astounded at the sight.

The word is used in the OT of the reaction of people to divine judgment (Lev. 26:32; 1 Kings 9:8; Jer. 18:16; 49:17; Ezek. 26:16). This may imply that, as the people of Jerusalem passed by, they thought Jesus was suffering for his own sins (cf. Isa. 53:4).

The Disfigurement of the Servant

The next two lines of the poem give a parenthetical reason for the horrified astonishment of the people.[96] Why were the people appalled, or horrified? The following lines explain, "**His appearance was so**[97] **disfigured**"[98] (HCSB). A number of English translations give the

---

[95] David Von Drehle, "Torn Asunder," *Time* (June 6, 2011): 26-32; Sharon Begley, "Are You Ready for More?" *Newsweek* (June 6, 2011): 40-45.

[96] Lindsey, *The Servant Songs*, 106.

[97] The majority of commentators do not take the כֵּן ("so," NASB) in verse 14b to be part of the apodosis in the comparison construction in verses 14-15. Rather, they take it in an adverbial way introducing an explanation why the "many" were appalled. The NET Bible's "he was so disfigured" captures the thought. Cf. Oswalt, *The Book of Isaiah, Chapters 40–66*, 379, n. 80.

[98] The word translated "disfigured" (NIV, REB, NET, HCSB) or "marred" (Darby, KJV, NASB, ESV, NRSV) is מִשְׁחַת and has caused considerable discussion. BDB, s.v. "מִשְׁחַת," 1008, identifies the form as a noun, "disfigurement," derived from the verb שָׁחַת, "to mar, ruin, spoil, destroy"; Smith (*Isaiah 40–66*, 438, n. 333) identifies it as a verb; and Oswalt (*The Book of Isaiah, Chapters 40–66*, 373, n. 54) as an adjective. As it stands in the MT, it is a noun in the construct state with the following adverbial phrase. According to *HALOT*, s.v. "מִשְׁחַת," 1:644, it is usually repointed to form a hophal [causative passive] participle (מָשְׁחָת), reflected in the above English translations (see also *Biblica Hebraica* [Stuttgart], note). All of these understandings of the word have precedent in the history of interpretation (cf. Dominique Barthélemy, *Critique Textuelle de l' Ancien Testament*, vol. 2, Isaïe, Jérémie, Lamentations [Göttingen: Vandenhoeck & Ruprecht, 1986], 385-86). The plot thickened a bit when it was discovered that 1QIsaᵃ added a *yod* to the word (משחתי). See *Discoveries in the Judaean Desert*, vol. 32: Qumran Cave 1, II. *The Isaiah Scrolls*, Part 1: *Plates and Transcriptions*, Column 44 (pp. 88-89).

impression that no one had ever been so disfigured before. The NASB has, "His appearance was marred more than any man and His form more than the sons of men" (also: Darby, KJV). Factually, of course, that is not true; one need only mention those incinerated in terrible fires or bomb explosions.

The adverbial phrases may be translated, "'from' or 'beyond' the human" and "'from' or 'beyond' human likeness."[99] The HCSB captures the idea, "His appearance was so disfigured that He did not look like a man, and His form did not resemble a human being."[100] The word "appearance" (מַרְאֶה, mar'eh) most likely refers to his face, while the word "form" (תֹּאַר, tō'ar) refers to his physical body in general.[101] To summarize the description of the disfigured Servant: "He was inhumanly deformed."[102] This disfigurement is an allusion to the physical sufferings leading up to and including the crucifixion of Jesus Christ.[103]

Ulrich and Flint note that 1QIsa[b] does not have the yod (idem., Part 2: Introductions, Commentary, and Textual Variants, 175). The reading of 1QIsa[a] led some scholars to argue that the word is a feminine noun (מִשְׁחָה, "anointing") derived from the verb (מָשַׁח) meaning "to smear, anoint" (e.g., John Goldingay, The Message of Isaiah 40–55 (London: T. & T. Clark, 2005), 490; Wm. H. Brownlee, "The Servant of the LORD in the Qumran Scrolls I," BASOR 132 [Dec., 1953]: 8-12). Most perhaps have defended "disfigured" in that it makes more sense. The imagery of anointing makes little sense here ("I anointed his appearance"—one anoints a person, not his appearance). Furthermore, the appalled response of the audience argues for "disfigured" and not the positive imagery of anointing (cf. the debate between Joseph Reider and Brownlee in, "On Mšḥty in the Qumran Scrolls," BASOR 134 (April, 1954): 27-28; also: Smith, Isaiah 40–66, 438, n. 323). Watts sums up his discussion with a classic understatement: "With so many possible roots, the Heb. word is a teaser" (John D. W. Watts, Isaiah 34–66, WBC, rev. ed. [Nashville: Nelson, 2000], 781, n.).

[99] The preposition מִן has here the local idea of separation rather than comparison. The thought is not that he was disfigured more than any other, but that he was so mistreated that he hardly looked human (Oswalt, The Book of Isaiah 40–66, 373, n. 55.

[100] As Lindsey observed, the Servant's appearance in verse 14 "is described in the context of His suffering and death (already implied in 49:4, 7; 50:6); it is not a reference to His normal appearance throughout life" (The Servant Songs, 106-107).

[101] Oswalt says "that all suffering is encompassed here: physical, mental, and spiritual" (The Book of Isaiah Chapters 40–66, 380). As Unger notes, Christ suffered in the spiritual realm as well as in the physical sphere. In this context, however, "only the brutality and inhumanity of the physical abuse heaped upon Him come into view" (Unger's Commentary on the Old Testament, 1294).

[102] HALOT, s.v. "מִשְׁחַת," 1:644. Cf. James Barr, Comparative Philology and the Text of the Old Testament (Oxford: Oxford University Press, 1968; reprint ed. [with corrections], Winona Lake: Eisenbrauns, 1987), 284-85.

[103] Cf. Lindsey, The Servant Songs, 107.

Nations will be Purified and Kings Astonished as a Result of the Servant's Disfigurement, verse 15

The Sprinkling of the Nations

In verse 15 Yahweh leaves the recital of his Servant's degradation and turns to his exaltation. He begins by speaking of the consequence of the Servant's sufferings. First, many will experience spiritual deliverance because of his death. They will be cleansed of their sins. Second, there will be "a great reversal"[104] in the attitude of the world's rulers; the One they had once despised they will reverence. Just as many in Israel were appalled at the Servant's "inhuman treatment, disfigurement, and death, so kings will be astonished when they comprehend the meaning of His abasement"[105] and the universal benefits and deliverance resulting from that death.

Yahweh says of the Servant, **"He will sprinkle many nations."** The form of the verb **"sprinkle"** (נָזָה, *nāzāh*) used here (יַזֶּה, *yazzeh*)[106] speaks in the Old Testament of the work of a priest. That which was sprinkled was most often blood, although there were occasions when the priest sprinkled water or oil.[107] To understand the sprinkling of the nations one need only remember the usage of the term.[108]

---

[104] Muilenburg, "Isaiah 40–66: Introduction and Exegesis," 618.

[105] Lindsey, *The Servant Songs*, 105.

[106] The form used in verse 15 (יַזֶּה) is 3d pers. msc. sing. hiphil imperfect.

[107] Examples of the sprinkling of blood include Lev. 4:6, 17; 5:9; 14:7; 16:14, 19; of oil (Lev. 8:11; 14: 16, 27); of water (Num. 19:18, 19); of blood and oil (Exod. 29:21; Lev. 8:30); of blood and water (Lev. 14:51). Cf. BDB, s.v. "נָזָה," 633.

[108] The reading of the Masoretic text (יַזֶּה, "he will sprinkle") is contested today by many scholars. The objection to "sprinkle" is fivefold: (1) In other occurrences of נָזָה in the Old Testament the object of the verb [in the accusative case] is the liquid that is being sprinkled. It is absurd to think of the Servant sprinkling the nations onto something. (2) In other occurrences of the verb the thing being sprinkled (e.g., the altar, Lev. 5:9) is prefixed by a preposition such as עַל- ['al], but there is no preposition with "sprinkle" in Isa. 52:15. (3) The parallelism between verses 14 and 15 demands that this phrase should express a change in those who formally abhorred the Servant. As a parallel to the words "just as many were astonished," there is the clause "he shall startle [or cause to tremble] many nations." (4) Any reference to the Servant as a priest or to his sufferings as of an expiatory or purifying nature would be out of place here. (5) The Hebrew may be a cognate of an Arabic homonym (*nāzāh*) meaning "to leap" [i.e., "in joyful surprise" or "reverence"] or "to startle." Proponents of this or other emendations of the text include: LXX; Darby, *New Translation*; NRSV; REB; TEV; NET; Wilhelm Gesenius, *Hebrew*

Fausset wrote:

"But the word [יַזֶּה, from *nāzāh*] universally in the Old Testament means either *to sprinkle (with blood)*; to *atone for guilt*—as the high priest makes an *expiation* (Lev. 4:6; 16:14, 19); or to *sprinkle (with water)*, as synonymous with *purifying* (Num. 19:18, 21) or *cleansing* (cf. Ezek. 36:25, where sprinkle (a different Hebrew word [זָרַק, *zāraq*, lit. "to toss") means to *cleanse*). Cf. as to the Spirit, Acts 2:33. [After Christ's ascension, he poured forth the Holy Spirit who would have a role in cleansing]. Both *atoning* for guilt and *purifying* by the Spirit are

---

and Chaldee Lexicon to the Old Testament Scriptures, ed., Samuel Prideaux Tregelles (London: Samuel Bagster, 1847; reprint ed., Grand Rapids: Baker, 1987), s.v. "נָזָה," 541; Delitzsch, *Biblical Commentary on the Prophecies of Isaiah*, 2:308-309; BDB, s.v. "נָזָה," 633; *HALOT*, s.v. "נזה," 1:683 [which emends the text to יִרְגְּזוּ (*yirg^ezû* ["astonished"])]; Whybray, *Isaiah 40–66*, 170; Westermann, *Isaiah 40–66*, 253 [in agreement with *HALOT*]; Oswalt, *The Book of Isaiah, Chapters 40–66*, 374, n. 56. A. B. Davidson went so far as to say, "It is simply treason against the Hebrew language to render 'sprinkle.' The interpreter who will so translate will 'do anything'" ["The Book of Isaiah—Chapters 40–66, Part 7: The Work of the Servant of the LORD," *Exp*, 2d Series, 8 (1884): 430-51 (esp. 443)]. Others have argued in favor of the reading of the Masoretic text ["sprinkle"]. They note the following: (1) The Masoretic text, with the weight of its ancient authority, reads "sprinkle." (2) Other ancient texts have "sprinkle" [Aquila, Theodotion, Vulgate] or "purify" [Syriac]. These translators seemed to sense that this was a unique usage of נזה without the usual object or preposition. (3) As Kay noted, those who make their case on the basis of the lack of the liquid object or the preposition introducing it "forget that in the passage before us the verb refers, not to a literal process of *sprinkling*, but to an act of purification *analogous* to that which was effected by ceremonial sprinkling," i.e., cleansing. (4) There are a number of references to the Servant's priestly work later in the this fourth Servant song [cf. 53:10-12] (5) Hebrew usage for the translation "to startle" is unattested, i.e., this view imports a root into the Hebrew language. (6) The real parallelism between the verses is between "Just as many were appalled at you" and "Kings shall shut their mouths." Proponents of the reading of the Masoretic text ("sprinkle") include: KJV, NASB, NIV, ESV, HCSB; W. Kay, "Isaiah: Introduction, Commentary and Critical Notes," in *The Holy Bible According to the Authorized Version (AD 1611), with an Explanatory and Critical Commentary*, ed. F. C. Cook [New York: Scribner's, 1893), 5:266, note A; Urwick, *The Servant of Jehovah*, 103-4; North, *The Second Isaiah*, 228; Young, *The Book of Isaiah*, 3: 338; idem., *Studies in Isaiah* [Grand Rapids: Eerdmans, 1954], 199-206; Lindsey, *The Servant Songs*, 108-109; Smith, *Isaiah 40–66*, 440; Goldingay and Payne, *Isaiah 40–55*, 2:294-295; Barthélemy, *Critique Textuelle de l' Ancien Testament*, 2:384-87. The essay of Young is still noteworthy.

appropriate to Messiah (John 13:8; Heb. 9:13, 14; 10:22; 12:24; 1 Pet. 1:2)."[109]

As Lindsey noted, "that the Servant will 'sprinkle many nations' is a metonymy of cause (sprinkling) for effect (cleansing)."[110] Yahweh, speaking through Isaiah, was here prophesying that through the atoning work of the Servant, which is set forth in great detail in chapter 53, people from many nations would have their sins expiated, i.e., blotted out, wiped away, or purged.

Lindblom translated the line, "He (the servant) will (at some time in the future) besprinkle many peoples, i.e., purify many peoples from their sins."[111] That "some time in the future" refers to the period following the disfigurement of the Servant. It refers to the present age leading up to the time when the kings of the earth show him honor. Looking ahead to the inter-advent period, the church age, Paul described it poetically as a time when Christ would be **"proclaimed among the nations,"** and **"believed on in the world"** (1 Tim. 3:16). Looking back, the future worshippers in heaven sing a new song that alludes to that same inter-advent era, **"Worthy are You to take the book and to break its seals; for You were slain, and purchased for God with Your blood men from every tribe and tongue and people and nation"** (Rev. 5:9). The present age from Pentecost to the second advent can surely be described as a time when the Servant "sprinkled the nations."[112]

---

[109] A. R. Fausset, *Job–Isaiah*, in *A Commentary Critical, Experimental, and Practical on the Old and New Testaments*, eds., Robert Jamieson, A. R. Fausset, and David Brown (1866; reprint ed., Grand Rapids: Eerdmans, 1967), 3:728.

[110] Lindsey, *The Servant Songs*, 109.

[111] Johannes Lindblom, *The Servant Songs in Deutero-Isaiah* (Lund: C. W. K. Gleerup, 1951), 41.

[112] Merrill F. Unger also sees an eschatological application of the sprinkling. He says the Servant shall sprinkle nations—that is millennial nations. They shall be sprinkled expiatorily and cleansed "for their role (as nations) in the Davidic-Messianic earthly Kingdom (2 Sam. 7:8-15)." See *Unger's Commentary on the Old Testament*, 1295.

The Reaction of the Kings

The concluding lines of the first stanza are eschatological.[113] They look to the end-time when kings and nations "will see, hear, and understand new things that they had never known before."[114]

> Yahweh's speech "draws attention to the Servant's future, his exaltation. It displays him before all the nations of the world, and it envisages the precise moment at which they will become aware of the true position of the man who has been despised and mutilated beyond human semblance. Greatly astonished, they become acquainted with something 'that had never been told them.'"[115]

The exaltation of the Servant appears to be two-fold in the poem: (1) his exaltation at the time of his ascension (52:13), and (2) his yet future exaltation on earth before kings (52:15; 53:12).

The second line of verse 15 completes the comparison or comparative contrast between the astonished Israelites of verse 14 and the reverent kings of verse 15. "Now comes a sharp contrast," says Westermann, "called in v. 15b 'something unheard of'—the effect of the Servant's exaltation on those who had part in it or learned of it."[116] **"Kings shall shut their mouths on account of Him."** This gesture parallels the millennial scene in Isaiah 49:7 when the kings of the earth arise and bow down before the Servant in deep respect.[117] The shutting of their mouths indicates that the kings of the millennial nations will be "silent in reverential awe and honor before the servant."[118]

---

[113] "The strophe as a whole is an excellent example of the motif of the great reversal especially common in eschatological contexts" (Muilenburg, "Isaiah 40–66," 618).

[114] Smith, *Isaiah 40–66*, 440.

[115] von Rad, *The Message of the Prophets*, 222-223; idem., *Old Testament Theology*, 2:256.

[116] Westermann, *Isaiah 40–66*, 259. Goldingay sees this as the fulfillment of Isaiah 52:7-10. "Verse 15b declares that this is the moment when Yhwh indeed reigns and people are caused to hear of it, and when all the ends of the earth are to see God's deliverance (52:7, 10)" (*Isaiah 40–55*, 494).

[117] Unger, *Unger's Commentary on the Old Testament*, 1279, 1295.

[118] Lindsey, *The Servant Songs*, 110.

The study of bas reliefs on stone by archeologists illustrates what this means. One such relief that still exists portrays King Darius the Great of Persia (521–486 BC). He sits majestically on his throne with his son, Crown Prince Xerxes, behind him. Before him stands a Median dignitary, and the right hand of this visiting official is raised to his mouth in a gesture of respect.[119]

In the ancient Near East, when someone recognized another as an authority over him, he would acknowledge that authority in his presence by putting his hand to his mouth. He, as it were, shut his mouth in submission to his superior.[120] This explanation is confirmed in the book of Job in chapter 29 where Job reflects on his glorious past. He says, **"As I was in the prime of my days, when the friendship of God was over my tent; when the Almighty was yet with me, and my children were around me; when my steps were bathed in butter, and the rock poured out for me streams of oil! When I went out to the gate of the city, when I took my seat in the square, the young men saw me and hid themselves, and the old men arose and stood. The princes stopped talking and put their hands on their mouths"** (vv. 4-9; cf. Job 40:4; Ps. 107:42; Ezek. 16:63; Micah 7:16).[121]

Baltzer notes an interesting parallel between Isaiah 45:14 and 52:15.[122] The former passage is a throne scene in which Cyrus receives the homage paid to him by representatives of foreign countries. The LORD says to Cyrus, **"They pass above you"** (עָלַיִךְ יַעֲבֹרוּ, *'ālayik ya'ăḇōrû*), the preposition "above" (עַל, *'al*) indicating that Cyrus is seated on his throne. The foreigners come in chains, bringing him products of their countries and prostrating themselves before him.

The scene in Isaiah 52:15 is similar in one significant point, yet different in others. Here again the preposition עַל is used. Although a

---

[119] James B. Pritchard, *The Ancient Near East in Pictures Relating to the Old Testament*, 2d ed. (Princeton: Princeton University Press, 1969), figure 463, p. 159, cf. p. 303. This bas relief is from Persepolis, an ancient capital of Persia, the ruins of which are in what is today S. Iran.

[120] Waltke, "The Real Value of Jesus Christ," 5 (pagination is that of transcribed manuscript).

[121] Cf. Benjamin Wills Newton, "Notes on Isaiah LII.13 to end, and on Isaiah LIII," in *Thoughts on Scriptural Subjects* (London: Houlston and Sons, 1871), 175-225 (esp. 185).

[122] Klaus Baltzer, *Deutero-Isaiah*, trans. Margaret Kohl, Hermeneia (Minneapolis: Fortress, 2001), 399-400. He translates 45:14, "[They] pass in front of you" (238). Of this usage *HALOT*, s.v. "עַל," 1:825, says, "in front of, before: used whenever one person stands and the other sits."

number of the versions have **"Kings will shut their mouths on account of him,"** or words to that effect (NASB, NIV, ESV), Baltzer translates, "Above/over him kings will shut their mouths."[123] The use of the preposition "above him" (עָלָיו, 'ālāyw) is important because it "implies that the Servant is now sitting on a throne."[124] The scene here differs, however, with that in Isaiah 45. The kings here do not prostrate themselves before the Servant; nor do they bring him gifts; or come in chains. The scene depicted here is "a friendly reception of foreigners." They show reverential awe in the Servant's presence, yet they are there "without compulsion." The picture is of the kings of redeemed ("sprinkled") Gentiles who appear before the King of Kings to pay him honor.[125]

The reason for the positive response of the kings is the "sprinkling of the nations which results in a new understanding of the Servant."[126] **"For what had not been told them they will see, and what they had not heard they will understand."**[127] The Septuagint renders the perfect verbs "see" (רָאוּ, rā'û)[128] and "understand" (הִתְבּוֹנָנוּ, hitbônānû)[129] in the future tense, "will see" (ὄψονται, opsontai) and "will understand" (συνήσουσιν, sunēsousin).[130] Goldingay and Payne conclude that the verbs "surely do refer to future events; the seeing and considering have not yet taken place, but their being qatal reflects the fact that they will precede and lead to the shutting of the mouth."[131] Koole translates,

---

[123] Baltzer, *Deutero-Isaiah*, 398.

[124] Baltzer, *Deutero-Isaiah*, 400.

[125] Cf. Unger, *Unger's Commentary on the Old Testament*, 1295.

[126] Smith, *Isaiah 40–66*, 440.

[127] The apostle Paul applies these words to the mission to the Gentiles during the present age. As Lindsey suggested, however, the ultimate fulfillment of verse 15 relates to "Gentiles of the end time who understand and accept the Servant's person and redemptive work, resulting in their salvation and entrance into the blessing of the millennial kingdom" (*The Servant Songs*, 110).

[128] The form רָאוּ is 3d per. pl. qal perf. of רָאה.

[129] The form הִתְבּוֹנָנוּ is 3d pers. pl. hithpolel perf. of בִּין.

[130] The qatals (perfects) are taken to be futures in most English versions (e.g., KJV, Darby, NASB, NIV, NRSV, TEV, HCSB, NET).

[131] Goldingay and Payne, *Isaiah 40–55*, 2: 296. As noted above, the perfect tense is also referred to as the qatal. In verse 15 the verbs are future perfects "(a future state ['will see'…'will understand'] resulting from an action ['will sprinkle'] that will have been completed by that time." See: Ronald J. Williams, *WHSB*, 67, § 162.4; cf. P. Joüon and T. Muraoka, *JMGBH*, 335, § 112 g-i.

"Kings will shut their mouth...for they will have seen what was not told to them and understood what they had not heard."[132]

The REB grasps the significance of what the kings will see and understand. They will see "what they had never been told," and their minds will be full "of things unheard of before." Westermann agreed with this interpretive rendering. "The event in question is literally 'unheard of.'" Isaiah, he writes, "does more that just accentuate the high degree of astonishment. Instead, the Servant's exaltation is a thing without precedent. It is epoch-making in its importance."[133]

He explains:

> "That a man who was smitten, who was marred beyond human semblance, and who was despised in the eyes of God and men should be given such approval and significance, and be thus exalted, is in very truth something new and unheard of, going against tradition and all men's settled ideas. Verse 15b also makes clear that the thing reported in this servant song is thought of as something absolutely unique."[134]

CONCLUSION

In the first stanza of the fourth servant song, Yahweh announces the exaltation of his servant because he has successfully carried out his mission. The servant's task was accomplished at a horrible cost—his physical disfigurement—causing those who saw it to be appalled. As a result of his disfigurement, however, many were to be spiritually delivered and cleansed of their sins.

In the end time the kings of the earth will appear before the Servant and pay him honor. They will understand what he has accomplished through his sufferings. The response of the kings can only be described as

---

132 Koole, *Isaiah III*, 271.

133 Westermann, *Isaiah 40–66*, 259-60.

134 "It cannot therefore be explained as arising out of anything that recurs, such as the cult of a dying and rising God" (Westermann, *Isaiah 40–66*, 260). Westermann here alludes to the view of Engnell and others that the Servant's resurrection and exaltation are notions borrowed from the liturgies of the Sumero-Akkadian god Tammuz, who died and rose annually. The Servant's exaltation, however, is unique and unheard of, while the Tammuz cult was well-known. See Engnell, "The 'Ebed Yahweh Songs and the Suffering Messiah in 'Deutero-Isaiah,'" 54-93 (esp. 55-59).

a complete reevaluation of the values that prevail in the world today. As one commentator notes, such reevaluation "is relevant for peoples and kings, but it is relevant too and above all for 'the many' at all times."[135]

Such a reevaluation of values is imperative in the present era of secularism, relativism, atheism, and pervasive unbelief—unbelief that has made great inroads into the professing church itself. What would Isaiah encourage his modern readers to do? He would, no doubt, echo the words of the Lord, **"Behold My servant."** "Behold him in his horrific sufferings, and behold him in his glorious exaltation.

The great Puritan theologian John Owen (1616–83) says that all of the prophecies and predictions of Jesus Christ in the Old Testament may be grouped under two headings: his sufferings, and the glory that resulted from them.[136] In this assessment he followed the apostle Peter, who said the prophets spoke of **"the sufferings of Christ and the glories to follow"** (1 Pet. 1:11). The Lord Jesus himself expressed the same thought, **"Was it not necessary for the Messiah to suffer these things and to enter into His glory?"** (Luke 24:26). The apostle Paul, surely echoing Isaiah 52:13–53:12, says that Christ Jesus **"humbled Himself by becoming obedient to the point of death,"** and, as a result, **"God highly exalted Him"** (Phil. 2:8-9). Somber reflection upon this text in Isaiah 52 should lead believers to a deeper understanding of the work of Christ, a more joyful adoration of the person of Christ, and a more hope-oriented obedience to Christ's call **"Follow Me"** (Matt. 16:24), for **"if we died with Him, we will also live with Him; if we endure, we will also reign with Him"** (2 Tim. 2:11-12).

---

[135] Baltzer, *Deutero-Isaiah*, 400.

[136] John Owen, "Meditations and Discourses on the Glory of Christ, In His Person, Office, and Grace" in *The Works of John Owen*, ed. William H. Gould (London: Johnstone and Hunter, 1850–53; reprint ed., London: Banner of Truth, 1965), 1: 273-415 (see esp. chapter 7, "The Glory of Christ in His Exaltation," 342-47).

CHAPTER 2

ISRAEL'S REJECTION

OF THE SERVANT OF THE LORD:

ISAIAH 53:1-3

INTRODUCTION[1]

Old Testament scholar, Bruce Waltke, tells a story about one of his cousins in New York. His cousin told Bruce of his family's vacation in Maine. They were all "rock hounds" and had gone to Maine to look for tourmaline crystals, which are semiprecious stones. One day they were searching in an abandoned granite quarry, the bottom of which was covered with water. They were standing on stones in the water chipping away at the granite and limestone looking for the crystals. As they worked, his wife saw the gleam of a crystal. She took a hammer, carefully worked around the crystal, and at last the gem popped out. It was the largest tourmaline stone that everyone working there had ever seen. The crystal was several inches long and worth hundreds of dollars.

She gave the crystal to her seven-year-old son and told him to take it back to the car and put it in the box where they were to keep any gems that they might find. The boy began to walk across the rocks toward the car when he saw a frog. He took the gem and threw it at the frog, and the gem sank into the water. The family spent the rest of the day fruitlessly looking in the muck for the crystal. So far as they know, it is still at the bottom of an old abandoned granite quarry somewhere in Maine. Obviously, the little boy had no appreciation for the value of that stone, and he just threw it away.

---

[1] The introduction to this essay is adapted from Bruce K. Waltke, "The Real Value of Jesus Christ: An Exposition of Isaiah 52:13–53:12" (Dallas: Believers Chapel Tape Ministry, n.d.), 1. The pagination is that of the writer's own typed transcription of Dr. Waltke's sermon. The introduction is used with permission from Bruce K. Waltke, Distinguished Professor of Old Testament at Knox Theological Seminary, Fort Lauderdale, Florida.

One of the most challenging tasks in raising children is helping them to develop an appreciation for those things that are truly valuable and excellent in life. Every parent has known the frustration of seeing his or her child reject that which is really valuable for that which is not valuable—that which is, in fact, "junk."

Sadly most adults show less discernment than that little seven-year-old boy. Far more valuable than any gem is the person and work of Jesus Christ, which is immeasurable; its value cannot be measured in terms of silver, gold, diamonds, or crystals. Yet thousands and thousands of people are taking this most precious of gifts that God has provided and are literally throwing it away. The reason the great majority of people bypass it, reject it, or throw it away is that they have no appreciation for who Jesus Christ really is and what he has done.

The goal of this monograph is to assist writer and reader alike to understand the real value of Jesus Christ. In Isaiah 52:13–53:12, God the Father tells us the inestimable value he places upon Jesus Christ.

Chapter 1 of our study was an exposition of the prologue, the first strophe or stanza of Isaiah's great "Servant Song." In those verses (52:13–15) Isaiah gave Yahweh's summary of the Servant's successful work. He accomplished the work of the cross and was exalted in reward for his work. In verse 15 Isaiah wrote that Christ will **"sprinkle many nations,"** i.e., he will carry out his priestly work of cleansing their sins. Then he said that at Christ's second advent the kings of the nations will be silenced in awe and veneration before him. They will understand and accept the truth of the gospel resulting in their salvation and enjoyment of kingdom blessings in the millennial age.[2]

Following this summary of the Servant's career, the poem continues with the second strophe in chapter 53, verses 1-3. The chapter break in our English Bibles is unfortunate in one sense, because chapter 53 continues the poem begun in 52:13-15. Yet the break is justified in another sense in that verses 13-15 are the prologue to the poem. Those verses are the introduction, while chapter 53 is the main body of the fourth Servant Song.[3]

---

[2] Merrill F. Unger, *Unger's Commentary on the Old Testament* (Chicago: Moody, 1981; reprint ed., Chattanooga, TN: AMG Publishers, 2002), 1295.

[3] Henri Blocher, *Songs of the Servant: Isaiah's Good News* (London: Inter-Varsity, 1975; reprint ed., Vancouver, BC: Regent College, 2005), 62.

The second strophe is written from the vantage point of the Servant's exaltation in his yet future kingdom. The speakers are the future remnant of Israelites,[4] who will turn in faith to the Messiah at his second advent.[5] They confess or lament that their countrymen did not

_____

[4] There have been at least seven explanations as to the identity of the speaker or speakers in verse 1: (1) The Gentile kings and nations of 52:15, who, in their confession, reveal their new understanding of the Servant's suffering. [James Muilenburg, "Isaiah: Introduction and Exegesis," in *IntB*, 5:619; Roy F. Melugin, *The Formation of Isaiah 40–55* (Berlin: Walter de Gruyter, 1976), 167]. This view is unlikely; the kings and nations are surprised by the Servant's atoning work and exaltation because they had not previously heard of it, whereas the speakers in verse 1 have heard of it and the redemptive actions are already accomplished facts when they speak. Furthermore, whenever there is an abrupt introduction of "we" [1st pers. pl.] into a prophecy in Isaiah, it is always Israel that speaks [16:6; 24:16; 42:24; 64:5-6]. Cf. J. Skinner, *The Book of Isaiah the Prophet, Chapters XL–LXVI*, CBSC [Cambridge: Cambridge University Press, 1954], 136; Franz Delitzsch, *Biblical Commentary on the Prophecies of Isaiah*, trans. James Martin [Edinburgh: T. & T. Clark, 1877], 2:309–10; Brevard S. Childs, *Isaiah*, OTL (Louisville: Westminster John Knox, 2001), 413]. (2) The prophet Isaiah, who expresses dismay over the widespread unbelief of the Servant's redemptive message [E. W. Hengstenberg, *Christology of the Old Testament*, trans. Theodore Meyer and James Martin (Edinburgh: T. & T. Clark, 1878), 2:275; Edward J. Young, *The Book of Isaiah*, NICOT (Grand Rapids: Eerdmans, 1972), 3:340]. The problem with this view is that the speakers are spoken of in the third person plural. (3) The "prosecuting counsel" ["Satan'?] who formulates objections to Yahweh's speech in 52:14-15. [This peculiar view takes its clues from two Old Testament "law court scenes," viz., Zechariah 3 and Job 1; see Klaus Baltzer, *Deutero-Isaiah*, Herm, trans. Margaret Kohl (Minneapolis: Fortress, 2001), 401–402]. (4) The prophet, i.e., the unknown author of "second Isaiah." [Christopher North, *The Second Isaiah* (London: Oxford University Press, 1964), 236]. (5) The prophet's disciples or friends, exiles in Babylon, here write retrospectively of the servant's [Deutero-Isaiah's] death, [Peter Wilcox and David Paton-Williams, "The Servant Songs in Deutero-Isaiah," *JSOT* 42 (1988): 79–102 (esp. 98)] or his deliverance from trouble. [R. N. Whybray, *Thanksgiving for a Liberated People*, JSOTSS 4 (Sheffield: University of Sheffield, 1978), 134; idem., *Isaiah 40–66*, NCBC (London: Marshall, Morgan, and Scott, 1981), 171–72]. The view of Wilcox and Paton-Williams assumes that the death of a sinful prophet would bring forgiveness to the people, and Whybray unsuccessfully sidesteps and denies the passage's clear description of substitutionary atonement. (6) The believing remnant of Israelites in the period immediately after the cross and Pentecost. [H. C. Leupold, *Exposition of Isaiah* (Grand Rapids: Baker, 1971), 2:225–226]. (7) The future remnant of Israel who will turn in faith to Messiah at his second advent. [Moses Margoliouth, *The Penitential Hymn of Judah and Israel After the Spirit: An Exposition of the Fifty-Third Chapter of Isaiah*, 2d ed. (London: Longman, Brown, Green, and Longmans, 1856), 12–13; Delitzsch, 2:311; Unger, *Unger's Commentary on the Old Testament*, 1295]. Delitzsch wrote, "All that follows is the confession of the Israel of the last times."

[5] "When the chorus which now follows describes the events of which the Servant is the center, it does so in retrospect; it therefore expresses insights which could only be seen

appreciate the real value of the Servant of the LORD when he appeared on earth. Their superficial estimation of him led them to reject him. He was "totally misunderstood because of his seeming insignificance."[6] This strophe (vv. 1-3) focuses on Israel's rejection of the Servant during his lifetime. They failed to recognize the value of the Servant and his work.

ISRAEL REJECTED THE MESSAGE OF THE SERVANT, VERSE 1[7]

Who has believed our message?
And to whom has the arm of the LORD been revealed?

THE ESCHATOLOGICAL LAMENT THAT SO FEW BELIEVED THE MESSAGE IN WORDS

The strophe begins with two rhetorical questions. The first question is, **"Who has believed our message?"** (NASB, NIV). This wording suggests that it is the prophets speaking. However, it is better rendered, "Who has believed the things heard by us?" or "Who has believed what we have heard?" (NRSV, HCSB), or "Who has believed the report we have heard?"[8] The implied answer to this rhetorical question is, "No-one."[9]

---

from an eschatological standpoint" (Gerhard von Rad, *The Message of the Prophets*, trans. D. M. G. Stalker [New York: Harper and Row, 1965], 223; idem., *Old Testament Theology*, trans. D. M. G. Stalker [New York: Harper and Row, 1965], 2:256).

[6] Leupold, *Exposition of Isaiah*, 2:225.

[7] The outline of this exposition is adapted from Robert D. Culver, *The Sufferings and Glory of The LORD's Righteous Servant* (Moline: Christian Service Foundation, 1958), 39–59. Also see F. Duane Lindsey, *The Servant Songs: A Study in Isaiah* (Chicago: Moody, 1985), 112–117.

[8] *HALOT*, s.v. "שְׁמוּעָה," 2:1156. As Goldingay and Payne note, the noun שְׁמוּעָה "always denotes a report received rather than one given" (John Goldingay and David Payne, *Isaiah 40–55*, ICC [London: T. & T. Clark, 2006], 2:297). Cf. Delitzsch, *Biblical Commentary on the Prophecies of Isaiah*, 2:311. Delitzsch says the noun "signifies the hearing...the tidings...i.e., the hearsay which we have heard." Cf. John N. Oswalt, *The Book of Isaiah, Chapters 40–66*, NICOT (Grand Rapids: Eerdmans, 1998), 374; Blocher, *Songs of the Servant*, 62.

[9] GKC, 476–77, § 151a; North, *The Second Isaiah*, 236; Goldingay and Payne, *Isaiah 40–55*, 2:297. That "No-one" is the implied answer to the question is clear. Yet the text contains a *"double intimation"* that some [the remnant] believed, while the majority did not. Cf. Carl Wilhelm Eduard Nägelsbach, *The Prophet Isaiah*, trans. Samuel T. Lowrie and Dunlop Moore, in *CHS (L)*, 11: 574. Goldingay concurred, "By implication, things have changed now, but the words look back to the moment when no one believed" (John Goldingay, *The Message of Isaiah 40–55* [London: T. & T. Clark, 2005], 494).

The substance of the report is the preaching that was common among the Jewish people in the aftermath of Golgotha, namely, "the exaltation of the servant of God from a state of deep degradation."[10] The content of the report is set forth in [greater] detail in the following stanzas of the poem (vv. 1-11).[11]

It is not the prophet who is speaking, but the Israelites of the end time who look back to their ancestors in Jesus' time and wonder that so few of them believed[12] the message of the Servant.[13] In his epistle to the Romans, the apostle Paul expressed the same sorrow and grief over the Israelites of his day who would not believe (Rom. 9:1-5). The number of Jewish believers was "vanishingly small" when compared with the mass of unbelievers in the nation (Rom. 10:16).[14]

This entire prophecy is filled with sadness and lamentation over Israel's reception of the Servant. George Adam Smith noted that the Servant himself is only mentioned twice (52:13; 53:11).

> Most wonderful and mysterious of all is the spectral fashion in which the prophecy presents its Hero. He is named only in the

---

[10] Delitzsch, *Biblical Commentary on the Prophecies of Isaiah*, 2:311.

[11] Goldingay and Payne, *Isaiah 40–55*, Volume II, 297.

[12] The verb אָמַן in the hiphil stem when followed as here by ל means "to regard something as trustworthy, to believe in, to give credence to." See *HALOT*, s.v. "אָמַן," 1:64. Goldingay notes, "Most significantly, the theme of (dis)belief in Yhwh's word is a recurrent one through chs. 40–55, and it is one that consistently relates to the people of God, not to the nations" (*The Message of Isaiah 40–55*, 494).

[13] Some take the verb הֶאֱמִין (3d msc. sg. hiphil perf. אָמַן) as a subjunctive, "Who could have believed what we heard?" (REB; cf. NET, TEV). The thought communicated by such an understanding of the verb is that the message contained such astonishing elements that it would be hard for anyone to believe (Joseph Blenkinsopp, *Isaiah 40–55*, AncB [New York: Doubleday, 2002], 345; Gary V. Smith, *Isaiah 40–66*, NAC [Nashville: Broadman, Holman, 2009), 443–44). This view would be more likely if the issue at stake was the astonishment of the nations (so: G. W. Wade, *The Book of the Prophet Isaiah*, WC [London: Methuen, n.d.], 338). However, the speakers are Israelites who confess that their knowledge came from divine revelation and was trustworthy, and they believed it (Brevard S. Childs, *Isaiah*, OTL [Louisville: Westminster John Knox, 2001], 413–14). Another argument in favor of the translation favored here is the Septuagint's aorist ἐπίστευσε ("who believed?").

[14] Delitzsch, *Biblical Commentary on the Prophecies of Isaiah*, 2:311. In Paul's quotation of Isaiah 53:1 in Romans 10:16 it is the prophet Isaiah who laments that his hearers will not believe, while in the Hebrew original it is those who hear the good tidings who lament the unbelief of their countrymen. Cf. Christopher R. North, *The Second Isaiah* (London: Oxford University Press, 1964), 236.

first line and once again: elsewhere He is spoken of as He. We
never hear or see Himself. But all the more solemnly is He there:
a shadow upon countless faces, a grievous memory on the hearts
of the speakers. He so haunts all we see and all we hear, that we
feel it is not Art, but Conscience, that speaks of Him.[15]

THE ESCHATOLOGICAL LAMENT THAT SO FEW BELIEVED THE MESSAGE IN WORKS

The second rhetorical question is: **"And to whom has the arm of the
LORD** (יהוה, Yahweh) **been revealed?"** This translation, that of the
NASB, is similar to many English versions (Darby, KJV, NIV, ESV,
HCSB, NRSV). Goldingay and Payne offer a more compelling
translation,[16] "Upon whom[17] did the arm of the LORD reveal itself?"
This indicates that there was another message which Israel rejected
besides the spoken one. The second line of verse 1 refers "to facts or
works, as the first does to words."[18]

   The expression "arm (זְרוֹעַ [$z^erôa'$, literally "forearm"],[19] of the
LORD" is generally taken as "a metaphor of military power; [picturing]
the LORD as a warrior who bares his arm, takes up his weapon, and
crushes his enemies (cf. 14:26-27; 30:30; Isa. 51:9-10; 63:5-6).[20] That
interpretation does not fit the present context. What is described is not
warlike activity. Here "Yahweh bares his arm 'like a man setting out to
do a job.'"[21] In the present context it speaks of Yahweh's power to save

---

[15] George Adam Smith, *The Book of Isaiah*, ExpB (New York: Armstrong, 1903), 2:341–42.

[16] Goldingay and Payne, *Isaiah 40–55*, Volume II, 296–298.

[17] The prepositional phrase עַל־מִי is best rendered here "upon whom" (BDB, s.v. "עַל," 757). "To" is a possible translation of עַל, but עַל "is not the obvious preposition to use to convey this meaning" (Goldingay and Payne, *Isaiah 40–55*, 2:297).

[18] William Urwick, עֶבֶד יְהוָה: *The Servant of Jehovah: A Commentary, Grammatical and Critical Upon Isaiah LII.13 to LIII.12* (Edinburgh: T. & T. Clark, 1877), 109.

[19] A. S. van der Woude, "זְרוֹעַ," in *TLOT*, 1:392.

[20] NET Bible, note on Isaiah 53:1. Cf. Baltzer, *Deutero-Isaiah*, 403; F. J. Helfmeyer, "זְרוֹעַ," *TDOT*, 4:131–40; Manfred Dreytza, "זְרוֹעַ," *NIDOTTE*, 1:1146–47.

[21] Helfmeyer, "זְרוֹעַ," 136. Dreytza notes that when used metaphorically it always involves a dynamic connotation: "It is the instrument of human working (Isa. 17:5; 40:10) and fighting (Gen. 49:24; Ps. 18:34). See "זְרוֹעַ,"1146.

or deliver his people (cf. 40:10; 52:10; 63:12).[22] Specifically, the arm of the LORD was revealed in the works of the Servant.[23]

How was God's power revealed in the Servant's life? This has reference to the miracles that Jesus performed. His contemporaries saw him feeding thousands (Matt. 14:21; 15:38), raising the dead (John 11:38-44), and healing many (Matt. 4:24-25). The Lord pointed to his many miracles as evidence that he was the promised Messiah (Luke 7:18-23). The Jewish leaders would accept none of it. When Jesus healed a

---

[22] Cf. *HALOT*, s.v. "זְרוֹעַ," 1:280. See Smith, *Isaiah 40–66*, 444, n. 349. So also: Delitzsch, *Biblical Commentary on the Prophecies of Isaiah*, 2:311; Young, *The Book of Isaiah*, 3:341; J. Ridderbos, *Isaiah*, trans. John Vriend, BSC (Grand Rapids: Eerdmans, 1985), 473. Calvin's editor noted, "All commentators of antiquity refer 'arm' to Christ." In the sixteenth century, Calvin and others rejected the ancient view. Cf. John Calvin, *Sermon's on Isaiah's Prophecy*, ed. T. H. L. Parker (London: James Clarke, 1956), 46, n. 2; idem., *Commentary on the Book of the Prophet Isaiah*, trans. William Pringle (Edinburgh: Calvin Translation Society, 1850), 3:112. A small but significant number of modern commentators have resurrected the ancient view and have argued that Isaiah here hypostatized (i.e., treated the idea as a real person) "the Arm" and identified the Arm of the LORD as the Servant himself. See Edward J. Kissane, *The Book of Isaiah* (Dublin: Browne and Nolan, 1943), 2:185; J. Alec Motyer, *The Prophecy of Isaiah: An Introduction and Commentary* (Downers Grove: Inter Varsity Press, 1993), 427; Oswalt, *The Book of Isaiah, Chapters 40–66*, 375; H. G. M. Williamson, *Variations on a Theme: King, Messiah and Servant in the Book of Isaiah* (Carlisle, UK: Paternoster, 1998), 164; Eugene Robert Ekblad Jr., *Isaiah's Servant Poems According to the Septuagint* (Leuven, Belgium: Peeters, 1999), 197; Goldingay and Payne, *Isaiah 40–55*, 2:298. Among early writers who identified the arm of the LORD as the Servant are: Tertullian (Against Praxeas 13), Jerome (Homilies on the Psalms 67, Alternate Series [Psalm 90]), Augustine (Sermon 363.2; Tractates on the Gospel of John 48.7; 53.2, 3), Caesarius of Aries (Sermon 163.2). For documentation, see Thomas C. Oden, *Ancient Christian Commentary on Scripture*, Old Testament XI: *Isaiah 40–66*, ed., Mark W. Elliott (Downers Grove: Inter Varsity Press, 2007), 157–58. For documentation of the same view in Eusebius (334, 30-32) and Cyril (70, 1169 D), see Johanna Manley, ed., *Isaiah Through the Ages* (Menlo Park, CA: Monastery Books, 1995), 782, n.5. See the following texts: Tertullian, *Against Praxeas* 13, in *ANF*, 3:607–8. Jerome, *Homilies on the Psalms* 67 [on Psalm 90 (LXX Ps. 89)], trans. Sister Marie Liguori Ewald, in *FC*, 57:80. Augustine, Sermon 363 [on Ex. 15:1-21], trans. Edmund Hill, in WSA III/10, 272–73. Idem., *Tractates on the Gospel of John* 48.7 [on John 10:22-42], in *FC*, 88:233–34. On p. 234 Augustine writes, "The hand of the Father is the Son himself." Idem., *Tractates on the Gospel of John* 53.2-3 [on John 12:37-43], in *FC*, 88:290–92. On p. 290 he writes, "Here he shows well that the Son of God was himself called the arm of God." On p. 292 he writes, "Therefore, let them understand how the Son has been called the arm of the Father, through which the Father effected all his works." Caesarius of Arles, Sermon 163.2 [on Luke 15:11-32], *FC*, 47:386–87.

[23] Helfmeyer, "זְרוֹעַ," 136.

demon-possessed man, they said he did so with the power of the devil (Matt. 12:24).

That this interpretation of the "arm of the LORD" is correct is evident because of John 12:37-38, **"But though He had performed so many signs before them, yet they were not believing in Him. This was to fulfill the word of Isaiah the prophet which he spoke: 'LORD, who has believed our report? And to whom has the arm of the LORD been revealed?'"**[24]

The contrast between this verse and the one that precedes it is significant. The Gentiles receive with faith things which they had never heard or seen before, whereas Israel has to lament that she put no faith in the good news she had heard long before—not only from the lips and works of Jesus, but from her own prophets and Scriptures. The prophets foretold the Servant of the LORD, his place of birth, his lowly birth, his substitutionary sufferings, and his glorious exaltation. Yet Israel did not believe.

As has been noted in chapter 1, the Jews in the Talmud and other writings of the Rabbis universally agreed that Isaiah 53 was a prophecy of the Messiah. For over 1,000 years after the death of Christ—from the second to the twelfth centuries—they gave this interpretation. After terrible persecutions at the time of Crusades, they gradually gave up the interpretation and began to teach that Israel was the Servant of Isaiah 53. Another reason they gave up the Messianic interpretation is that many Jews had become convinced that it was a cogent and strong argument for the Christian position and had converted to the Christian faith.[25] Avoidance of the passage altogether has led to its being called *carnificina Rabbinorum* (Lat., "the torture chamber, or rack, of the Rabbis").[26]

---

[24] Culver, *The Sufferings and Glory of The LORD's Righteous Servant*, 45. Others have argued that the arm of the LORD is a reference to the content of "our message" "(i.e., God's salvation provided through the sacrificial, substitutionary death of the Servant) or to the power of Yahweh in the Holy Spirit effecting faith in those who respond to the message (i.e., efficacious grace)." Lindsey, *The Servant Songs*, 114; cf. Calvin, *Commentary on the Book of the Prophet Isaiah*, 4:112–13; Young, *The Book of Isaiah*, 3:341.

[25] Joel E. Rembaum, "The Development of a Jewish Exegetical Tradition Regarding Isaiah 53," *HTR* 75 (1982): 289–211 (esp. 292–93); Victor Buksbazen, *The Prophet Isaiah: A Commentary* (Collingworth, NJ: Spearhead Press, 1971; reprint ed., Bellmawr, NJ: Friends of Israel Gospel Ministry, 2008), 402. Buksbazen notes that after fighting the pagan Muslims in Palestine, the Crusaders turned upon "the Christ-killing Jews" of Europe.

[26] Delitzsch, *Biblical Commentary on the Prophecies of Isaiah*, 2:311.

In August of each year, the synagogue Scripture reading from the prophets is taken from the book of Isaiah. Around the third Sabbath in August, the reading ends at Isaiah 52:12, just three verses before the end of that chapter. On the next Sabbath the reading picks up at Isaiah 54:1, omitting Isaiah 52:13–53:12 from the readings of the prophets in the synagogue. [This] important passage is *never* read in the synagogue.[27]

Jewish-Christian commentator, Victor Buksbazen explains, "Because of the striking parallel between the suffering Messiah of the amazing prophecy and its remarkable fulfillment in the person of Jesus, Isaiah 53 has been excluded from the Sabbath readings of the Prophets in the synagogue, known as the Haftorah. Some have called Isaiah 53 'the secret chapter,' or 'the guilty conscience of the synagogue.'"[28]

The writer notes these things because this passage suggests that Israel will one day again see Christ in Isaiah 53. The prophet Zechariah agreed. He wrote prophetically the words of Jesus in the end-time: "**They will look on Me whom they have pierced; and they will mourn for Him, as one mourns for an only son, and they will weep bitterly over Him like the bitter weeping over a firstborn**" (Zech. 12:10).[29] Isaiah 53, says Delitzsch, is "one of the greatest prophecies of the future conversion of the nation, which has rejected the servant of God, and allowed the Gentiles to be the first to recognize him. At last, though very late, it will

---

[27] Will Varner, "Of Whom Speaketh the Prophet This?" *Israel My Glory* (December, 1994), 16–18 (esp. 16); idem., *The Messiah: Revealed, Rejected, Received* (Bloomington, Author House, 2004), 82; cf. Risto Santala, "The Suffering Messiah 53 in the Light of Rabbinic Literature," *The Springfielder* 39 (March, 1976): 177–82 (esp. 177–78). McCaul argued that four expressions in three verses from Isaiah 52:13–53:12 are distinctly quoted in the synagogue every year at the feast of Passover: (1) "He shall deal prudently" ["shall act wisely"], 52:13. (2) "He shall be exalted, extolled, and be high," 52:13. (3) "He shall sprinkle many nations, 52:15. (4) "[He that is now] despised," 53:3. See A. McCaul, *The Doctrine and Interpretation of the Fifty-Third Chapter of Isaiah* (London: London Society's House, 1888), 22–23. Cf. David Levi, מכל השנה כמנהג פלין מחזור: *The Festival Prayers, According to the Ritual of the German and Polish Jews*, vol. 5: מחזור של פסח: *Service for the Feast of Passover* (London: H. Abrahams, 1859), 55.

[28] Buksbazen, *The Prophet Isaiah*, 409.

[29] The parallels between Zechariah 12 and Isaiah 53 have been noted by a number of commentators. See David Baron, *The Visions and Prophecies of Zechariah* (London: Hebrew Christian Testimony to Israel, 1918; reprint ed., Grand Rapids: Kregel, 1972), 450; Merrill F. Unger, *Zechariah: Prophet of Messiah's Glory* (Grand Rapids: Zondervan, 1963), 218.

feel remorse. And when this shall once take place, then and not till then will this chapter…receive its complete historical fulfillment."[30]

ISRAEL REJECTED THE PERSON OF THE SERVANT, VERSE 2

> For He grew up before Him like a tender shoot,
> And like a root out of parched ground;
> He has no stately form or majesty
> That we should look upon Him,
> Nor appearance that we should be attracted to Him.

In verse 2 Israel explains the cause of their unbelief. It was the ordinariness of the Servant, "his unassuming appearance," and his lack of outward attractiveness.[31] Israel laments and confesses that they did not place any value on Jesus as he grew up before them.

It should be noted that there have always been Jews who have believed and have borne witness to Christ. Paul called them "a remnant" (Rom. 11:5), and that remnant included Matthew, Mark, John, Peter and others in the first century, and many others down to the present day.

It should also be noted that while Israel did not place any value on the Servant, there was One who did. Verse 2 reads, "**He grew up before Him.**" The "him" in question is, of course, Yahweh, the LORD of whom they have just spoken in verse 1.[32] "God the Father had his eye ever fixed upon the Son with watchfulness and tenderness and love."[33]

In any case, Israel confesses that *they* were not impressed with the Servant during his earthly life. "There was nothing," Israel says, "that attracted us to Him."

THEY WERE UNIMPRESSED WITH HIS RUSTIC ORIGINS, VERSE 2A

In the confession/lament/report that follows, there is unfolded the whole earthly life story of the Servant, beginning with his youth, developing

---

[30] Delitzsch, *Biblical Commentary on the Prophecies of Isaiah*, 2:311.

[31] C. von Orelli, *The Prophecies of Isaiah*, trans. J. S. Banks (Edinburgh: T. & T. Clark, 1895), 291.

[32] "The obvious meaning of this phrase (לְפָנָיו, *lepānâw*, "before him") is "in Yahweh's presence" (Whybray, *Isaiah 40–66*, 173).

[33] G. Rawlinson, "Isaiah: Exposition," in *PC*, 10:294.

into his manhood of suffering, and culminating in his violent death, royal burial, and glorious resurrection.[34]

"For He grew up before Him like a tender shoot (כַּיּוֹנֵק, *kayyônēq*), and like a root (וְכַשֹּׁרֶשׁ, *wᵉkaššōreš*) out of parched ground." The expression "tender shoot" is from the word (יוֹנֵק, *yônēq*) meaning "suckling." It is used several times in the OT of a suckling, a baby that is breast-fed (Num. 11:12; Deut. 32:25; 1 Sam. 15:3, etc.),[35] but here it is used in a horticultural sense of "a tender twig that sucks up its nourishment from the root and stem."[36] The word translated "root" (שֹׁרֶשׁ, *šōreš*) probably has here the sense "shoot," "stock" or "stem."[37] **"For he grew up before him like a tender plant, like a stem from dry soil."** This suggests the lowly character of his origins. During the "hidden years" of Christ, i.e., the years before his public ministry, "He was known by Yahweh though unknown by the world."[38]

His origins were not what Israel expected of the coming Messiah. He was born of a mother, to use her own words, of **"humble state"** (NASB, NIV) or "humble condition" (Luke 1:48, HCSB). He did not grow up in the capital city in a royal palace like Moses. He grew up in a remote village, in a carpenter's home, with a carpenter's vocation. Culver says, He was "a 'back-woods' character—just another little bush from the back side of the blackberry patch" so far as his countrymen were concerned.[39] Even his fellow townspeople were unimpressed. In fact, Luke says they were **"filled with rage"** (Luke 4:28) that the carpenter's son (Luke 4:22) would dare preach to them in a confrontational way. "Who," they no doubt thought, "does he think he is?"

---

[34] Baron, *The Servant of Jehovah*, 69; Smith, *Isaiah 40–66*, 443.

[35] Cf. *HALOT*, s.v. "יוֹנֵק," 1:402.

[36] Delitzsch, *Biblical Commentary on the Prophecies of Isaiah*, 2:312.

[37] The Hebrew word שֹׁרֶשׁ is commonly translated "root" in Isaiah 53:2 (Darby, NRSV, REB, NET, NASB, ESV, NIV, HCSB). H. L. Ginsberg has argued that שֹׁרֶשׁ is not to be understood solely as the root of a plant or tree, but also as its stock or stem ("'Roots below and Fruit Above' and Related Matters," in *Hebrew and Semitic Studies Presented to Godfrey Rolles Driver*, eds. D. Winton Thomas and W. D. McHardy [Oxford: Oxford University Press, 1963], 72–76). A. R. Millard has applied this observation to Isaiah 53:2, arguing that "stem" or "stock" better conveys the idea of a new growth from the ground than does "root." See "Notes: Isaiah 53:2," *TynB* 20 (1969): 127. The TEV's "taking root in dry ground" also conveys the idea of newness.

[38] Lindsey, *The Servant Songs*, 114.

[39] Culver, *The Sufferings and Glory of The LORD's Righteous Servant*, 48.

When Israel described a king, they would use the metaphor of a flourishing tree. The dynasty of King David was portrayed as a cedar (Ezek. 17:22-23); in Judges 9 the king is portrayed as a fig tree covered with sweet fruit or an olive tree covered with olives (vv. 9-10); and in the Song of Solomon the beloved is described as a fruitful apple tree.

The Jews expected that splendor from the beginning, and because he didn't have it, they despised him.[40] All they saw in Jesus was a tiny, helpless twig. Robert Culver draws an important spiritual lesson from the fact that Jesus spent most of his lifetime living in an obscure place working as a common man in an ordinary trade. He wrote, "Though [his] hidden life...was an offense to them, it should be a blessing to us, for it sanctified forever the obscure tasks that common people do and the humble places in which common people dwell." Jesus came to do his father's will, and his father's will for thirty years was that he work in an out-of-the-way village as a carpenter.[41] Francis Schaeffer's observation is to the point: "With God there are no little people,...there are no little places."[42] This is an important lesson in a world where status, wealth, power, and celebrity are the things that are truly esteemed.

He was "like a stem from dry soil." Anything planted in fertile well-watered soil will thrive abundantly. But something that is rooted in parched ground, ground without nutrients and moisture, derives very little from the soil. No one attaches much importance to a plant in such an environment. "It seems doomed to wither away early."[43] He derived nothing from the soil in which he was planted. He derived nothing from *natural descent*.[44] He was of the Davidic line, but his family had fallen into obscurity. Position, wealth, and reputation were gone, and a usurper sat on the throne. His birth in a stable suggests that he derived nothing from *human society*. He derived nothing from *his followers*. He did not populate his apostolate with graduates of the leading schools. There were no famous philosophers, experts on political power and oratory. Instead, he chose men who were for the most part uncultured and uneducated.

---

[40] Hengstenberg, *Christology of the Old Testament*, 2:278.

[41] Culver, *The Sufferings and Glory of The LORD's Righteous Servant*, 49.

[42] Francis Schaeffer, "No Little People, No Little Places," in *No Little People: Sixteen Sermons for the Twentieth Century* (Downers Grove: Inter Varsity Press, 1974), 13, 18.

[43] Leupold, *Exposition of Isaiah*, 2:226.

[44] The writer is here indebted to Charles Haddon Spurgeon, "A Root Out of a Dry Ground," in *The Treasury of the Bible* (reprint ed., Grand Rapids: Baker, 1981), 3:720–25 (esp. 721).

It should be added that these men changed the world. Whatever they became after meeting Jesus, he made them that. As Spurgeon said, "Peter did not make Christianity, but Christianity made Peter. Paul brought nothing to Christ, but Christ gave everything to Paul.... This wondrous root fertilized the soil in which it grew."[45]

Although his unbelieving countrymen could not see it, the Servant was nourished by the inner reservoir of the Spirit of God. He was like one of those desert plants "which have a large succulent root full of liquid though the surrounding earth seems utterly devoid of moisture."[46]

He derived nothing from *his nationality*. No race was hated more by the Romans than the Jews. And even his fellow Israelites were spiritually burned out. The very parched ground of Jewry, the believing Israelites of the end-time seem to say, was antithetical to the spiritual discernment needed to properly identify and receive the Servant of the LORD. The dry ground, says Delitzsch, was "the existing state of [an] enslaved and degraded nation; i.e., he was subject to all the conditions inseparable from a nation that had been given up to the power of the world, and was only enduring all the consequent misery, but was in utter ignorance as to its cause; in a word, the dry ground is the corrupt character of the age."[47]

Charles Spurgeon wrote:

> Mentally, among the Jews nothing was left; no harp resounded with psalms like those of David; no prophet mourned in plaintive tones like [Jeremiah], or sang in the rich organ tones of Isaiah; there remained not even a Jonah to startle, or a Haggai to rebuke. No wise man gave forth his proverbs, nor preacher took up his parable. The nation had mentally reached its dregs, its scribes were dreaming over the letter of Scripture, insensible to its inner sense, and its elders were driveling forth traditions of the fathers, and sinking lower and lower in an inane superstition.[48]

---

[45] Spurgeon, "A Root Out of a Dry Ground," 722.

[46] W. Kay, "Isaiah: Introduction, Commentary, and Critical Notes," in *The Holy Bible According to the Authorized Version (A.D. 1611), With an Explanatory and Critical Commentary*, ed. F. C. Cook (New York: Scribner's, 1893), 5:267.

[47] Delitzsch, *Biblical Commentary on the Prophecies of Isaiah*, 2:312; Lindsey, *The Servant Songs*, 115.

[48] Spurgeon, "A Root Out of a Dry Ground," 721.

THEY WERE UNIMPRESSED WITH HIS HUMBLE APPEARANCE, VERSE 2B

The speakers make three statements about his appearance, "emphasizing three times that he did 'not' look like royalty."[49] **"He didn't have an impressive form or majesty,…no appearance that we should desire Him"** (HCSB). The word "form" (תֹאַר, *tōa'r*) is rendered "stately form" in the NASB. It is used to describe the physical attractiveness ("beauty," NIV, REB) and royal bearing of Joseph (Gen. 39:6) and David (1 Sam. 16:18).[50] The word "majesty" (הָדָר, *hādār*) speaks here of the splendor and majesty of a king (Ps. 21:5 [MT 21:6]; Ps. 45:3-4 [MT 4-5]).[51] The word "appearance" (מַרְאֶה, *mar'eh*) is used by Solomon to describe the lovely appearance of his beloved (Song 2:14).[52] King Saul was chosen because of his tall and imposing stature (1 Sam. 9:2); King David was **"ruddy, with beautiful eyes and a handsome appearance"** (1 Sam. 16:12).

Yet the Servant had none of these things.[53] In short, they say, he was easy to miss. There was nothing about him that made him stand out. He did not look like a king. There was nothing about his bearing that was striking. He looked so ordinary and human.

Old Testament scholar Bruce Waltke spent time in Israel many years ago working on an archeological excavation. He says that one of the highlights was the opportunity to spend an hour alone with Moise

---

[49] Gary V. Smith, *Isaiah 40–66*, 445. The three words ("form," "majesty," "appearance") are all preceded by the negative particle לֹא (*lō'*, "not").

[50] *HALOT*, s.v. "תֹאַר," 2:1676–77. Gary Smith (*Isaiah 40–66*, 446) notes that the same word (תֹאַר) is used in 52:14 and draws the conclusion that the Servant's form "was disfigured in some way." However, 52:14 refers to the disfigurement caused by the events surrounding Jesus' crucifixion, while 53:2 has reference to his earthly life before the cross.

[51] *HALOT*, s.v. "הָדָר," 1:240.

[52] *HALOT*, s.v. "מַרְאֶה," 1:630.

[53] Claus Westermann comments on the prerequisite of beauty (תֹאַר) in the cases of Joseph and David. In order to understand the importance of this in the life of the Servant "we have to remember two things: First, in the Old Testament beauty of the person is a concomitant of the blessing; Joseph's beauty thus indicates that he is a man with a blessing. Of the Servant, however, it is said that there was nothing beautiful about him; he was a man without a blessing. Secondly, in the Old Testament beauty is first and foremost something that comes about—here clearly a person's beauty is experienced as something conjoined with what happens to him. Thus, for the Servant lack of beauty means that no regard will be paid to him" (*Isaiah 40–66*, trans. David M. G. Stalker, OTL [Philadelphia: Westminster, 1969], 261).

Dayan, the hero general of Israel's "Six-Day War" in 1967. Dayan was one the twentieth century's great military geniuses. Waltke writes,

> One thing that struck me about him was his intelligence—he was one of the most observant people I had ever been with. Another thing that struck me was that I was disappointed. This great general of Israel—I thought he would have a great physique. Instead he was kind of like me—kind of dumpy! He just didn't have the bearing of a great general. [Waltke adds:] I'm sure that our Lord wasn't as bad off as me, but neither was he striking in appearance.[54]

The point here is not that the Servant had a physical defect; rather, the point is that he did not impress the people as their king. He had no aura, no halo, no splendor. He was ordinary. Would this Jesus, born in the back stable of a village inn, shake the Roman Empire? His contemporaries did not think so.[55] "They would have welcomed a plumed and mail-clad warrior," said David Baron, "riding forth to battle against the oppressor, [and they] would have shouted before him, '[Gird your sword on your thigh, O Mighty One, in your splendor and your majesty!'] They [had] no admiration and no welcome for One who [came], meek and lowly, to make His soul an offering for sin, and to be God's salvation to the end of the earth."[56]

> They all were looking for a king
> > To slay their foes and lift them high:
> Thou cam'st a little baby thing
> > That made a woman cry.[57]

Many of our modern representations of the LORD Jesus are very misleading. If one could go back to the time of Christ and see him in

---

[54] Waltke, "The Real Value of Jesus Christ."

[55] Oswalt, *The Book of Isaiah, Chapters 40–66*, 382.

[56] Baron, *The Servant of Jehovah*, 73; James Culross, *The Man of Sorrows and the Joy that was Set Before Him* (Stirling, UK: Drummond's Tract Depot, n.d.), 80–81.

[57] George MacDonald, "That Holy Thing," in *The Gifts of the Child Christ: Fairytales and Stories for the Childlike*, ed., Glenn Edward Sadler (Grand Rapids: Eerdmans, 1973), 261.

Judea or Galilee, the modern time traveler would be surprised. If someone pointed to a group of men and said, "There is Jesus of Nazareth and his disciples," what would one say? Most likely he would ask, "Which one is Jesus?" Modern artists who produce pictures of Jesus for Sunday school materials, books, or wall decorations present no questions as to his identity. Jesus is easy to spot in an artist's group portrait with his disciples. He's the tall handsome man dressed in white with handsome Anglo-Saxon features (blue eyes, light brown hair). The disciples, on the other hand, are shorter, dressed in earth tones, and bear Middle Eastern features. Lost is the sense that Christ's was an inner beauty perceived only by the eyes of faith.[58]

"They wanted a king, but they got a carpenter."[59] There is a lesson here. **"God sees not as man sees, for man looks at the outward appearance, but the LORD looks at the heart"** (1 Sam. 16:7). In light of contemporary models of celebrity leadership and the "'Christian stardom' of some pastors and Christian television personalities one wonders if this Servant would have appeared as someone desirable according to modern leadership criteria. Would people recognize him for who he really was or would they ignore him or reject him?"[60] Old Testament commentator John Oswalt wrote, "Deliverers are dominating, forceful, attractive people, who by their personal magnetism draw people to themselves and convince people to do what they want them to do.

---

[58] Theologian Karl Barth warned all who would attempt to portray the face of Christ. He affirmed that Jesus, the eternal Son of God incarnate, is the full manifestation of God's resplendent beauty, but only under the veil of human nature. He wrote, "And this is the crux of every attempt to portray this face, the secret of the sorry story of the representation of Christ. It could not and cannot be anything but a sorry story. No human art should try to represent—in their unity—the suffering God and triumphant man, the beauty of God which is the beauty of Jesus Christ. If at this point we have one urgent request to all Christian artists, however well-intentioned, gifted or even possessed of genius, it is that they should give up this unholy undertaking—for the sake of God's beauty. This picture, the one true picture, both in object and representation, cannot be copied, for the express reason that it speaks for itself, even in its beauty." See Karl Barth, *Church Dogmatics*, II/1, trans. T. H. L. Parker, W. B. Johnston, Harold Knight, and J. L. M. Haire (Edinburgh: T. & T. Clark, 1957), 658–666 (esp. 666). "To follow Barth's logic, God's beauty is paradoxically revealed and hidden concomitantly in the life, and especially in the death, of the Son" (Scott Jackson, "Worship and the Hidden Beauty of Christ," *PTR* 13 (Autumn, 2007): 87–89 (esp. 89).

[59] Culver, *The Sufferings and Glory of The LORD's Righteous Servant*, 52.

[60] Gary Smith, *Isaiah 40–66*, 446.

People who refuse to follow that leadership frequently find themselves crushed and tossed aside. This man does not fit that picture at all."[61]

ISRAEL DESPISED AND DEVALUED THE SERVANT, VERSE 3

HE WAS DESPISED BECAUSE HE WAS ASSOCIATED WITH SUFFERING

> He was despised and forsaken of men,
> A man of sorrows and acquainted with grief;
> And like one from whom men hide their face
> He was despised, and we did not esteem Him.

In verse 3 the end-time Israelites continue their report—their lamentation—that "their nation despised and devalued the Servant." "He was despised and rejected by men" (HCSB). While verse 2 speaks of his childhood, "verse 3 signals that the Servant has come of age."[62] From this point on, his adult life is described. The word "despised" (נִבְזֶה, nibzeh)[63] means "to consider something or someone to be worthless, unworthy of attention."[64] It speaks of an inner attitude, but one that can affect behavior, as was seen in the abusive treatment of the Servant. The word appears both at the beginning and the end of the verse "to emphasize the contemptible treatment this Servant will receive."[65] A related Arabic word (bazā) means "to raise the head loftily and

---

[61] Oswalt, *The Book of Isaiah, Chapters 40–66*, 382.

[62] Baltzer, *Deutero-Isaiah*, 406.

[63] The word נִבְזֶה is msc. sg. niphal (simple passive) ptc. of בָּזָה. The same form appears twice in the verse. The NKJV, following the KJV and Darby, renders the first occurrence with the English present passive ("is despised") and the second occurrence with an English past passive ("was despised"). Most other versions translate both occurrences as "was despised" (NASB, NIV, NRSV, REB ["was despised…we despised him"], NET, ESV, HCSB). The context favors the same rendering ("was despised") in both occurrences.

[64] Oswalt, *The Book of Isaiah, Chapters 40–66*, 383. See also M. Görg, "בָּזָה," *TDOT*, 2:60–65 (esp. 65). Görg says, "The Servant of Yahweh is almost the archetype of the *nibzeh* and of the *bazuy*, "the one despised."

[65] Michael A. Grisanti, "בָּזָה," in *NIDOTTE*, 1:628–30.

disdainfully."[66] The people had a vaunting, dismissive, and mocking attitude toward him.[67]

He was "forsaken" (NASB), "rejected" (KJV, NIV, ESV, HCSB), "shunned" (REB), "left alone" (Darby), or "abandoned" by men.[68] Franz Delitzsch argued that commentators generally err when they understand the term *men* (אִישִׁים, *'îšîm*) to mean people generally, i.e., common people. In the only other texts where the form appears (Prov. 8:4; Ps. 141:4) it means "persons of rank."[69] That he was rejected by such people meant that he had no respectable men with him, to support him with their authority. "The chief men of His nation who towered above the multitude, the great men of this world, withdrew their hands from Him, drew back from Him: He had none of the men of any distinction at His side."[70]

David Baron (1857–1926) was a Jewish convert to Christianity, a missionary to the Jews, and an able writer of books on the Bible and biblical themes. He noted that the great and mighty still ignore and despise Christ. Celsus (2d century Greek philosopher) and other pagan writers reproached Christianity as the religion of slaves. The Jewish rabbis of Baron's day taunted believers from among their people that it is to poor people that the gospel is preached, and that those drawn to Christ are from the "common people." The same argument was used in New Testament days. When officers were sent to seize Jesus, they returned without him. When the Pharisees saw that they were impressed with him, they asked, **"No one of the rulers or Pharisees has believed in**

---

[66] BDB, s.v. "בָּזָה," 102.

[67] J. Alec Motyer, *The Prophecy of Isaiah: An Introduction and Commentary* (Downers Grove: InterVarsity Press, 1993), 428.

[68] The adjective חָדֵל is translated "abandoned" in Koehler and Baumgartner, *Hebrew and Aramaic Lexicon*, s.v. "חָדֵל," 1:293. Some (e.g., North, *The Second Isaiah*, 237) have taken the adjective to mean "ceasing," i.e., "ceasing from men." In other words, the Servant turned away from men because of their refusal of his message. The more common view, however, is that people shunned him. Gary Smith (*Isaiah 40–66*, 446) says this suggests "a major difference in their theological perspectives." It calls to mind the harsh reaction to Jesus after his synagogue message in Nazareth (Luke 4:28-29).

[69] Delitzsch (*Biblical Commentary on the Prophecies of Isaiah*, 2:313) drew a distinction between the expressions בְּנֵי־אָדָם and בְּנֵי־אִישׁ, which in such verses as Ps. 49:2 (v. 3 in MT) and 62:9 (v. 10 in MT) respectively mean "men of low degree" and "men of rank." Cf. also: Young, *The Book of Isaiah*, 3:343; T. R. Birks, *Commentary on the Book of Isaiah*, 2d ed. (London: Macmillan, 1878), 263.

[70] Delitzsch, *Biblical Commentary on the Prophecies of Isaiah*, 2:313–14.

Him, has he? But this crowd [of common people] which does not know the Law is accursed" (John 7:48-49).[71]

No doubt his disciples took note of this. He didn't spend time with influential people like the Pharisees, the Sadducees, or the Roman authorities. Instead, he spent his time with sinners, prostitutes, and hated tax collectors. In the Rock opera *Jesus Christ Superstar*, Judas is puzzled at Jesus' kindness to Mary Magdalene. "It seems to me a strange thing, mystifying that a man like you can waste his time on women of her kind."[72] His unspoken conclusion: "The kingdom cannot be built on scum like that."

HE WAS DESPISED BECAUSE HE WAS CONSIDERED OFFENSIVE, CONTEMPTIBLE, AND OF NO ACCOUNT

The next two cola (lines) of verse 3 speak of another reason why the Servant was considered unworthy of respect and attention. Not only did he lack physical attractiveness, he appeared to be full of problems. "He [was] not one of the winners, He [was] one of the losers," or so men thought.[73] He was "a man of sorrows and acquainted with grief." The word "sorrows" (מַכְאֹבוֹת, *mak'ōbôt*) literally means "pains" or "sufferings."[74] The word "grief" (חֳלִי, *ḥŏlî*) literally means "sickness" (HCSB).[75]

Most versions say he was **"acquainted with"** (NASB) or "familiar with" (NIV) **sickness**.[76] Hengstenberg said that this speaks of "one who is intimately acquainted with it, who has, as it were, entered into a covenant of friendship with it."[77] Smith said that sickness/suffering "was

---

[71] Baron, *The Servant of Jehovah*, 78.

[72] *Jesus Christ Superstar: A Rock Opera*, Lyrics by Tim Rice, Music by Andrew Lloyd Webber (New York: Decca Records, 1970 [libretto, London: Leeds Music, 1970]), 7.

[73] Oswalt, *The Book of Isaiah, Chapters 40–66*, 383.

[74] *HALOT*, s.v. "מַכְאֹב," 1:579.

[75] *HALOT*, s.v. "חֳלִי," 1:318.

[76] Smith notes that the verb is passive, which communicates the idea "that the Servant 'was known' (יָדוּעַ, *yadûa'*) for His painful experiences." Others connected his life and reputation to a time of great suffering. He does concede that Isaiah's thought is best expressed in English with and active idea ("he knew suffering"). This leaves us with the question, "In what way did he know suffering? See Smith, *Isaiah 40–66*, 447.

[77] Hengstenberg, *Christology of the Old Testament*, 2:280.

a pivotal factor in his life."[78] The words "pains" and "sickness" might suggest to the reader one who is a sick man or a man sick at heart (cf. Jer. 15:18). Derek Kidner suggested another category, "that of the physician's voluntary involvement; he is also a man of pain and sickness in the sense that he gives himself to these things and their relief. This is the sense defined in Matthew 8:17, quoting Isaiah 53:4."[79]

There were a number of reasons for Christ's sufferings while on earth. First, he suffered on the cross, but those sufferings do not come into view until verses 4b-6. Second, he suffered because of the rejection of his Jewish brethren, actually the very leaders of the people ("rejected by men"). Third, as in this passage, the Great Physician suffered due to "His association with the sick and suffering class in contrast to the dignitaries."[80] To be surrounded by the ill and the dying as he was continually brought great physical and emotional anguish to this sympathetic and empathetic man.[81]

The Servant was despised and treated as worthless. He was **"like one from whom men hide their face."** People could not endure him. He was

---

[78] Smith, *Isaiah 40–66*, 447. Pieper wrote, "Before all others, the Servant was the object of suffering, sought out to speak, by suffering as the one object on earth to whom suffering pertained. All the suffering that pertained to this cursed world, He attracted to Himself" (August Pieper, *Isaiah II: An Exposition of Isaiah 40–66*, trans. Erwin E. Kowalke [Milwaukee, WI: Northwestern Publishing House, 1979], 437.

[79] Derek Kidner, "Isaiah," in *New Bible Commentary*, 4th ed., eds. G. J. Wenham, J. A. Motyer, D. A. Carson, and R. T. France (Downers Grove: IVP Academic, 1994), 663.

[80] Cf. Lindsey, *The Servant Songs*, 116.

[81] Commentators differ in their interpretations. (1) Some suggest that the Servant suffered due to his own illnesses, possibly including leprosy [Muilenburg, "Isaiah 40–66: Introduction and Exposition," 5:620–21]. (2) Others take the passage in a metaphorical sense. Most people find illness in others embarrassing and frustrating due to their helplessness to do anything about it. Hence, most avoid any contact with the ill. The point here is that the Servant was treated as if he was ill, and he experienced what the sick experience: avoidance [Oswalt, *The Book of Isaiah, Chapters 40–66*, 383–84]. (3) Still others link the sufferings to the cross where the guilt of sin, the wrath of God, the curse, the punishment that were taken from us and laid upon him (Pieper, *Isaiah II*, 437–38). (4) Some see in his sufferings his indignation and wrath against the sin and powers that cause sin and suffering in the world. "The zeal of self-sacrifice [Ps. 69:10] burnt like the fire of a fever in His soul and body." His conflict with the powers of destruction that were innate in humanity in consequence of sin was self-consuming [Delitzsch, *Biblical Commentary on the Prophecies of Isaiah*, 2:314]. (5) Finally, there is the view expounded in this monograph. The Servant was a man of "pains" and "sickness," "in the sense that he [gave] himself to these things and their relief" (Kidner, "Isaiah," 663). Coupled with this is the Servant's own anguish as he sympathetically and empathetically dealt with those under his care.

an object of displeasure._There are those who lift our spirits and bring a gleam to our eyes. We are happy to see them. However, we all remember a time when we knew an obnoxious person, someone whose strangeness, crudeness, or "geekiness" made him/her hard to be around. When such a one would approach, we would think or say, "Oh, oh, here comes that weirdo; let's hide before he sees us and comes over to us."[82]

Christians are often treated like that; not because they are strange, crude, or geeky, but because they speak openly of Christ and his salvation. "Look out," people say, "here comes that Christian; if I hear one more Bible verse I'm going to be sick." That's how Jesus was treated. He was avoided; in fact he was despised to the point that men would eventually set up a kangaroo court and have him executed.

"He was despised, and we did not esteem Him." The word "despised" is here repeated for emphasis. One of the most hated and despised villains in Hebrew history was Antiochus Epiphanes, a pagan Hellenist. Among other things he put to death women who had their sons circumcised, and he hung their infants from their necks (c. 165 BC). In addition he robbed the Jerusalem temple of all its furnishings, its gold and silver utensils, and ordered that swine and unclean animals be offered on the altar of burnt offering (1 Macc. 1:20-24, 41-61). The prophet Daniel uses this very Hebrew word (בָּזָה, *bāzāh*) to describe Antiochus. In the NASB he is called **"a despicable person"** (Dan. 11:21).[83] As Robert Culver observed, in the minds of his contemporaries Jesus "was in the same class with the reprobate who desecrated the holy altar with the carcass of a sow!"[84]

The second stanza of the Servant song ends with the end-time Israelites lamenting on behalf of their first century countrymen, "We did not esteem him." The verb "esteem" (חָשַׁב [*ḥāšab*]) means "to respect," "hold in high regard,"[85] "value."[86] Instead of counting him precious and worthy; instead of recognizing in his words and works the mighty arm of the LORD, we formed a very low estimate of him. We missed him; we did not appreciate the real value of the Servant. To tell the matter

---

[82] Cf. Baron, *The Servant of Jehovah*, 81; Culross, *The Man of Sorrows*, 83–84.

[83] The form used in Daniel 11:21 is נִבְזֶה (msc. sg. niphal ptc.), precisely the same form used in Isaiah 53:3.

[84] Culver, *The Sufferings and the Glory of the LORD's Righteous Servant*, 56–57.

[85] *HALOT*, s.v. "חָשַׁב," 1:360.

[86] BDB, s.v. "חָשַׁב," 363.

truthfully, we did not esteem him at all. As Luther put it in his German translation, "We have estimated him as nothing."[87]

CONCLUSION

In the two thousand years since Jesus lived upon this earth, much has been said about the culpability of the Jews in his death. Horrid customs developed in the Christian church that made the Jews objects of hatred and insult, especially during the ceremonies of Easter week. The famous German "Passion Plays" (in Oberammergau, Bavaria) were undeniably anti-Semitic in character. In various parts of Europe, Jews were charged with deicide, i.e., with being "Christ killers."

But what if Christ humbled himself again and appeared visibly among us in secular America? How would he be greeted by Gentiles—even by many baptized Gentiles? He would be met in the same way as he was in the first century. He would be "crucified again and put to open shame" (Heb. 6:6). As an older writer put it, "He would again have to listen to the dogmas of insolent reasoning; he would once more be disgusted with the fiend-like sneers of reprobate men, and the polished cavils of fashionable contempt."[88]

As to "insolent reasoning," one need only mention the various books of John Shelby Spong, retired Episcopal bishop of New Jersey, who openly denied the inspiration of the Scriptures, the doctrine of original sin, the virgin birth, the deity of Christ, the substitutionary atonement, the Holy Trinity, and Christ's role as the only Savior of mankind.[89] As to the "sneers of reprobate men," one need only listen to the media elites in their hostile reaction to the governor of Texas when he called his fellow citizens to a day of prayer and fasting for their country (July, 2011)—or their reactions to any other public figure who speaks openly in favor of Christ and his church. As to the "polished cavils [sham arguments] of fashionable contempt," one need only consider the current

---

[87] Cf. Delitzsch, *Biblical Commentary on the Prophecies of Isaiah*, 2:315.

[88] Margoliouth, *The Penitential Hymn of Judah and Israel After the Spirit*, 33.

[89] E.g., see John Shelby Spong, *Why Christianity Must Change or Die: A Bishop Speaks to Christians in Exile* (San Francisco: Harper, 1999); idem., *Here I Stand: My Struggle for a Christianity of Integrity, Love, and Equality* (San Francisco: Harper, 2000).

wave of atheistic university professors who are putting forth the same old arguments answered by Christian apologists time and time again.

But the primary issue facing the reader of this text is this: Isaiah 53:1-3 confronts us with this question: What value do you place on the Servant of the LORD, Jesus Christ? Do you esteem him as God's Son, the Savior sent into the world to atone for your sins? Or do you bypass him, reject him, and throw him aside as having no value at all? Do you embrace him as your Savior and Redeemer, or do you regard him as of no value at all? It is the most important question that any human being will ever face. It is a question that Holy Scripture assures us every single human being must answer.

CHAPTER 3

THE VICARIOUS SUFFERINGS OF THE

SERVANT OF THE LORD:

ISAIAH 53:4-6

INTRODUCTION

It has been said that we are a generation of people concerned with getting what we deserve.[1] We deserve childcare, health care, good schools, good jobs, easy commutes, and generous pension plans. We deserve smoke-free air, a strong stock market, happy marriages, and well-behaved kids who remember our birthdays. Politicians, think-tanks, and experts of various sorts exist solely for the purpose of seeing to it that we get what we deserve. We deserve our money's worth, to be treated respectfully, to get good customer service. We deserve a good vacation, to eat and not grow fat, to be heard and have all our questions answered.

A powerful response to our self-centered attitudes comes at the end of a classic Western film.[2] Two men are waiting outside the frontier town of Big Whiskey, Wyoming, in 1880. Someone will soon bring them payment for murders they have committed. The older man, standing and looking toward the town, is William Munny, a notoriously vicious criminal who has blown up trains, killed peace officers, and murdered a variety of other men, women, and children. The younger man, nicknamed "the Schofield Kid"—not for a Scofield Bible he doesn't carry, but for the Schofield model Smith and Wesson pistol he *does* carry—sits by a tree, drinking whiskey. He is filled with remorse, vowing never to commit such crimes again. He tries to rationalize his

[1] Cf. Lori Borgman [Knight Ridder Newspapers], "Did we really get what we deserve when it comes to Christ?" *Dubuque Telegraph Herald* (April 15, 2006), 1–D.

[2] *Unforgiven*, written by David Webb Peoples, directed by Clint Eastwood (Warner Brothers Pictures, 1992).

deeds, "Well, I guess they had it coming." The older and harder man, William Munny, who is deeply afraid of death, knows what people really deserve. He responds like the Old Testament prophet himself, "We all have it coming, kid."

The outlaw, William Munny, has put his finger on the most critical problem of life. It is not the prevalence of war (both religious and secular), the increase of violent crime, the rampant immorality of the 21st century with its pornography, sexually transmitted diseases, dysfunctional families, and divorce. It is not the deficit problem, the energy problem, and our consumeristic society, characterized by a pervasive avarice and greed. It is the age-old moral and spiritual problem: How can a righteous God forgive sinful man? We have all sinned against this holy God (Rom. 3:23); the Bible says we face divine judgment (Heb. 9:27); and in our hearts we know, "We all have it coming" (Rom. 6:23a; cf. 1:28-32; Ezek. 18:4). Job asked plaintively, **"In truth I know that this is so; but how can a man be in the right before God?"** (Job 9:2).

In his great "Servant Song" (Isa. 52:13–53:12), Isaiah, who has been called "the Old Testament evangelist" and whose book has been called "the fifth Gospel,"[3] provides the key to the problem. The solution to the problem of unforgiven sin and the punishment we surely deserve is found in the ministry of the "Suffering Servant of the LORD," whom the New Testament identifies as the Lord Jesus Christ. To be more precise, the solution is to be found in the death of Christ, which was an act of penal satisfaction through substitution. This means that God's holy wrath against our sin was satisfied by the penalty Christ bore on the cross in our place (2 Cor. 5:21; Gal. 3:10-13). The nature of Christ's atonement as substitutionary and penal was not understood by the Jewish leaders of Jesus' day, and it is not understood—in fact, it is repudiated—by many religious leaders and biblical scholars in our day.[4]

---

[3] Cf. John F. A. Sawyer, *The Fifth Gospel: Isaiah in the History of Christianity* (Cambridge: Cambridge University Press, 1996), 86. Sawyer notes that Isaiah was called "a fifth Evangelist" by Jerome, Augustine, and Isidore of Seville.

[4] "I believe that the recent merging of Holiness in Love, and the practical denial that Righteousness is fundamental in God's nature, are responsible for the utilitarian views of law and the superficial views of sin which now prevail in some systems of theology. There can be no proper doctrine of the atonement and no proper doctrine of retribution, so long as Holiness is refused its preeminence. Love must have a norm or standard, and this norm or standard can be found only in Holiness. The old conviction of sin and the sense of guilt that drove the convicted sinner to the cross are inseparable from a firm belief in the self-affirming attribute of God [holiness] as logically prior to and as conditioning the

Isaiah 53:4-6 is the third strophe or stanza in Isaiah's great servant song or poem. In the previous strophe (vv. 1-3) Israel—specifically, the remnant of Israel who will turn in faith to the Messiah at his second advent—lament that their countrymen did not appreciate the real value of the Servant of the LORD when he lived among them in the first century AD. Their superficial estimation of him led them to reject him. He was "totally misunderstood because of His seeming insignificance."[5]

In this strophe (vv. 4–6), the lament of End-time redeemed Israel continues. They confess their people's initial confusion over the miraculous works the Servant performed (v. 4a), the true nature of his sufferings (v. 4b), acknowledge that they (i.e., believing Jews at the time of Israel's end-time conversion, Rom. 11:26) now understand the substitutionary nature of Christ's sufferings (v. 5), and confess that it was their own personal iniquity that caused God's wrath to fall on the Servant (v. 6).[6]

ISRAEL'S CONFUSION OVER THE NATURE OF THE SERVANT'S SUFFERINGS, VERSE 4

Surely our griefs He Himself bore,
And our sorrows He carried;
Yet we ourselves esteemed Him stricken,
Smitten of God, and afflicted.

THE "GREAT REVERSAL" OF ISRAEL IN THE END-TIME, VERSE 4A

As has been noted earlier in this study, the fourth "Servant Song" is Israel's great penitential confession to be made in the future when the nation is converted at the second advent of Christ. It parallels Zechariah

---

self-communicating attribute [love]. The theology of our day needs a new view of the Righteous One. Such as view will make it plain that God must be reconciled before man can be saved, and that the human conscience can be pacified only upon condition that propitiation is made to the divine Righteousness" (Augustus Hopkins Strong, *Systematic Theology*, 5th ed. [Philadelphia: Griffith and Roland, 1907; reprint ed., Old Tappan, NJ: Revell, 1970], x–xi).

[5] H. C. Leupold, *Exposition of Isaiah* (Grand Rapids: Baker, 1971), 2:225.

[6] The speakers use an indeterminate "our" or "we," and in doing so they identify themselves with those who rejected Christ and speak for the people as a whole. Cf. John N. Oswalt, *The Book of Isaiah, Chapters 40–66*, NICOT (Grand Rapids: Eerdmans, 1998), 384, n. 4.

12:10, "I will pour out on the house of David and on the inhabitants of Jerusalem, the Spirit of grace and supplication, so that they will look on Me whom they have pierced;[7] and they will mourn for Him, as one mourns for an only son, and they will weep bitterly over Him like the bitter weeping over a firstborn." This will truly be a "great reversal" for Israel.[8] The sorrows and griefs (verse 3) that made Christ so unappealing to Jews in the first century will one day be understood by redeemed Israel to be for their benefit. "Those things were all for us!"[9]

In many of our English versions, verse 4 begins with the adverb "surely" (KJV, NASB, NIV, ESV). According to that translation, the word is emphatic and introduces a new thought. In this verse, however, the Hebrew word (אָכֵן ['āk̲ēn]) should probably be translated as an adversative, "yet" (HCSB), "but" (NET), or "however."[10] The thought is this: in verses 1-3 Israel confesses that they failed to value the Servant and his work. They misinterpreted it. "We did not esteem him, but the true story is this...."[11]

"Our griefs He Himself bore, and our sorrows He carried" (NASB). "Verse 4 has often been misunderstood because two quite specific nouns have been taken in a general sense."[12] The word "griefs" is a translation of a Hebrew word that literally means "sicknesses" (חֳלִי, ḥŏlî). The word translated "sorrows" (מַכְאֹבִים, mak̲'ōb̲îm) literally means "pains."[13]

The two verbs, on the other hand, do have a more general sense. The verb translated "to bear" in the NASB (נָשָׂא, nāśā') is a common Hebrew word (over 650 occurrences in the Old Testament, 597 in the qal stem) from the root "referring to the physical movement or raising, lifting up, and carrying." It has a wide semantic range "with every conceivable

---

[7] The verb translated in Zechariah 12:10 is דָּקָרוּ (3rd pers, pl qal perf. דָּקַר), while the verb used In Isaiah 53:5 is מְחֹלָל (msc. sg. polal [passive intensive] ptc. of חָלַל). On the former, see *HALOT*, s.v. "דָּקַר," 1:230. On the latter, see idem., s.v. "חָלַל," 1:320.

[8] Cf. James Muilenburg, "Isaiah, Chapters 40–66: Introduction and Exegesis," in *IntB*, 5:618.

[9] Oswalt, *The Book of Isaiah, Chapters 40–66*, 385–86.

[10] *HALOT*, s.v. "אָכֵן," 1:47.

[11] Robert D. Culver, *The Sufferings and the Glory of the LORD's Righteous Servant* (Moline, IL: Christian Service Foundation, 1958), 65, n. 1; F. Duane Lindsey, *The Servant Songs: A Study in Isaiah* (Chicago: Moody, 1985), 118.

[12] Allan A. MacRae, *The Gospel of Isaiah* (Chicago: Moody, 1977), 136.

[13] *HALOT*, s.v. "מַכְאֹב," 1:579; cf. BDB, s.v. "מַכְאֹב," 456.

association."[14] The verb translated **"to carry"** (סָבַל, *sābal*) literally means "to carry" in the qal stem.[15] It may be translated here, "to carry pain, aches."[16] In the present text, the two verbs involve the idea of lifting something up, removing it, and carrying it away.[17] The translation of the NET Bible has it about right: "But he lifted up [removed] our illnesses, he carried [away] our pain."[18]

It is significant that Matthew (8:17) quotes this verse in connection with Jesus' miracles of healing, **"[This was] to fulfill the prophecy of Isaiah: 'He took our illnesses from us and carried away our diseases'"** (REB). Matthew's Greek translation of Isaiah is very similar in meaning to Isaiah's Hebrew. Both nouns refer to physical ailments. The first noun (ἀσθενείας [*astheneias*]) here means "a state of debilitating illness, sickness, disease."[19] The second noun (νόσους [*nosous*]) speaks of a "physical malady, a disease or illness."[20] The distinction between the two

---

[14] See D. N. Freedman, B. E. Willoughby, Heinz-Josef Fabry, and Helmer Ringgren, "נָשָׂא," in *TDOT*, 10:24–25, 27–28; cf. *HALOT*, s.v. "נָשָׂא," 1:724. Among the meanings of the word in various contexts are "lift," "lift up," take," "take away [remove]," "bear," and "carry" (BDB, s.v. "נָשָׂא," 669–72). When defining נָשָׂא both major Hebrew lexicons have the meaning ""to bear guilt for others." They both cite Isaiah 53:12 as an example of that meaning, but only BDB cites verse 4 [BDB, s.v. "נָשָׂא," 671; *HALOT*, s.v. "נָשָׂא," 1:726].

[15] D. Kellermann, "סָבַל," in *TDOT*, 10:139–44 (esp. 141). In a number of contexts it refers to physically bearing a heavy load or burden (143).

[16] *HALOT* ("סָבַל," 1:741) has "to carry pain, aches" for both verses 4 and 11. BDB ("סָבַל," 687), on the other hand, asserts that in verse 4 it speaks of the Servant carrying a load of pain, while in verse 11 it speaks of his carrying a load of guilt (or punishment).

[17] MacRae, *The Gospel of Isaiah*, 136. It is worth noting that Isaiah did not put the verbs in the emphatic position (before the nouns). "It seems that what is really important is what the suffering servant has taken, not how he has taken it" (Millard J. Erickson, *Christian Theology*, 3d ed. [Grand Rapids: Baker, 1998], 766).

[18] See also the HCSB, "Yet He Himself bore our sicknesses, and He carried our pains."

[19] BDAG, s.v. "ἀσθένεια," 142. Matthew here follows the Hebrew text and not the LXX, which has τὰς ἁμαρτίας ἡμῶν ("our sins"). William Kelly wrote, "The wisdom of inspiration shines conspicuously here; for the Septuagintal Version is avoided when incorrect or equivocal, and employed only when exact" (*The Day of Atonement* [London: F. E. Race (C. A. Hammond), 1925], 184). Kelly notes that Isaiah 53:4 is not applied by any NT writer to the atonement. When his dying for our sins is meant, he adds, they refer to Isaiah 53:11, 12 (1 Pet. 2:24; Heb. 9:28). See idem., *An Exposition of the Book of Isaiah*, 4th ed. (London: C. A. Hammond, 1947; reprint ed., Denver: Wilson Foundation, 1975), 341.

[20] BDAG, s.v. "νόσος," 679.

is that the first emphasizes the idea of weakness and powerlessness; such an illness is debilitating or incapacitating.[21]

The first verb (ἔλαβεν [elaben]) is a common one and here means "to take away or remove [diseases]."[22] The second verb (ἐβάστασεν [ebastasen]) is very close in meaning to סָבַל. It means "to carry," and everywhere it is used there is the suggestion of a burden involved. In the present verse it means "to carry [disease] away," "to remove [illness]."[23] Isaiah was looking forward to (and the end-time Israelites will look back at) the Servant's earthly life and healing ministry. They will view the events of Jesus' earthly life with believing eyes. They will acknowledge that those who saw him perform his many miracles (their own first century countrymen) should have understood that only the Messiah could do these mighty works. The miracles he performed were on behalf of their brethren. Those were "our sicknesses" and "our pains" that he took away.

THE GREAT MISUNDERSTANDING OF ISRAEL IN AD 33 (THE YEAR OF JESUS' DEATH), VERSE 4B[24]

Having confessed their realization of the true nature of the Servant's mighty miracles, end-time Israel will look back to the first century and acknowledge that Israel at that time responded in unbelief. Their own leaders attributed his miracles to Satan, to **"Beelzebul the ruler of the demons"** (Matt. 12:24). Their chief priests and rulers **"delivered Him to the sentence of death and crucified Him"** (Luke 24:20). Even some of his followers wondered if their hopes that he was the Messiah were in vain (Luke 24:17-21). In the end many, if not most, of the people were convinced by their chief priests and elders that he was worthy of death (Matt. 27:20-23).

Many believers have read the second half of verse 4 as if it gives a correct interpretation of the cross. It does not.[25] Their interpretive error

---

[21] BDAG, s.v. "ἀσθενής," 142.

[22] BDAG, s.v. "λαμβάνω," 583.

[23] BDAG, s.v. "βαστάζω," 171.

[24] For the view that Christ died in AD 33, see Harold W. Hoehner, *Chronological Aspects of the Life of Christ* (Grand Rapids: Zondervan, 1977), 95–114 (esp. 113–14); Jack Finegan, *Handbook of Biblical Chronology*, rev. ed. (Peabody, MA: Hendrickson, 1998), 367–69.

[25] Culver, *The LORD's Righteous Servant*, 68–69.

does not concern the divine agency behind the sufferings of Christ. It *was* God's plan to deliver him over to death (Acts 2:23). Rather, their error is in misunderstanding whose perspective is being expressed in verse 4b. In context, verse 4b is not the expression of the view of believing Israel; it is the expression of the viewpoint of unbelieving Israel in the first century.

"Yet we ourselves esteemed Him stricken, smitten of God, and afflicted." The expression "yet we ourselves" (וַאֲנַחְנוּ, *wa'ănaḥnû*) is very emphatic,[26] because there is an antithesis between the two halves of the verse.[27] In the first half it is end-time Israel speaking. They will have a positive interpretation of the work of the Servant. In the second half it is unbelieving Israel speaking at the time of Jesus' death. The Jews of our Lord's day wrongly concluded that he was suffering afflictions sent by God for sins he had committed himself. They believed that Jesus of Nazareth was getting just what he deserved. They said in John 5:18 that he was a Sabbath breaker and a blasphemer, both capital offences.

In the world of Christ's day, "this attitude was the orthodox, correct, indeed the devout, one."[28] It is sometimes called the "Deuteronomic theory" of suffering. This view, exemplified in Deuteronomy 28, is that if one undergoes grief, suffering, and divine punishment, he deserves it. Job's friends (Eliphaz, Bildad, and Zophar) held this view. "You are suffering Job; you must have done something wrong."

> It is the view held by Lucy in Charles M. Schulz' comic strip, "Peanuts." Lucy, her brother Linus, and Charlie Brown are talking. Lucy asks Linus, "What's the matter with you?" He replies, "I have a sliver in my finger." She says, "Ah, Ha! That means you're being punished for something. What have done wrong lately?" "I haven't done anything wrong!" Linus protests. Lucy presses on, "You have a sliver, haven't you? That's a

---

[26] William Urwick, *The Servant of Jehovah: A Commentary, Grammatical, and Critical, Upon Isaiah 52:13–53:12* (Edinburgh: T. & T. Clark, 1877), 120.

[27] The antithesis is actually twofold. In addition to a change of perspective (between believing and unbelieving Israel) there is also a change in time. Verses 1-4a are concerned with the earthly sufferings and work of the Servant, while verses 4b-12 are concerned with the Servant's sufferings in death. Cf. Lewis Sperry Chafer, *Systematic Theology*, vol. 3: *Soteriology* (Dallas: Dallas Seminary Press, 1948), 39.

[28] Claus Westermann, *Isaiah 40–66*, OTL, trans. David M. G. Stalker (Philadelphia: Westminster, 1969), 262–63.

misfortune, isn't it?" You're being punished with misfortune because you've been bad!" Charlie Brown tries to intervene, "Now wait a minute, does…" Lucy cuts him off in mid-sentence: "What do you know about it, Charlie Brown? This is a sign! This is a direct sign of punishment! Linus has done something very wrong, and now he has to suffer misfortune! I know all about these things! I know that a …" Linus interrupts, "It's out! It just popped right out!" Lucy walks away, steaming mad. Linus has a happy look of victory as he says to his departing sister, "Thus endeth the theological lesson for today!"[29]

The Jews of Jesus' day, like the friends of Job, and like Lucy, had an orthodox view of suffering—some suffering. After all, Deuteronomy 28 does say that sin and disobedience will lead to punishment by God. But orthodoxy is sometimes not enough.[30] It is possible to have a truncated or incomplete orthodoxy—an orthodoxy that ignores other elements in Scripture.

Take the subject of suffering, for example: It is true that *some sufferers are sinners*, i.e., that some suffering is the result of personal sin. However, some *sufferers are saints*, i.e., their suffering is caused by the good they are doing or because the Lord has something important to teach them. Certainly the suffering of Job, Jeremiah, and Paul the apostle falls into this category. Finally *one sufferer is a Savior*. Jesus Christ suffered not for his own sins, but for those of others.[31] Hengstenberg adds, "The suffering of a perfect saint…involves a contradiction, unless it be vicarious."[32]

---

[29] Robert L. Short, *The Parables of Peanuts* (New York: Harper & Row, 1968), 288. For this reference to Charles Schulz' comic strip the writer is indebted to S. Lewis Johnson, Jr., "The Vicarious Messiah: An Exposition of Isaiah 53:4-6," *EmJ* 21 (Winter, 2012): 125–35 (esp. 128).

[30] T. M. Moore, "When Orthodoxy is Not Enough: Calvin on Job's Interlocutors," *RRJ* 12 (Winter, 2003), 11–21.

[31] John Paterson, *The Praises of Israel: Studies Literary and Religious in the Psalms* (New York: Scribner's, 1950), 225–27.

[32] E. W. Hengstenberg, *Christology of the Old Testament*, trans. Theodore Meyer and James Martin (1878; reprint ed., Grand Rapids: Kregel, 1956), 2:284.

It is true that the suffering of the Servant came from the hand of God; he was **"stricken, smitten of God and afflicted,"**[33] but the Jews were all wrong about the reason. He was suffering for their sins and not his own.

Thus our LORD Jesus Christ, the only sinless man who ever lived, is grouped with the *posh'e Yisrael—the sinners of Israel*—in Jewish literature.[34] In the Talmud he is linked with the Roman general Titus and the false prophet Balaam in hell.[35] Isaiah now goes on to record end-time Israel's understanding of the true meaning of the Servant's death.

---

[33] The words used here are of interest. The word "stricken" (נָגוּעַ, msc. sg. qal pass. ptc. נָגַע) means "to touch violently, strike." It can mean to strike with a disease, especially leprosy (as in the case of Miriam, Num. 12:9-10; and Uzziah, 2 Kings 15:5). The noun form of the word is used about sixty times in Leviticus 13–14 of an infection (lit. "stroke," "mark," "attack") of "leprosy" or "skin disease" (BDB, s.v. "נֶגַע," 619; *HALOT*, s.v. "נָגַע," 1:668). Among the Rabbis there was a tradition that the Messiah would be a leper: "His name is 'the leper scholar,' as it is written, 'Surely he hath borne our griefs, and carried our sorrows: yet we did esteem him a leper, smitten of God and afflicted" (Sanhedrin 98b, in *The Babylonian Talmud*, Seder Nezikin, ed. I. Epstein [London: Soncino, 1935], 3:668). According to Jerome, Aquila translated נָגוּעַ by ἀφημένον ["leprous"] and the Vulgate has *quasi leprosum* [Joachim Jeremias, "παῖς θεοῦ," in *TDNT*, 5:690]. There is no warrant here to go beyond the general translation, "stricken" (Urwick, *The Servant of Jehovah*, 120–21). On the cross, the Jews believed, the Servant was deservedly struck by God. He was "smitten of God" (מֻכֵּה אֱלֹהִים, *mukkēh 'ĕlōhîm*). The word "God" (אֱלֹהִים) appears between "smitten" (מֻכֵּה, *mukkēh*, msc. sg. hophal [causative passive] ptc. נָכָה, "to be beaten, struck dead") and "afflicted" (מְעֻנֶּה, *mᵉ'unneh*, msc. sg. pual [intensive passive] ptc. עָנָה, "to oppress, humiliate, afflict") in that it is logically connected with them both. See *HALOT*, s.v. "נָכָה," 1:697–98; idem., s.v. "עָנָה," 853. It is significant, says Delitzsch, that Isaiah uses "God" and not "Yahweh." His "evident intention is to point to the all-determining divine power." The picture is of one bowed down (by God), i.e., afflicted with suffering. The construction "smitten of God" signifies "one who has been defeated in conflict with God his LORD." (*Biblical Commentary on the Prophecies of Isaiah*, 2:317).

[34] Baron, *The Servant*, 87. Compare the clause וְאֶת־פֹּשְׁעִים נִמְנָה ("and was numbered with the transgressors") in verse 12.

[35] The relevant section of the Talmud with specific reference to Jesus may be found in Peter Schäfer, *Jesus in the Talmud* (Princeton: Princeton University Press, 2007), 84–85, 173, n. 11. As Schäfer notes, the standard English printed editions of the Talmud have "sinners of Israel" and delete the name of Jesus. See, for example: Giṭṭin 56b in *The Babylonian Talmud*, Seder Nashim, ed. I. Epstein (1936; reprint ed., London: Soncino, 1978), 4:260–61; Giṭṭin 5 (folio 56b) in *The Babylonian Talmud: A Translation and Commentary*, trans. Jacob Neusner (1999; reprint ed., Peabody, MA: Hendrickson, 2005), 11:244–45.

ISRAEL'S RECOGNITION OF THE SUBSTITUTIONARY PURPOSE OF the Servant's Sufferings, VERSE 5

But He was pierced through for our transgressions,
He was crushed for our iniquities;
The chastening for our well-being fell upon Him,
And by His scourging we are healed.

THE VIOLENT AND PAINFUL DEATH OF THE SERVANT

Verse 5 begins with the adversative "**but He**" (וְהוּא, *wᵉhû'*) to contrast with the "**and we**" or "**yet we**" in verses 3 and 4.[36] End-time Israel will "recognize the substitutionary redemptive purpose of the Servant's sufferings."[37] Four words (two passive verbs and two nouns) describe the sufferings of the Servant: "**He was pierced through for our transgressions.**" The KJV says, "wounded," but the Hebrew word in the form used here (מְחֹלָל, *mᵉḥōlāl*)[38] means "pierced." He was crucified, i.e., nailed up on a cross. His hands and feet were pierced with nails, his head was pierced with thorns, and his heart was pierced with a spear. New Testament scholar, Martin Hengel, says it was a "'barbaric' form of execution of the utmost cruelty."[39]

"**He was crushed for our iniquities.**" The word "crushed" (מְדֻכָּא, *mᵉduka'*)[40] means "broken to pieces, shattered." The word is consistently used (except Deut. 23:1) in a metaphorical sense, i.e., a "crushed spirit" (Isa. 57:15), a "crushed heart" (Ps. 51:17).[41] This speaks of "His emotional destruction in bearing sin as a substitute for guilty sinners."[42]

---

[36] Urwick, *The Servant of Jehovah*, 122.

[37] Lindsey, *The Servant Songs*, 121.

[38] The Hebrew form מְחֹלָל is msc. sg. polal (passive intensive) ptc. of חלל ("to pierce"). BDB, s.v. "חלל," 319. *HALOT*, s.v. "חלל," 1:320, has "to pierce" for the perfect and "wounded" for the participle.

[39] Martin Hengel, *Crucifixion* (Philadelphia: Fortress, 1977), 22.

[40] The Hebrew form מְדֻכָּא is msc. sg. pual ptc. of דָּכָה.

[41] *HALOT*, s.v. "דָּכָה," 1:221.

[42] Lindsey, *The Servant Songs*, 121.

The Servant's pain was excruciating. The etymology of that adjective, *excruciating*, is significant: *ex cruce*, "out of the cross." Patrick Reardon says:

> It is nearly impossible to exaggerate what the Savior suffered on the cross. Whether the cause of Jesus' death was asphyxiation [i.e., death by impaired breathing or suffocation], or hypercarbia [abnormally high levels of carbon dioxide in the circulating blood], or hypovolemic shock [a condition in which severe blood and fluid loss makes the heart unable to pump enough blood to the body], or heart failure, or exsanguination [to be drained of blood; severe loss of blood], or total physical exhaustion brought on by tetanic contractions [continuous muscular spasms brought on by a rapid series of nerve impulses] throughout his entire body—or any combination of these, or any other plausible suggestion—the astounding fact is that Jesus, at the very end, 'cried out again with a loud voice' [Luke 23:46]. From a medical perspective, this is surprising.[43]

"**The chastening for our well-being fell upon Him.**" The noun "**chastening**" (מוּסָר, *mûsar*) speaks of "the discipline of a child by a parent up to and including punishment."[44] The context here requires the thought of "punishment"—"**and by His scourging we are healed.**" The noun "**scourging**" (חַבּוּרָה, *ḥabbûrāh*) speaks of the torture that preceded the actual crucifixion. In addition to punching (Matt. 26:67), there was scourging or whipping (Matt. 27:26),[45] and this treatment left bruises, and welts, and bloody slashes.[46] Hengel says that sometimes the

---

[43] Patrick Henry Reardon, "From the Cross," *Touchstone* (May, 2011): 48. The "loud voice," Reardon suggests, demonstrated "the truth of the Savior's claim, 'I lay down my life that I may take it again. No one takes it from me, but I lay it down of myself. I have the power to lay it down, and I have power to take it again'" (John 10:17-18).

[44] Oswalt, *The Book of Isaiah 40–66*, 388; cf. *HALOT*, s.v. "מוּסָר," 1:557.

[45] The Roman scourge, the *horribile flagellum*, was made of leather, and the end thongs were interwoven with bones and bits of metal. Cf. Carl Schneider, "μάστιξ," *TDNT* 4: 517–19 (esp. 519); Josef Blinzler, *The Trial of Jesus*, trans. Isabel and Florence McHugh (Westminster, MD: Newman, 1959), 222–35 (esp. 222).

[46] Faith healer, Aimee Semple McPherson (1890–1944) gave an imaginary dialogue, "Was He whipped that my sins might be washed away?" "No, child, the blood of the Cross was sufficient for that." "Why, then, did they whip Him so?" "'Twas thus He bore our suffering, and 'By His stripes we are healed.' At the Whipping Post He purchased your healing." Quoted by William Edward Biederwolf, *Whipping-Post Theology or Did*

torture was so horrific that the condemned person died before he was crucified.[47]

In 2004 director Mel Gibson presented his film *The Passion of the Christ*, a moving portrayal of the last twelve hours of Jesus' life. It accurately portrayed crucifixion as a violent and bloody affair.[48] Franz Delitzsch says, "There were no stronger expressions to be found in the language, to denote a violent and painful death [than those used by Isaiah]."[49]

A seventeenth century Puritan preacher spoke of Isaiah 53 as "the prophet Isaiah's crucifix." He wrote:

> Now though the Papists dote upon artificial and wrought crucifixes, we may better study prophetical and apostolical crucifixes, their holy sermons, that, above all paint, lay clearly

---

Jesus Atone for Disease? (Grand Rapids: Eerdmans, 1934). The quote is on the frontispiece facing the title page. T. J. McCrossan, in a book very popular with Pentecostal preachers of an earlier generation, wrote, "Much of His precious blood was doubtless shed while receiving [those awful stripes] for our physical healing, but the rest of His precious blood was reserved to be shed on the cross for our sins" (*Bodily Healing and the Atonement* [Seattle, WA: T. J. McCrossan, 1930], 38). Along the same line British pastor, Colin Urquhart, wrote, "When Jesus stood bearing the lashes from the Roman soldiers, all our physical pain and sicknesses were being heaped upon him.... It is as if one lash was for cancer, another for bone disease, another for heart disease, and so on. Everything that causes physical pain was laid on Jesus as the nails were driven into his hands and feet (*Receive Your Healing* [London: Hodder and Stoughton, 1986], 38). There is nothing in Isaiah 53 that indicates that the piercing, crushing, chastening, and scourging represent different effects of the atonement. "In Isaiah 53, all that enters into His death as the immediate preparation for it, is included. He is there said to be *wounded, bruised, chastised,* and subject to *stripes* by which there is healing. In the minds of those who inflicted the death sufferings of Christ, it is probable that the scourging, the buffeting, the spitting, and the crown of thorns, like the nails and the spear, were but parts of the whole project. If this be true, the stripes are included in the death sufferings and it would be without controversy that 'with his stripes we are healed'" (Lewis Sperry Chafer, *Systematic Theology,* vol. 3: *Soteriology* [Dallas: Dallas Seminary Press, 1948], 38).

[47] Hengel, *Crucifixion,* 29, n. 21. Cf. *HALOT,* s.v. "חַבּוּרָה," 1:285.

[48] Hengel (*Crucifixion,* 31) describes as "incomprehensible" the statements of scholars who state that crucifixion was "by nature a bloodless form of execution" (e.g., Joachim Jeremias, *The Eucharistic Words of Jesus,* New Testament Library, trans. Norman Perris [London: SCM, 1966], 223). In response Hengel cites Josephus's description of a play in which two people were crucified and "thus a great quantity of artificial blood was shed." Cf. Josephus, *Jewish Antiquities* 19.94, trans. Louis H. Feldman, in *Josephus,* 10 vols., LCL (Cambridge: Harvard, 1965), 9:261.

[49] Delitzsch, *Biblical Commentary on the Prophecies of Isaiah,* 2:318.

before our eyes Christ crucified, and, which pictures cannot do, the excellent benefits of his passion. All the pictures and sculptures in the world cannot represent unto us justification, pardon, reconciliation with God, which issue from Christ's death, but the verbal crucifix can set out these to life. This chapter is so clear a crucifix, as if John that saw Christ crucified had writ it, and not Isaiah that prophesied some eight hundred years before Christ, and only saw it by the spirit of prophecy, and spirit of faith. This is a blessed perpetual crucifix of Isaiah's [illumination]; so plainly deciphering Christ's sorrows, scourgings, base usage, bruisings, condemnation, piercing, burial, death, that this chapter may well be called, and have this title over the head of it, "The Passion of Jesus Christ according to Isaiah."[50]

THE SUBSTITUTIONARY AND PENAL (I.E., A PENALTY) DEATH OF THE SERVANT

"He was pierced through for our transgressions (מִפְּשָׁעֵנוּ, *mippᵉšāʿēnû*).**"**[51] The word *transgression* is the noun form of a verb (פָּשַׁע, *pāšaʿ*) "to pass over or beyond; to cross over any rule prescribed as the limit of duty; to break or violate the law, whether civil or moral."[52] It is commonly defined, "to break with," "to behave as a criminal," or "to rebel."[53] The noun used here (פֶּשַׁע, *pešaʿ*) and ninety-two other times in the OT is generally defined as "offence" (as in stealing property) or "crime" (cf. Gen. 31:36; Exod. 22:9 [MT = v. 8]). The word is a theological word because this is God's world and he is sovereign over it. Whoever commits a transgression "breaks with Yahweh, takes away what is his, robs, embezzles, misappropriates it."[54] Because these acts are

---

[50] Thomas Calvert, *Mel Cæli, Medulla Evangelii; or, The Prophet Isaiah's Crucifix, Being An Exposition of the Fifty third Chapter of the Prophecie of Isaiah* (London: Tho. Pierrepont, 1657), 3.

[51] The form מִפְּשָׁעֵנוּ is msc. pl. of פֶּשַׁע. See *HALOT*, s.v. "פֶּשַׁע" and "פָּשַׁע," 2:981–82.

[52] David Roberts Dungan, "Transgression," *ISBE*, 5 (1939): 3006–7.

[53] BDB, s.v. "פֶּשַׁע," 833.

[54] R. Knierim, "פֶּשַׁע," *TLOT*, 2:1036; H. Seebass, "פֶּשַׁע" and "פָּשַׁע," in *TDOT*, 12:144–45.

against the authority of God, some prefer a stronger translation than "transgressions," viz. "rebellious deeds" (NET).[55]

The end-time Israelites, here speaking for their first-century countrymen, are confessing that that the grievous physical afflictions suffered by the Servant are punishments they deserved and not the Servant. He was punished because of their transgressions.[56] And so it is of us. We have transgressed in all kinds of ways, and God's Servant, Jesus, was punished because of those transgressions or rebellious actions.

"He was crushed for our iniquities" (מֵעֲוֹנֹתֵינוּ, mēʿăwōnōtênû). The word iniquity (עָוֹן, ʿāwôn) is from the verb (עָוָה, ʿāwāh) meaning "to bend, twist." When used of human sin, it means "to act wrongly, to do wrong, to go astray." The noun means "bending, curving, turning, twisting" and is usually translated "misdeed, guilt, iniquity (resulting in guilt)." It speaks of human perversity.[57] The end-time Israelites confess that God's Servant was crushed because of all the bent and twisted misdeeds of the people.[58] And applying the text to modern day readers, we may say that he was crushed because of all our wrong doing as well.

When we consider the sufferings of Christ, we learn something of the magnitude of our sins in the eyes of God. If transgressions and iniquities are merely the failure to live up to human standards, and if they are simply human errors that we have made, it is very difficult to understand why such failures led to the death of the Servant as our substitute. If, however, Isaiah is speaking of "something far more serious, namely iniquities and transgressions that God regards as such, then the profundity of the passage immediately becomes clear."[59]

[55] Smith, Isaiah 40–66, 450–51, n. 376.

[56] The preposition מִן prefixed to the noun פֶּשַׁע here has a causal sense, i.e., "because of our transgressions" (BDB, s.v. "פֶּשַׁע," 833; cf. Bruce K. Waltke and M. O'Connor, IBHS, § 11.2.11d [213]; HALOT, s.v. "מִן," 598).

[57] R. Knierim, "עָוֹן, ʿāwōn, perversity," in TLOT, 2:862–66. See also HALOT, s.v. "עָוָה," and "עָוֹן," 1:796 and 800.

[58] As with פֶּשַׁע, the noun עָוֹן is prefixed with a causal מִן.

[59] Edward J. Young, The Book of Isaiah, NICOT (Grand Rapids: Eerdmans, 1972), 3:347.

THE BENEFICIAL AND HEALING DEATH OF THE SERVANT

The first half of verse 5 sets forth the reason for the Servant's sufferings.[60] **"He was pierced because of our transgressions, crushed because of our iniquities"** (HCSB). The believing Israelites of the end-time confess that the Servant suffered the consequences of their sinful acts (**"our transgressions," "our iniquities"**). In short, his sufferings were substitutionary and penal. They were penal in that they were "a just punishment for rebellious acts." And they were substitutionary in that the punishment that should have fallen on the sinful Israelites fell on him instead.[61] The entire passage supports the substitutionary, penal view of the atonement.[62] He bore the punishment of sin as our substitute, and God was satisfied.[63]

---

[60] Smith, *Isaiah 40–66*, 450–51.

[61] Smith, *Isaiah 40–66*, 451.

[62] The evidence is four-fold: First, there are close similarities to the terminology of the Day of Atonement in Leviticus 16. Second, there is the contrast of pronouns ("he" vs. "us/our"). Third, the Servant is called a guilt offering or reparation offering in verse 10. Fourth, scholars have noted several expressions in the chapter that describe the vicarious or substitutionary nature of the Servant's sufferings: (1) "He Himself bore our griefs," (2) "He carried our sorrows," (3) "He was pierced through for our transgressions," (4) "He was crushed for our iniquities," (5) "The chastening for our well-being fell upon Him," (6) "We are healed by His scourging," (7) "The LORD has caused the iniquity of us all to fall on Him," (8) "He was cut off out of the land of the living for the transgression of my people, to whom the stroke was due," (9) "The LORD was pleased to crush Him, putting Him to grief," (10) "He rendered Himself as a guilt offering," (11) "He will bear their iniquities," (12) "He poured out his soul to death [for many]." (13) He was [wrongly] numbered with the transgressors." (14) "He Himself bore the sin of many." See J. S. Whale, *Victor and Victim: The Christian Doctrine of Redemption* (Cambridge: Cambridge University Press, 1960), 69; W. Kay, "Isaiah: Introduction, Commentary and Critical Notes," in F. C. Cook, ed., *The Holy Bible According to the Authorized Version (1611), with an Explanatory and Critical Commentary* (New York: Scribner's, 1893), 5:266. The present writer would omit numbers one and two from the list in that they refer not to the Servant's bearing of sin but to his healing of the sick during his earthly ministry. He has added numbers 12 and 13 in that the other expressions all indicate that the Servant's actions were for others, i.e., he identified with them and stood in their place.

[63] Much contemporary scholarship is opposed to the idea of vicarious atonement. Harry M. Orlinsky says the idea of vicarious suffering is "a theological and scholarly fiction." The concept "is not to be found either here or anywhere else in the Bible." "Nothing could be farther from this basic concept of *quid pro quo*, or from the spirit and letter of biblical law, or from the teachings of the prophets, than that the just and faithful should suffer vicariously for the unjust and faithless; that would have been the greatest injustice of all, nothing short of blasphemy" ("The So-Called 'Servant of the Lord' and 'Suffering Servant' in Second Isaiah," in *Studies on the Second Part of the Book of Isaiah*, by Harry M.

The second half of verse 5 describes the benefits of the substitutionary penal atonement accomplished by the Servant.[64] The first benefit is "our well-being," or "our peace." The Israelites say, "The chastening for our well-being fell upon Him." This has been more accurately translated, "[The] punishment[65] for our peace was on Him" (HCSB) or "the punishment that brought us peace was upon him"

Orlinsky and Norman H. Snaith (Leiden: Brill, 1967), 51, 54–55). Also see: R. N. Whybray (*Isaiah 40–66*, NCBC [Grand Rapids: Eerdmans, 1981], 175), who argues that verse 4 speaks of the Servant's "identification with them in their suffering: there is nothing to suggest that he suffered in their place." He adds, "The Servant shared with others a penalty which was appropriate for them but not for him." Three assertions are made, especially by Orlinsky: (1) Vicarious suffering is not found in Isaiah 53. (2) Vicarious suffering is not found in the Bible. (3) The idea of vicarious atonement is unjust, unrighteous, and blasphemous. To respond briefly: (1) To say vicarious suffering is not found in Isaiah 53 is a mere assertion that flies in the face of the text itself, as well as its best interpreters. (2) To say that vicarious suffering is not found in the Bible is to ignore the Hebrew Bible. Blood sacrifices [an innocent victim dying in the place of a guilty sinner] go back to the fall of man [the sacrifice for Adam and Eve and the sacrifice for Abel]. The Mosaic law itself is "a system of atonement. Blot out the passages relating to atonement and sacrifice, and how much of the whole law remains? Take away the doctrine of atonement and what becomes of that tribe [Levi] set apart to the priestly office? Take away the doctrine of atonement, and what use is the high priest with all his holy garments, and all the laws peculiar to him alone. Take away the doctrine of atonement, and where is the necessity for the Holy of Holies, into which the high priest went once a year; the Holy of Holies, the most sacred object in the whole Mosaic constitution and the most signal mark of the Divine favor to Israel? Take away the doctrine of atonement, and what becomes of the Day of Atonement, the most solemn day in the whole Jewish year?" [A. McCaul, *The Doctrine and Interpretation of the Fifty-Third Chapter of Isaiah* (London: London Society's House, 1888), 3–4]. (3) To say that the doctrine of vicarious atonement is unjust or unrighteous assumes that one has a standard of righteousness outside of Scripture. We have no way of knowing what is unjust or unrighteous apart from the Word of God. Orlinsky "cannot possibly determine, *a priori*, any general truth respecting the right or the wrong of God's dealings, independently of the revelation which He has given" (McCaul, 4–5). Cf. also: William D. Barrick, "Penal Substitution in the Old Testament," *TMSJ* 20 (Fall, 2009): 149–69.

[64] Smith, *Isaiah 40–66*, 451.

[65] The LXX softens immediate context of the Hebrew מוּסַר to παιδεία ("education"). Goldingay and Payne also fly in the face of the context and argue that punishment is not in view. "It is more a word for the disciplining of a pupil by a teacher or a child by a parent with a view to the recipient's growth or reform" (John Goldingay and David Payne, *Isaiah 40–55*, ICC [London: T & T Clark, 2006], 2:307). Surprisingly, Young agrees and argues that מוּסַר here refers to "corrective discipline"…and…contains the thought of remedy or correction" (*The Book of Isaiah*, 3:348).

(NIV).[66] In Hebrew grammar the words "punishment" and "peace" (מוּסַר שְׁלוֹמֵנוּ, *mûsar šᵉlômēnû*) are said to be in a construct relationship, specifically, a construct-genitive relationship. Here that relationship or "construct chain" expresses purpose.[67] It was the purpose of God in punishing the Servant to secure "our peace."[68]

The peace (שָׁלוֹם, *šālôm*) Isaiah speaks of is "peace with God."[69] The Servant endured "a beating for our salvation."[70] Because of their sins the people were in a state of hostility toward God and deserving of his punishment. However, that punishment did not fall on the transgressors, but on the Servant, and peace was restored.[71] Therefore the peace

---

[66] "Here for the first time we encounter explicit reference to the vicarious suffering of the righteous [one]." F. J. Stendebach, "שָׁלוֹם," *Theological Dictionary of the Old Testament*, 15:34.

[67] GKC § 128q, p. 417. Others have argued that the construct chain here expresses effect, that is, the punishment had the effect of securing "our peace." See Waltke and O'Connor, *IBHS*, § 9.5.2 (p. 146). Either understanding of the syntax is possible; the first view underscores the divine intention behind the sufferings of the Servant.

[68] Smith, *Isaiah 40–66*, 451. The first use of שָׁלוֹם ("peace") in Isaiah also refers to Christ. The royal child in Isaiah 9:6 (MT, v. 5) is called שַׂר־שָׁלוֹם (*śar šālôm*), "Prince of Peace." His rule will be marked by endless שָׁלוֹם (v. 7 [MT, v. 6]). The future king will establish his rule upon righteousness and justice. In this context שָׁלוֹם means "the total divine order of the world, which it is the king's duty to protect" (F. J. Stendebach, "שָׁלוֹם," *TDOT*, 15:34).

[69] BDB, s.v. "שָׁלוֹם," 1023.

[70] *HALOT*, 2:1510.

[71] Young, *The Book of Isaiah*, 3:348–49. Isaiah 53:5 anticipates the New Testament doctrine of reconciliation, which has been defined as "a finished work of God by which man is brought from an attitude and position of enmity with God to an attitude and position of amity and peace with God by means of the removal of the enmity through the cross" (S. Lewis Johnson, Jr., "From Enmity to Amity," *BibSac* 119 [April, 1962], 139–49 [esp. 144]). The word שָׁלוֹם in Isaiah 53:5 is translated εἰρήνη in the LXX. In the New Testament εἰρήνη is used in a number of contexts where peace with God is linked with Christ's atoning death, which has done away with the enmity between God and man. See the following expressions: "preaching peace through Jesus Christ" (Acts 10:36, 39-40); "peace with God" (Rom. 5:1, 8-9); "the God of peace" (Heb. 13:20); "he himself is our peace," "thus establishing peace," "he came and preached peace to you" (Eph. 2:14, 15, 17). On the Ephesians 2 passage Foerster wrote, "Hence in verse 14, αὐτὸς γὰρ ἐστιν ἡ εἰρήνη ἡμῶν, is to be taken in a comprehensive sense. When Christ abolished the Law, he set aside the twofold disorder of the race both among men and toward God. Εἰρήνη means peace with God and within humanity" (Werner Foerster, "εἰρήνη," *TDNT*, 2:415). For a full discussion of "peace" in the context of the doctrine of reconciliation, see Leon Morris, *The Apostolic Preaching of the Cross*, 3d ed. (London: Tyndale, 1965), 237–44.

accomplished by the Servant's suffering "must include the forgiveness of sins and the annulment of their consequences."[72]

Oswalt has illustrated this with peace in a home:

> The child has rebelled against the parent; not only has the relationship been disrupted, but justice is offended. There is no *šālôm*, well-being, because things are out of order, unbalanced. Until punishment has been meted out, all the good intentions in the world cannot restore that broken order. But when the parent's authority has been recognized, when justice has been done, then both sides of the equation are balanced again, which is what shalom is all about.[73]

The punishment **"fell upon Him."** There is no verb in the Hebrew text, so translators add one, such as "fell" (NASB) or "was" (Darby, KJV, NIV, ESV, HCSB).[74] In any case, the idea of substitution is clearly expressed; the punishment that secured our peace was endured by him in our place.

The second benefit of the Servant's sufferings is expressed in the last colon or line of verse 5: **"And by His scourging we are healed."** The Hebrew word for scourging (חַבּוּרָה [*ḥabbûrāh*]) occurs twice in Isaiah, here and in chapter 1 (1:6). In chapter 1, Israel is described as sick unto death, covered with **"bruises, welts, and raw wounds."** The context makes it clear that the prophet is speaking of the nation's sin: **"Alas, sinful nation, people weighed down with iniquity, offspring of evildoers, sons who act corruptly!"** (1:4). It is evident that God's punishment is represented using the imagery of disease.

---

[72] F. J. Stendebach, "שָׁלוֹם," *TDOT*, 15:34. Hengstenberg wrote, "Peace stands as an individualizing designation of salvation; in the world of contentions, peace is one of the highest blessings. Natural man is on all sides surrounded by enemies...and peace with God renders all other enemies innocuous, and at last removes them altogether. The peace is inseparable from the substitution. If the Servant of God has borne our sins, he has thereby, at the same time, acquired peace; for, just as he enters into our guilt, so we now enter into his reward. The justice of God has been satisfied through him; and thus an open way has been prepared for his bestowing peace and salvation (*Christology of the Old Testament*, 2:284).

[73] Oswalt, *The Book of Isaiah, Chapters 40–66*, 388.

[74] The REB has "the chastisement he bore," and the NET has "he endured punishment."

Likewise in chapter 53, the problem of the people is their rebellious deeds and iniquities. Just as their problem is a spiritual one, so also is the remedy. Just as their punishment is described as scourging, so their deliverance from it is described as healing. The only relief from the "bruises, welts, and raw wounds" is the healing that comes when the Servant of the LORD takes these bruises, welts, and raw wounds upon himself.[75] When Jesus Christ submitted to divine justice at the cross, his voluntary death became the source of our healing.[76] Delitzsch wrote:

> We were sick unto death because of our sins; but He, the sinless one, took upon himself a suffering unto death, which was, as it were, the concentration and essence of the woes that we had deserved; and this voluntary endurance, this submission to the justice of the Holy One, in accordance with the counsels of divine love, became the source of our healing.[77]

ISRAEL'S CONFESSION OF THEIR PERSONAL INIQUITY AS THE CAUSE OF THE SERVANT'S SUFFERINGS, VERSE 6

All of us like sheep have gone astray,
Each of us has turned to his own way;
But the LORD has caused the iniquity of us all
To fall on Him.

ISRAEL CONFESSES THAT THEY WENT ASTRAY, TO THEIR RUIN

The Corporate Guilt of Israel
In verse 6 the believing remnant of Israel in the last days will declare what Yahweh has done with their guilt. Before they do, they will confess their guilt, both corporate and individual, and compare themselves to

---

[75] Oswalt, *The Book of Isaiah, Chapters 40–66*, 388. As Smith notes (*Isaiah 40–66*, 451), the passage can be given a "more holistic eschatological interpretation," which includes spiritual healing in the present and physical healing in the resurrection life to come.

[76] BDB says that נִרְפָּא (3d msc. sg. niphal perf. רָפָא) is here used figuratively of the healing of national hurts...involving forgiveness and Israel's blessing. The figurative use of healing as forgiveness is confirmed in 1 Peter 2:24: "And he himself bore our sins in his body on the cross, so that we might die to sin and live to righteousness; for by his wounds you were healed."

[77] Delitzsch, *Biblical Commentary on the Prophecies of Isaiah*, 2:319–20.

wayward sheep. He first speaks of their corporate guilt. **"All of us like sheep have gone astray."** This emphasizes the "extent of the problem."[78] "All of us" (כֻּלָּנוּ [*kullānû*])—there are no exceptions. Unlike Jesus' parable of the lost sheep, in which a man loses one out of a flock of one hundred (Luke 15:4), the picture here is of the scattering of the whole flock.

Sheep are notoriously prone to getting lost. "They do not behave as individuals in moving from one area to another." As a friend of the writer, who knows something of sheep has said, "They follow a leader and move as a flock."[79] The remnant confesses that they all have "gone astray" (תָּעָה, *tā'āh*)[80].

This has been interpreted in at least three ways, all of which have merit. First, some have argued that it speaks of inborn, Adamic sin,[81] i.e., original sin.[82] This very verb is used in Psalm 58:3, **"The wicked are estranged from the womb; these who speak lies go astray from birth."** In this verse the verb "go astray" does not involve reflective thought or decision of the will. Original sin is ours without any actions of our own. We receive it at conception even before we can think. As David wrote, **"In sin my mother conceived me"** (Ps. 51:5), i.e., from the moment of conception David had a sinful nature or disposition.

---

[78] Oswalt, *The Book of Isaiah, Chapters 40–66*, 389.

[79] Culver, *The Sufferings and the Glory of the LORD's Righteous Servant*, 78.

[80] The form used in the text is תָּעִינוּ (1st pers. pl. qal perf.). Cf. *HALOT*, s.v. "תָּעָה," 2:1766; BDB, s.v. "תָּעָה," 1073.

[81] Culver, *The Sufferings and the Glory of the LORD's Righteous Servant*, 78.

[82] In defining original sin theologians have differed. Hodge, for example, defined it broadly and included three elements: (1) the guilt of Adam's first sin, (2) the loss of original righteousness, and (3) the corruption of our whole nature. Berkhof, on the other hand, argues for a narrower definition that eliminates original guilt. Original sin is inherited; original guilt is imputed [Rom. 5:12]. He limited his definition to the inherited corrupt nature of each human being. It is "the sinful state and condition in which men are born." It is called "original sin" for three reasons: (1) It is derived from our first parents or, as Berkhof puts it, "the original root" of the human race. (2) It is present in the life of every individual from the time of his birth. It is original equipment and cannot be the result of imitation. (3) It is the source ("inward root") of all the personal sins that defile a man's life. Berkhof adds this caveat: One must not make the mistake of assuming that the term "original sin" implies that such sin belonged to the original constitution of human nature. Adam was fully human, yet he was sinless for a time. See Charles Hodge, *Systematic Theology* (New York: Scribner, 1972; reprint ed., Grand Rapids: Eerdmans, 1975), 2:227; Louis Berkhof, *Systematic Theology*, 4th ed. (Grand Rapids: Eerdmans, 1949), 244.

Second, others have said that it describes the universality of sin. The figure of wandering, or lost sheep, is common in the Old Testament "to denote alienation from God and the misery which is its necessary consequence" (Jer. 10:21; 23:2; 50:6-7; Ezek. 34:5).[83] Repentant Israel here looks back at the exile as the final state of punishment before its deliverance. "Israel in its exile resembled a scattered flock without a shepherd; it had lost the way of Jehovah (Isa. 63:17)."[84] Isaiah, of course, could not have distinguished the Babylonian exile from Israel's inter-advent exile which will end with Christ's second coming and Israel's final deliverance.

A third opinion, expressed by Theodoret (c. AD 393–c. 466), Bishop of Cyrrhus in Syria, is that the verb "go astray" is used here of going after false gods as exemplified in various idols.[85] It is noteworthy that the verb תָּעָה (tāʿāh) is used in a number of places of Israel's idolatry (Ezek. 44:10, 15; 48:11).[86] Should this be uppermost in Israel's mind, they here confess that they have not kept the first commandment and have gone after false gods (cf. Exod. 20:2-3). In the context of Israel's apostasy in Isaiah, this third view is most probable (cf. Isa. 40:19, 20; 44:10; 45:20; 48:5; 66:3).[87]

The Individual Guilt of Israelites

In the next line "the confession turns from the flock to the individual sheep."[88] "Each of us has turned to his own way." If the previous line speaks in some way of corporate sin (original sin, universal sin, idolatry), this line speaks of personal sins. All people are individually sinners by choice. The sinful nature or inclination of man expresses itself in decisions of the will.[89] Each of them deliberately (not accidentally) "turned to his own way" or "strayed off on his own path" (NET).

Both the Old Testament and the New Testament affirm that each and every human being is a sinner. **"The LORD has looked down from**

---

[83] Joseph Addison Alexander, *Commentary on the Prophecies of Isaiah*, rev. ed. (T. & T. Clark, 1875; reprint ed., Grand Rapids: Zondervan, 1974), 2:296–97.

[84] Delitzsch, *Biblical Commentary on the Prophecies of Isaiah*, 2:320.

[85] Theodoret, cited by Alexander, *Commentary on the Prophecies of Isaiah*, 2:297.

[86] Cf. U. Berges, "תָּעָה," *TDOT*, 15:732–36 (esp. 735).

[87] From a theological perspective, of course, all three views are true.

[88] Lindsey, *The Servant Songs*, 123.

[89] Culver, *The Sufferings and the Glory of the LORD's Righteous Servant*, 79.

heaven upon the sons of men to see if there are any who understand, who seek after God. They have all turned aside, together they have become corrupt; there is no one who does good, not even one" (Ps. 14:2-3). "For all have sinned and fall short of the glory of God" (Rom. 3:23; cf. vv. 10-18). It is significant that the verb "to turn" (פָּנָה, *pānāh*) is used to speak of both turning to God in worship (Isa. 45:22) and turning to false religion, viz., mediums and spiritists (Lev. 19:31; 20:6), other gods (Deut. 31:18-20; Hos. 3:1), and idols (Lev. 19:4).[90]

There is not a person alive who has perfectly kept the first commandment. All have gone after the tinsel and junk of this world—possessions of which we are proud and in which we find security: money (silver, gold, or paper), stocks, and bonds. Our own way has caused us to stray down the path to sophistication, pride, and prestige.[91]

At a gathering of Christians in a lovely home, someone (speaking somewhat enviously and judgmentally) told a friend of the writer that the owner, a fellow Christian, lived in a mansion. My friend gently responded, "Yes, and isn't it wonderful the way he uses it for the Lord?" He then added, "We all have our mansions!" He did not mean that we all have grand homes; rather, he meant that we all have something that can become an idol—something that turns us away from God in our hearts and minds. None of these things is necessarily an idol, but any of them can become an idol.

Retrospectively, the repentant Israelites will realize that their own way was not God's way, and they will turn back to God.[92]

ISRAEL CONFESSES THAT THE SERVANT WAS PUNISHED FOR THEIR GOOD

The verse closes with the Israelites confessing/reporting that the punishment for all of their transgressions and iniquities was transferred from "us" to "him," i.e., the Servant, the Lord Jesus Christ. They say, no doubt in amazement, **"But the LORD has caused the iniquity of us all to**

---

[90] The form used in Isaiah 53:6 is פָּנִינוּ (1st pers. pl. qal perf.). Cf. *HALOT*, s.v. "פָּנָה," 2:937–38; BDB, s.v. "פָּנָה," 815; J. Schreiner, "פָּנָה," *TDOT*, 11:578–85 (esp. 583–84).

[91] Bruce K. Waltke, "The Real Value of Jesus Christ: An Exposition of Isaiah 52:13–53:12" (cassette tape, Dallas: Believers Chapel Tape Ministry, n.d.), 8 (pagination is that of the writer's transcribed manuscript of the sermon).

[92] Cf. Berges, "תָּעָה," *TDOT*, 15:735.

fall on Him." Men could crucify him, but only Yahweh could cause iniquity to fall on him so that he could bear it as a divine penalty.[93]

Many of our translations follow the KJV's mild rendering, "The LORD hath laid on him the iniquity of us all" (cf. NIV, ESV, NRSV, REB). The verb translated "laid" in these versions (פָּגַע, *pāga'*)[94] usually suggests a violent, hostile action, "to fall upon someone intending to kill [him]."[95] The NET Bible gets to the point with, "The LORD caused the sin of all of us to attack him."

A few quotations from the Old Testament will illustrate this usage. **"The sons of Dan said to him [Micah], 'Do not let your voice be heard among us, or else fierce men will fall upon you and you will lose your life'"** (Judg. 18:25). **"So King Solomon sent Benaiah the son of Jehoida; and he fell upon him [Adonijah] so that he died"** (1 Kings 2:25). **"Then Benaiah the son of Jehoida went up and fell upon him [Joab] and put him to death"** (1 Kings 2:34). Cambridge professor T. R. Birks wrote that the word suggests, "many shafts aimed at one common target. Each sin of every sinner would be like a separate wound in the heart of this Man of Sorrows."[96]

The word "iniquity" has been defined above, but it should be added that it is a word with a variety of nuances.[97] It can refer to the misdeed or sin itself (2 Sam. 22:24; Ps. 18:23 [M.T. v. 24]; Jer. 11:10; Ezek. 4:5); it can refer to the guilt incurred because of the sin (Num. 14:19; Isa. 59:3; Ezek. 9:9); and it can refer to the punishment that results from the sin (Gen. 4:13; Jer. 51:6; Ezek. 4:4-6). The ideas "are so closely related that they are not always clearly distinguishable."[98] In the present context it is wise not to distinguish too finely among these various nuances.[99] In short, the word translated "iniquity" has the meaning of "misdeeds," "guilt," and "punishment." It must be stressed, however, that it is *vicarious punishment* (*poena vicaria*). The word *vicarious* means "standing

---

[93] Lindsey, *The Servant Songs*, 124.

[94] The form used in Isaiah 53:6 is הִפְגִּיעַ (3d pers. msc. sg. hiphil perf.).

[95] *HALOT*, s.v. "פָּגַע," 2:910.

[96] T. R. Birks, *Commentary on the Book of Isaiah Critical, Historical, and Prophetical*, 2d ed. (London: Macmillan, 1878; reprint ed., Delhi, India: Pranava Books, 2008), 264.

[97] *HALOT*, s.v. "עָוֹן," 1:800; BDB, s.v. "עָוֹן," 730–31; cf. Delitzsch, *Biblical Commentary on the Prophecies of Isaiah*, 2:322.

[98] J. C. Motyer, "Iniquity," in *ISBE*, rev, 2:825.

[99] Cf. Oswalt, *The Book of Isaiah, Chapters 40–66*, 389, n. 10.

in the place of another."[100] Yahweh caused the punishment for the iniquity (עָוֹן) of Israel to strike against (בְּ) the Servant of God, so that he suffered vicariously for the people.[101]

The Servant of the LORD submitted to God in all of this; he took the sin of men upon himself; as a result he stood before God as a guilty man, and divine punishment was inflicted upon him.

> He took my sins and my sorrows,
>   He made them His very own;
> He bore the burden to Calv'ry,
>   And suffered and died alone.[102]

Delitzsch wrote, "the Servant of God cannot become the object of punishment, either *as a servant of God* or *as an atoning Savior*; for *as servant of God* he is the beloved of God, and *as atoning Savior* he undertakes a work which is well pleasing to God, and ordained in God's eternal counsel. So that wrath which pours out upon him is not meant for him as the righteous One who voluntarily offers up himself; but indirectly it relates to him, so far as he has vicariously identified himself with sinners, who are deserving of wrath."[103]

Lewis Johnson asked, "Would a loving God forsake the only good man who ever lived (cf. Matt. 3:17; Ps. 37:25)? The answer to that question must be 'no'.... Would a loving God injure the only innocent man who ever lived? The answer must be the same."[104] How, then, could Christ be punished? The apostle Paul answered, **"He [God] made Him [Christ] who knew no sin to be sin on our behalf"** (2 Cor. 5:21).

On the cross Christ vicariously became the guilty one. He was **"numbered with the transgressors [and]...bore the sin of many"** (Isa. 53:12). As Luther commented, Christ became guilty (vicariously), and

---

[100] Richard A. Muller, *Dictionary of Latin and Greek Theological Terms* (Grand Rapids: Baker, 1985), 327 [on *poena*, see p. 229].

[101] P. Maiberger, "פָּגַע," *TDOT*, 11:470–76 (esp. 474). When the verb denotes a hostile action it is often accompanied, as here, by the preposition בְּ. See John Goldingay and David Payne, *Isaiah 40–55*, ICC (London: T. & T. Clark, 2006), 2:308. Cf. *HALOT*, s.v. "פָּגַע," 2:910.

[102] Charles H. Gabriel, "My Savior's Love," Hymn 512 in *The Hymnal for Worship and Celebration* (Waco, TX: Word, 1986).

[103] Delitzsch, *Biblical Commentary on the Prophecies of Isaiah*, 2:321.

[104] S. Lewis Johnson, Jr., "The Death of Christ," *Bibliotheca Sacra* 125 (Jan., 1968): 17.

bore sin and the curse of God. He wrote, "Paul therefore doth very well allege this general law out of Moses as concerning Christ: 'Everyone that hangeth upon the tree is the accursed of God' [Gal. 3:13]. Christ hath hanged upon the tree, therefore Christ is the accursed of God."[105] Speaking typically, David, in a psalm interpreted Christologically by the author of Hebrews, has Christ say, "**For evils beyond number have surrounded me; my iniquities have overtaken me, so that I am not able to see; they are more numerous than the hairs of my head, and my heart has failed me**" (Ps. 40:12; cf. Heb. 10:5-7). Here Christ takes our sins upon himself and confesses them as his own.[106]

In the midst of his exhortation to perseverance, the author of Hebrews says of Jesus that he "**endured the cross, despising the shame**" (12:2).[107] The shame inflicted on Christ was twofold.[108] First, there was

---

[105] Martin Luther, *A Commentary on St. Paul's Epistle to the Galatians*, the Middleton edition, ed., Philip S. Watson (London: James Clarke, 1953), 271. Luther's comments on Galatians 3:13 are marked by a profound understanding of the substitutionary, penal doctrine of the atonement and should be read (esp. 269–73).

[106] Commentators have debated this point. Those objecting to a Messianic interpretation of Psalm 40:12 include Perowne, Maclaren, and Delitzsch. Those advocating a Messianic interpretation include Spurgeon, Murphy, Darby, Fausset, Grant, and Lewis. See: J. J. Stewart Perowne, *The Book of Psalms*, 3d ed. (London: George Bell, 1878; reprint ed., Grand Rapids: Zondervan, 1966), 1:46, 338; Alexander Maclaren, *The Psalms* (New York: Doran, 1892), 2:27–28; Franz Delitzsch, *Biblical Commentary on the Psalms*, trans. Francis Bolton (Edinburgh: T. & T. Clark, 1871; reprint ed., Grand Rapids: Eerdmans, n.d.), 2:35, 41; C. H. Spurgeon [quoting John Frame with approbation], *The Treasury of David* (New York: Funk, 1882; reprint ed. [7 vols. in 3], Grand Rapids: Zondervan, 1963), 1, pt. 2: 250 [orig. 2:250]; James G. Murphy, *A Critical and Exegetical Commentary on the Book of Psalms* (Andover, MA: Draper, 1876; reprint ed., Minneapolis: James, 1977), 261; J. N. Darby, "Psalm 40," in *The Collected Writings of J. N. Darby*, ed., William Kelly (reprint ed., Oak Park, IL: Bible Truth Publishers, 1971), 30:75–80 (esp. 76–78); A. R. Fausset, *Job–Isaiah*, in Robert Jamieson, A. R. Fausset, and David Brown, *A Commentary Critical, Experimental, and Practical on the Old and New Testaments* (Glasgow: W. Collins, 1870; reprint ed., Grand Rapids: Eerdmans, 1945), 3:189; F. W. Grant, *The Numerical Bible: The Psalms* (New York: Loizeaux, 1895), 168; C. S. Lewis, *Reflections on the Psalms* (New York: Harcourt, Brace and World, 1958), 127. As Dodd noted, the New Testament authors did not cite OT quotations as isolated proof texts. These quotations were understood to be parts of whole contexts, and it is often the total OT context that provides the basis of the NT argument (C. H. Dodd, *According to the Scriptures* [New York: Scribner's, 1953], 126). Messiah's bearing of his peoples' sins and confessing them as his own certainly fits with the argument of Hebrews 10:9-12. The author of Hebrews clearly believed in a substitutionary atonement (cf. 2:9).

[107] Philip Edgcumbe Hughes wrote, "It is important to recognize that the shame of the cross, where Christ bore the sins of the world, is something infinitely more intense than

his shame before men. Crucifixion was the most barbaric form of execution known in antiquity. It was a "sign of shame" as well as an instrument of torture and death. Pagans called it the "infamous stake," the "barren" or "criminal" wood, "the terrible cross."[109] It was "a 'barbaric' form of execution of the utmost cruelty," the word "barbaric" suggesting it was suitable for barbarian people, not Romans.[110] "To die by crucifixion was to plumb the lowest depths of disgrace; it was a punishment reserved for those who were deemed most unfit to live, a

---

the pain of the cross" (*A Commentary on the Epistle to the Hebrews* [Grand Rapids: Eerdmans, 1977], 525).

[108] The author of Hebrews said, "He endured the cross, despising the shame" (ὑπέμεινεν σταυρὸν αἰσχύνης καταφρονήσας). The participle "despising" has been understood in two ways: (1) A small minority take it in a negative way, i.e., "He did not like it; he wanted to avoid it; this was anything but his choice" [George Wesley Buchanan, *To the Hebrews*, AncB (Garden City, NY: Doubleday, 1972), 209; possibly Hughes, *A Commentary on the Epistle to the Hebrews*, 524–25]. This interpretation has the advantage of taking seriously Jesus' actions and words in Gethsemane [Matt. 26:39; Mark 14:33; Luke 22:44; Heb. 5:7] and his cry of dereliction on Golgotha [Matt. 27:46]. Everywhere else in the N.T., it should be noted, the verb καταφρονέω does have a negative connotation. Cf. BDAG, s.v. "καταφρονέω," 529. (2) The majority of commentators take the participle in a positive way, "He considered it as nothing; He wasn't troubled by it" [Otto Michel, *Der Brief an die Hebräer*, 12th ed. (Göttingen: Vandenhoeck and Ruprecht, 1966), 436]. "Jesus' reaction was 'to scorn the shame' associated with it" [Peter T. O'Brien, *The Letter to the Hebrews*, PNTC (Grand Rapids: Eerdmans, 2010), 457]; F. F. Bruce, *The Epistle to the Hebrews*, rev. ed., NICNT (Grand Rapids: Eerdmans, 1990), 338; BDAG, s.v. "καταφρονέω," 529; Carl Schneider, "καταφρονέω," TDNT, 3:631–33 (esp. 632); David Arthur deSilva, *Despising Shame: Honor Discourse and Community Maintenance in the Epistle to the Hebrews*, rev. ed. (Atlanta: Society of Biblical Literature, 2008), 178–88. The second interpretation seeks to take seriously the immediate context in which Jesus serves as an example of one who was not overcome by his sufferings and society's norms of honor and shame, but bravely endured in obedience to God and for the honor that lay before him at God's right hand. It runs the risk, however, of suggesting that the crucifixion was not as horrific as the Gospels imply [cf. Buchanan's translation of Michel, "He sloughed it off as if it were nothing"]. The present writer believes that one must honor the context, and this one may do by stressing the verb "to endure" rather than by giving "despising" a good sense. Moffatt, who does give καταφρονήσας a good sense, does not deny Jesus' experience of shame. "Jesus was sensitive to such emotions; he felt disgrace keenly" (James Moffatt, *A Critical and Exegetical Commentary on the Epistle to the Hebrews*, ICC [Edinburgh: T. & T. Clark, 1924], 197). In short, it seems best to give καταφρονήσας its usual N.T. sense, i.e., a negative one.

[109] Martin Hengel, *Crucifixion in the Ancient World and the folly of the message of the cross*, trans. John Bowden (Philadelphia: Fortress, 1977), 7; J. Schneider, s.v. "σταυρός," TDNT, 7:573–77.

[110] Hengel, *Crucifixion in the Ancient World*, 22–23.

punishment for those who were subhuman."[111] "It was inflicted above all on the lower classes, i.e., slaves, violent criminals and the unruly elements.... By the public display of a naked victim at a prominent place...crucifixion also represented his uttermost humiliation."[112] From the Jewish point of view, a person put to death by crucifixion (hanging) was cursed by God (Gal. 3:10; cf. Deut. 21:22-23).[113]

Second, there was the shame of this sinless, perfect man before God. Francis Pieper, a devout and evangelical Lutheran theologian, caught the awful significance of this when he wrote:

> We can understand the meaning of Christ's [bearing our iniquities and] being forsaken by God only if we fully accept the central truth of Christ's substitution for us. Christ in himself indeed was no sinner. The transfer of our sin to him was a purely juridical [i.e., judicial] divine act: "God made Him to be sin for us who knew no sin" (2 Cor. 5:21). But this divine juridical act of God penetrated to the very heart and conscience of the suffering Christ. When Christ was forsaken of God, he felt the sin and guilt of all men in his soul as his own sin and guilt. This is clearly brought out in the Old Testament prophecy in which Christ speaks of his own sin and guilt in the words: ["O God, you are aware of my foolish sins; my guilt is not hidden from you," Ps. 69:5, NET]. With our sin and guilt, Christ also felt God's wrath, that is, God's verdict of condemnation and rejection, in His soul, just as if He had personally committed all sins of mankind.[114]

---

[111] F. F. Bruce, *The Epistle to the Hebrews,* rev. ed., NICNT (Grand Rapids: Eerdmans, 1990), 338.

[112] Hengel, *Crucifixion,* 87.

[113] Peter J. Gentry. "The Atonement in Isaiah's Fourth Servant Song (Isaiah 52:13–53:12)," *SBJT* 11 (Summer, 2007): 20–47 (esp. 33). Gentry notes that in the previous verses (Deut. 21:18–21) the procedure for dealing with a rebellious son (stoning) is given. "This makes our text ironic. The Servant was given a death penalty as if he were a rebellious son, but in fact, it is Israel that is the rebellious son. The servant dies in Israel's place."

[114] Francis Pieper, *Christian Dogmatics,* trans. Theodore Engelder and John Theodore Mueller (St. Louis: Concordia, 1951), 2:310.

Luther describes the scene as follows:

> Our most merciful Father, seeing us to be oppressed and
> overwhelmed with the curse of the law, and so to be holden
> under the same that we could never be delivered from it by our
> own power, sent his only Son into the world and laid upon him
> all the sins of all men, saying: "Be thou Peter that denier; Paul
> that persecutor, blasphemer and cruel oppressor; David that
> adulterer; that sinner which did eat the [fruit] in Paradise; that
> thief which hanged upon the cross; and briefly, be thou the
> person which hath committed the sins of all men; see therefore
> that thou pay and satisfy for them." Here now cometh the law
> and saith: "I find him a sinner, and that such a one as hath taken
> upon him the sins of all men, and I see no sins else but in him;
> therefore let him die upon the cross." And so he setteth upon
> him and killeth him. By this means the whole world is purged
> and cleansed from all sins, and so delivered from death and all
> evils. Now sin and death being abolished by this one man, God
> would see nothing else in the whole world, especially if it did
> believe, but a mere cleansing and righteousness.[115]

> Jehovah bade His sword awake:
>   O Christ, it woke 'gainst Thee;
> Thy blood the flaming blade must slake,
>   Thy heart its sheath must be.
> All for my sake, my peace to make:
>   Now sleeps that sword for me.[116]

The NIV retains the Hebrew word order regarding the *inclusio*
formed by the identical form, the emphatic "all" (כֻּלָּנוּ, *kullānû*) at the
beginning and end of the verse ("**We all, like sheep, have gone astray,
each of us has turned to his own way; and the LORD has laid on Him**

---

[115] Luther, *A Commentary on St. Paul's Epistle to the Galatians*, 272. He wrote, "And this
is a singular consolation for all the godly, so to clothe Christ with our sins, and to wrap
him in my sins, thy sins, and the sins of the whole world, and so to behold him bearing
all our iniquities" (271).

[116] Annie R. Cousin, "O Christ, what burdens bowed Thy head!" Hymn # 126, in
Hymns: The hymnal of Inter-Varsity Christian Fellowship, ed. Paul Beckwith (Chicago:
Inter-Varsity Press, 1950).

the iniquity of us all").[117] In the epistle to the Romans (3:19)[118] the apostle makes it clear that Israel is a test case for the whole human race. **"All of us like sheep have gone astray."** That includes not only all of Israel, but all others among the Gentiles as well. "The sinful alienation is *universal*, the modes of its manifestations are as various as men and their tendencies."[119] The "us all" at the end of the verse speaks of the *universal* provision made for sin in the vicarious death of the Servant. In its ultimate application, of course, it speaks of the redeemed—"primarily of all redeemed Israel, but inclusively also of all the redeemed from among all the nations."[120]

CONCLUSION

> The first thing that stands out in these verses is the basic Christian truth that Christ's sufferings were substitutionary,...[yet] countless modern theologians have rejected the biblical doctrine of propitiation, namely, that righteousness and justice are attributes of the divine being and must be satisfied by a proper substitute.[121]

This is illustrated by Steve Chalke, a well-known preacher, author, and broadcaster. He wrote:

> John's Gospel famously declares, "God loved the people of this world so much He gave His Son" (John 3:16). How then, have

---

[117] Isaiah 53:6 is one of many verses used in the perennial debate over the extent of the atonement. Lindsey notes that the group included in both occurrences of "all" must be the same. "[כֻּלָּנוּ...כֻּלָּנוּ] emphasizes the fact that those whose iniquity was borne by the Servant are identical to those who have corporately and individually wandered away like sheep." All of Israel, not just the elect, wandered away, and the Servant bore the iniquities of that same group. This would seem to suggest an unlimited atonement, i.e., the Servant in his death made provision for the forgiveness of all the people. The redeemed, of course, are God's elect who confess their sins and place their faith in the finished work of the Servant. Edward J. Young responds that such a conclusion as unlimited atonement is unwarranted (*The Book of Isaiah*, 3:350).

[118] "Now we know that whatever the Law says, it speaks to *those who are under the Law*, so that every mouth may be closed and *all the world* may become accountable to God."

[119] Baron, *The Servant of Jehovah*, 94.

[120] Baron, *The Servant of Jehovah*, 97.

[121] Johnson, "The Vicarious Messiah," 133.

we come to believe that at the cross this God of love suddenly decides to vent his anger and wrath on his only Son? The fact is that the cross isn't a form of cosmic child abuse—a vengeful Father, punishing his Son for an offence he has not even committed.... Such a concept stands in total contradiction to the statement, "God is Love." If the cross is a personal act of violence perpetuated by God towards humankind but borne by his Son, then it makes a mockery of Jesus' own teaching to love your enemies and to refuse to repay evil with evil.[122]

The view that the substitutionary view of the atonement is unjust and unloving is almost commonplace today.[123] Joel Green and Mark Baker, both professors at evangelical seminaries, wrote, "God takes on the role of the sadist, inflicting punishment, while Jesus, in His role as the masochist, readily embraces suffering."[124] John Spong, the infamous apostate Anglican bishop, said, "I would choose to loathe rather than to worship a deity who required the sacrifice of his son."[125] Responding to such views, Lewis Johnson quoted Luther's comment to Erasmus, "Your thoughts about God are all too human."[126]

---

[122] Steve Chalke, *The Lost Message of Jesus*, ed., Alan Mann (Grand Rapids: Zondervan, 2003), 182–83; cf. Brian D. McLaren, *The Story We Find Ourselves In: Further Adventures of a New Kind of Christian* (San Francisco: Jossey-Bass, 2003), 102–104.

[123] Such attacks on penal substitution are not new. In his Yale lectures, Methodist bishop G. Bromiley Oxnam tells a story of a father and son found in Hugh Walpole's book *Wintersmoon*. A minister read the Bible to his family one evening, and his reading was the account of the plagues in the Book of Exodus. Later that evening he passed his son's bedroom, and the boy called him in. He said, "Father, you hate Jehovah. So do I. I loathe him, dirty bully!" Oxnam said that he agreed with the boy that a God who is righteous and demands that sin be punished is "a loathsome God" and must be denounced by preachers in a revolutionary age. See G. Gromley Oxnam, *Preaching in a Revolutionary Age*, The Lyman Beecher Lectures on Preaching, 1943–44, Yale University Divinity School (New York: Abingdon-Cokesbury, 1944), 79.

[124] Joel B. Green and Mark D. Baker, *Recovering the Scandal of the Cross* (Downers Grove: IVP, 2000), 30.

[125] John Shelby Spong, *Why Christianity Must Change or Die* (San Francisco: Harper, 1999), 95.

[126] Martin Luther, *De Servo Arbitrio*, in *Luther and Erasmus: Free Will and Salvation*, eds., E. Gordon Rupp and Philip S. Watson, Library of Christian Classics (Philadelphia: Westminster, 1969), 125. Cf. Johnson, "The Vicarious Messiah," 133.

A complete response to modern objections to the doctrine of the penal substitutionary atonement cannot be given here,[127] but a brief review of the contribution of Isaiah 53:4-6 can be. Three observations may be made. First, Isaiah's pronouns referring to the people ("our," "we," "us"—"our transgressions," "our iniquities," etc.) contrast with those used of the Servant ("he," "him"—"he was pierced," "He was crushed," "the iniquity of us all to fall on Him, etc.") and clearly imply substitution. Second, God inflicted this punishment upon him. He was "smitten of God." "The LORD has caused the iniquity of us all to fall on him." Verse 10 reinforces this point. "The LORD was pleased to crush Him, putting him to grief." Finally, this was a voluntary act on the part of the Servant. "He was oppressed and He was afflicted, yet He did not open His mouth" (v. 7).

In conclusion, it must be asked, how can someone become one of the redeemed (one of God's people) and be able to say with confidence, "The LORD has caused all of my iniquity—my sins, my guilt, my punishment to fall on him"? The answer is illustrated in Aaron's actions on the Day of Atonement, when he would lay both of his hands on the head of the live goat and confessed all of the iniquities of the people, thus transferring their guilt to the goat (Lev. 16:21). The same process occurred when an Israelite offered a burnt offering (Lev. 1:4) or a sin offering (Lev. 4:4). He placed his hand on the head of the offering, making that animal his substitute.

One of England's most famous evangelical ministers was Charles Simeon (1759–1836), who ministered in one church in Cambridge for over fifty years. The story of his conversion is well-known and wonderful. It was during his first year as a student at King's College, Cambridge. The college required that he attend the Lord's Supper on Easter Sunday. He was not a believer, but he began to read a book on the Lord's Supper and became very depressed as he thought of his many sins.

---

[127] A number of recent defenses have been published. For example, see John R. W. Stott, *The Cross of Christ* (Downers Grove: Inter Varsity Press, 1986), esp. 87–163; Charles E. Hill and Frank A. James III, eds., *The Glory of the Atonement*, Essays in Honor of Roger Nicole (Downers Grove, IL: Inter Varsity Press, 2004); J. I. Packer and Mark Dever, *In My Place Condemned He Stood: Celebrating the Glory of the Atonement* (Wheaton: Crossway, 2007); Steve Jeffery, Mike Ovey, and Andrew Sach, *Pierced for Our Transgressions: Rediscovering the Glory of Penal Substitution* (Nottingham, UK: Inter-Varsity Press, 2007); Richard D. Phillips, ed., *Precious Blood: The Atoning Work of Christ* (Wheaton: Crossway, 2009). See also appendix 3 at the end of this monograph.

He then began to read a book by Bishop Thomas Wilson on the Lord's Supper and came across the words, "The Jews knew what they did when they transferred their sin to the head of their offering." Simeon wrote:

> The thought came into my mind, "What, may I transfer all my guilt to another? Has God provided an Offering for me, that I may lay my sins on His head? Then, God willing, I will not bear them on my own soul one moment longer." Accordingly I sought to lay my sins upon the sacred head of Jesus; and on the Wednesday began to have a hope of mercy; on the Thursday that hope increased; on the Friday and Saturday it became [stronger]; and on the Sunday morning, Easter-day, April 4, I awoke early with those words upon my heart and lips, "Jesus Christ is risen today! Hallelujah! Hallelujah!" From that hour peace flowed in rich abundance into my soul; and at the Lord's Table in our Chapel I had the sweetest access to God through my blessed Savior.[128]

> "Sweetest rest and peace have filled us,
>   Sweeter praise than tongue can tell;
>   God is satisfied with Jesus,
>   We are satisfied as well."[129]

---

[128] H. C. G. Moule, *Charles Simeon*, rev. ed. (London: Inter-Varsity Fellowship, 1948), 25–26.

[129] Frances Bevan, trans., "On the Lamb Our Souls are Resting," Hymn # 115 in *Hymns of Worship and Remembrance* (Dubuque, IA: Emmaus International, 1960).

CHAPTER 4

THE IGNOMINIOUS YET VOLUNTARY DEATH

OF THE SERVANT OF THE LORD

ISAIAH 53:7-9

INTRODUCTION

In the opening line of Isaiah's great "Servant Song" the LORD describes Jesus Christ as his "servant" (Isa. 52:13). The Old Testament word (עֶבֶד, *'ebed*) speaks of a person who belongs to another, a slave. He does his work in complete submission to his master. According to Hebrew law, the Hebrew slave was not to be treated as ruthlessly as in the surrounding nations because he shared in the religious life of his owner and because the Israelites were never to forgot that they had themselves been slaves in Egypt.[1]

Furthermore, the submission of a Hebrew slave was not forced submission, but willing submission.[2] A man might become an unwilling slave of another (e.g., in order to pay a debt), but the law stipulated that such servitude could only last six years and no more. At the end of that time he was set free (Ex. 21:1-2). However, if he wished, he could stay with his master in willing submission. Exodus 21:5-6 sets forth the conditions: **"But if the slave plainly says, 'I love my master, my wife and my children; I will not go out as a free man,' then his master shall bring him to God** [i.e., the judges who acted in God's name, NASB mg.], **then he shall bring him to the door or the doorpost. And his master shall pierce his ear with an awl; and he shall serve him permanently."**

---

[1] W. Zimmerli and J. Jeremias, *The Servant of God* (Naperville, IL: Allenson, 1957), 9–34; idem., "παῖς θεοῦ," *TDNT*, 5:654–677. Cf. U. Rutersworden, H. Simian-Yofre, H. Ringgren, "עֶבֶד," *TDOT*, 10:376–405; *HALOT*, "עֶבֶד," 1:774–775.

[2] In this discussion I am following Robert D. Culver, *The Sufferings and the Glory of The Lord's Righteous Servant* (Moline, IL: Christian Service Foundation, 1958), 85–86.

Our Lord did not have to become a "slave" (cf. Phil. 2:7, "δοῦλος," *doulos*); he was **the Lord of Glory** (1 Cor. 2:8). But God the Father wanted a slave (or bond-servant) to rescue lost humanity. So the Son of God, in submission to and out of love for his Father, went to heaven's door, as it were, and, figuratively speaking, had his ear bored through, becoming Yahweh's servant forever.[3] Everything that Jesus experienced and endured while on earth he did in complete submission to his Master's will. Of him the Psalmist wrote, **"I delight to do Your will, O my God; Your Law is within my heart"** (Ps. 40:8; cf. Heb. 10:7).

In this chapter we continue our meditation on this great passage concerning the Suffering Servant of the LORD, which has been called "The Gospel in Five Words," since it contains five poetic strophes, or stanzas (52:13-15; 53:1-3, 4-6, 7-9, 10-12).[4] As we do, we shall see that his submission to his Master's will led him to suffering, death, and burial. Once he took the **"form of a servant,"** the apostle says, there was no turning back—no avoiding death (Phil. 2:7-8).[5]

In verses 7-9 the speakers are believing Israelites in the end-time, i.e., Jews who have believed in Christ at the time of his second coming to the earth. They are lamenting the treatment that Messiah (Christ, "the Anointed One") received at the hands of their unbelieving countrymen at the time of his first coming. They report that (1) like a lamb, the mistreated Servant silently submitted to the sufferings imposed on him; (2) his contemporaries did not comprehend or care to know that he was unjustly put to death because of other peoples' sins; and (3) his death was followed by an honorable burial, which was not the intention of his enemies.[6] As Patrick Reardon observed, the verses offer a "graphic depiction" and theological interpretation of the events of "Good Friday."[7]

---

[3] Culver, *The Sufferings and the Glory of The Lord's Righteous Servant*, 86.

[4] Cf. S. Lewis Johnson, Jr., "The Submissive Messiah: An Exposition of Isaiah 53:7-9," *BBB* (Dallas: Believers Chapel, n.d.): 1–7 (esp. 1).

[5] Culver, *The Sufferings and the Glory of The Lord's Righteous Servant*, 87.

[6] F. Duane Lindsey, *The Servant Songs: A Study in Isaiah* (Chicago: Moody, 1985), 125. Cf. Gary V. Smith, *Isaiah 40–66*, NAC (Nashville: B & H, 2009), 452. Delitzsch's outline is more succinct: (1) the patience with which He suffered, v. 7; (2) the manner in which He died, v. 8; and (3) a retrospective glance at His burial, v. 8. Cf. Franz Delitzsch, *Biblical Commentary on the Prophecies of Isaiah*, trans. James Martin (Edinburgh: T. & T. Clark, 1877; reprint ed., Grand Rapids: Eerdmans, 1965), 2:326.

[7] Patrick Henry Reardon, "Isaiah's Good Friday," *Touchstone* (March, 2008): 48.

THE UNCOMPLAINING SUBMISSION OF THE MISTREATED SERVANT, VERSE 7

> He was oppressed and He was afflicted,
> Yet He did not open His mouth;
> Like a lamb that is led to slaughter,
> And like a sheep that is silent before its shearers,
> So He did not open His mouth.

THE UNSPARING MISTREATMENT OF THE SERVANT IN HIS FINAL HOURS[8]

First, they "report that the Servant patiently endured mistreatment."[9] **"He was oppressed and He was afflicted, yet He did not open His mouth."** The word "oppressed" (נִגַּשׂ, *niggaś*)[10] has been interpreted in different ways.[11] Here it most likely has the sense "He has been hard pressed (1 Sam. 13:6): He is driven or hunted (1 Sam. 14:24), treated tyrannically and unsparingly; in a word plagued."[12] Robert Culver translates "harassed."[13] TEV has "He was treated harshly." "The word implies the use of physical violence."[14] After he was arrested, he was

---

[8] It is evident from verses 7-9 that Isaiah gives here a description of events in the last hours ("closing portion") of the Servant's earthly life. Cf. Delitzsch, *Biblical Commentary on the Prophecies of Isaiah*, 2:323.

[9] Lindsey, *The Servant Songs*, 125.

[10] The word נִגַּשׂ is 3rd msc. sg. niphal (passive) perfect of נָגַשׂ. *HALOT* ("נָגַשׂ," 1:670) supports the rendering "he was oppressed."

[11] Bishop Robert Lowth translated, "It was exacted, and he was made answerable" (*Isaiah. A New Translation with a Preliminary Dissertation, and Notes Critical, Philological, and Explanatory* [London: J. Nichols, 1795], 171). Kay has "oppressed as by an unrelenting creditor (Deut. 15:2-3)," cf. W. Kay, "Isaiah," in *The Holy Bible According to the Authorized Version (A.D. 1611), with an Explanatory and Critical Commentary*, ed. F. C. Cook (New York: Scribner's, 1893), 5:268. In like manner, Moses Margoliouth paraphrased, "He was rigorously demanded to pay the debt, but He submitted *Himself*, and opened not His mouth." (*The Penitential Hymn of Judah and Israel After the Spirit: An Exposition of the Fifty-Third Chapter of Isaiah*, 2d ed. [London: Longman, Brown, Green, and Longmans, 1856], 85).

[12] Delitzsch, *Biblical Commentary on the Prophecies of Isaiah*, 2:322.

[13] Culver, *The Sufferings and the Glory of The Lord's Righteous Servant*, 87–88.

[14] Christopher R. North, *The Second Isaiah* (London: Oxford University Press, 1964), 240. John N. Oswalt writes, "Oppressed" carries with it the idea of harsh physical

pushed around, spit upon, punched, whipped (John 19:1; cf. Matt. 26:67; 27:26), and crowned with thorns (John 19:1-3).

"**And He was afflicted.**"[15] This participle (נַעֲנֶה, na‘ᵃneh) may be translated "though He submitted humbly"[16] or "suffered voluntarily."[17] TEV has "[He] endured it humbly." "The Servant did not fight against this fate; rather, he gave himself willingly to it. Thus he was not a victim caught in the great gears of a remorseless destiny, but a person of worth and dignity even in the most degrading of circumstances. One thinks of Jesus 'setting his face' to go to a Jerusalem where even the densest of his disciples understood that death awaited him (Luke 9:51)."[18]

THE SUBMISSIVE RESPONSE OF THE SERVANT IN HIS FINAL HOURS

The lamenting end-time Israelites add, "**And**[19] **He did not open His mouth.**" The silence here "pertains to the legal accusations against Him" at his trials. It does not relate to what he said to Judas or to the soldiers in Gethsemane (Matt. 26:50), or to his responses to the High Priest (Matt. 26:64), or to his comments to Pontius Pilate (John 18:33-38;

---

treatment at the hands of others" (*The Book of Isaiah, Chapters 40–66*, NICOT [Grand Rapids: Eerdmans, 1998], 391).

[15] The participle נַעֲנֶה (msc. sg. niphal [passive] ptc. עָנָה) is translated "afflicted" in a number of the versions (Darby, NASB, NIV, NKJV, ESV, NRSV, NET, HCSB). For a defense of the translation "afflicted," see William Urwick, עֶבֶד יְהוָה *The Servant of Jehovah: A Commentary, Grammatical and Critical on Isaiah 52:13–53:12* (Edinburgh: T. & T. Clark, 1877), 132.

[16] North, *The Second Isaiah*, 240. North observes that it can also be taken as a circumstantial clause, "while he submitted Himself."

[17] Delitzsch (*Biblical Commentary on the Prophecies+ of Isaiah*, 2:323), Joseph Addison Alexander, *Commentary on the Prophecies of Isaiah*, rev. ed., ed., John Eadie (Edinburgh: T. & T. Clark, 1875; reprint ed., Grand Rapids: Zondervan, 1974), 2:299, and Oswalt (*The Book of Isaiah, Chapters 40–66*, 391) reject the translation "afflicted" (NASB) and translate the Hebrew participle נַעֲנֶה as reflexive meaning here "to bend oneself," "to submit oneself," or "to humble oneself." *HALOT*, s.v. "עָנָה," 1:853, has "to bend, submit" for Isaiah 53:7. Also see: TEV, REB. On the reflexive use of the niphal, cf. GKC § 51c (137).

[18] Oswalt, *The Book of Isaiah, Chapters 40–66*, 391.

[19] The conjunction וּ preceding the particle לֹא (*lo'*, "not") is here rendered "and" rather than by the adversative "yet" or "but." The REB has, "He was submissive and did not open his mouth." Translating the participle נַעֲנֶה with the word "afflicted" requires the adversative, while the translation "he submitted humbly" requires "and." Cf. Oswalt, *The Book of Isaiah, Chapters 40–66*, 389.

19:11).[20] Rather, it speaks of his response to the verbal attacks and accusations that were leveled at him.

The New Testament accounts give a full picture of his silent submission to the charges against him. When Caiaphas presented the charges, "**He kept silent and did not answer**" (Mark 14:61; cf. Matt. 26:63). When the chief priests accused him before Pilate, "**Jesus made no further answer**" (Mark 15:5). To Pilate's inquiry, Matthew says, "**And He did not answer him with regard to even a single charge, so the governor was quite amazed**" (Matt. 27:14). When Herod Antipas questioned him at length, Jesus "**answered him nothing**" (Luke 23:9). When Jesus faced Pilate the second time, the governor asked him, "'**Where are you from?' But Jesus gave him no answer**" (John 19:9). On an earlier occasion the temple guards had said, "**Never has a man spoken the way this man speaks**" (John 7:45), but now He "condemned their hopeless moral condition by baffling silence!"[21]

Victor Buksbazen, a Jewish-Christian commentator, says:

> This kind of submissive behavior can in no way be attributed to Israel as a nation. Whatever the virtues of Israel are, suffering in silence and submission to her tormentors is not one of them [— even when they are accusing God, 40:27; 49:14; 63:15].[22]

He also adds, "Whenever the Jews were able, they resisted with all their might, and when they were unable to do this because of unfavorable circumstances, they protested vigorously and vociferously against their oppressors. In fact, they never considered suffering in silence as a virtue."[23] As another has written, "The Apostle Paul may cry out in complaint to the priest, but Jesus will not (cf. Acts 23:3; Matt. 7:6)."[24]

---

[20] Lindsey, *The Servant Songs*, 125.

[21] Johnson, "The Submissive Messiah," 3.

[22] Buksbazen is here responding to the modern Jewish view that the Servant of Isaiah 53 is "not an individual." He is the "the ideal Israel or the faithful remnant [of the nation of Israel]" (Victor Buksbazen, *The Prophet Isaiah: A Commentary* [Collingswood, NJ: Spearhead Press, 1971; reprint ed., Bellmawr, NJ: The Friends of Israel, 2008], 419). Cf. I. W. Slotki, *Isaiah*, SBB (London: Soncino, 1949), 260. Also Oswalt, *The Book of Isaiah, Chapters 40–66*, 392.

[23] Buksbazen, *The Prophet Isaiah*, 419. Buksbazen is here echoing what other scholars have said. Alexander McCaul, for example, wrote, "Another characteristic ascribed to the person here described is equally inapplicable to the Jewish nation: it is this, a patient endurance of injuries, as non-resistance of evil, (verse 7). McCaul cites as examples Jewish

As Buksbazen notes, "Even in the infamous extermination camps and in the ghettoes of the Nazis, they resisted whenever they were able, or sent messages of protest and alarm to the rest of the world. This was an understandable reaction on the part of the Jews."[25]

We all respond the same way. "'When we suffer, how hard we find it to be still!' The flames of resentment—how they leap up in our [chests], and flush our cheeks with an angry red! What impatience there often is, what [an] outcry, what [a telling everyone who will listen] of our sorrow!"[26]

But the Servant **"did not open His mouth."** Why? Because Yahweh willed it![27] As Jesus prayed in the Garden of Gethsemane, **"Your will be done"** (Matt. 26:42). From the beginning of his ministry, this was his determination: **"Behold I have come (in the scroll of the book it is written of Me) to do Your will, O God"** (Heb. 10:7). I believe we should go a step further. It was not only his obedience to the Father; it was also his love for his people; and it was "His acquiescence [to] the justice of God in the punishment of sin, the whole burden of which He bore."[28]

The lamenting Israelites now use a simile that would be very familiar to them. **"Like a lamb that is led to slaughter, and like a sheep that is silent before its shearers, so He did not open His mouth."** It is significant—and surely not accidental—"that the only extended metaphor in the poem involves sheep, the primary animals of sacrifice."[29] It is especially meaningful when one considers that the

---

resistance to the Romans, the rebellion of the Jews of Cyrene (AD 115), the rebellion of Jews in Mesopotamia (AD 116), the rebellion of Ben Kokba in which the learned Rabbi Akiva took part (AD 132–136), the revolt of the Jews of Alexandria (AD 522), the rebellion of the Jews in Caesarea (AD 535), the rebellion of the Jews in Antioch (AD 602), the armed opposition to Mohammed by the Jews in Arabia (AD 624). McCaul does not deny the right of the Jews to fight oppression; he simply notes that they did so, unlike the Servant of Isaiah 53. See A. McCaul, *The Doctrine and Interpretation of the Fifty-Third Chapter of Isaiah* (London: London Society's House, 1888), 15–16.

[24] Johnson, "The Submissive Messiah," 3.

[25] Buksbazen, *The Prophet Isaiah*, 419–20.

[26] James Culross, *The Man of Sorrows and the Joy that was Set Before Him* (London: Drummond's Tract Depot, 1896), 121; cf. David Baron, *The Servant of Jehovah* (New York: Doran, 1921), 100.

[27] Culross, *The Man of Sorrows*, 121; Baron, *The Servant of Jehovah*, 100.

[28] Baron, *The Servant of Jehovah*, 100–101.

[29] Oswalt, *The Book of Isaiah, Chapters 40–66*, 391–92.

events of this strophe occur on the day when the Passover sheep were to be slaughtered. Some of our leading New Testament scholars agree that this verse is a primary source of John the Baptist's exclamation, "**Behold, the Lamb of God who takes away the sin of the world!**" (John 1:29).[30]

One of the friendships I have made in recent years (actually, he befriended me) was with Dr. Robert Culver, a revered evangelical scholar who in a long career taught at Grace Seminary, Wheaton Graduate School, and Trinity Evangelical Divinity School. He died on February 7, 2015 at the age of ninety-eight. Bob Culver grew up on a farm and knew a lot about sheep. He saw many sheep and lambs led to slaughter. He observed that you must carry or lead a lamb to slaughter; you cannot drive or beat them, because it has no effect. Never once did he hear one of those animals utter any noise of protest.

And when the traveling sheep-shearers would come to the farm—they were fast working, impatient men—they might gouge, scratch, cut, or bruise a sheep, and the most you might hear from the animal was a subdued sigh. Even a coyote or sheep-killing dog arouses no protest. Sheep can express hunger and thirst, or a frolicking mood, but they simply do not or cannot express vocal protest at mistreatment.

He said that the nature of a hog is quite different. A hog will squeal to the last drop of its blood when it is being slaughtered. "Be thankful," he said, "[that] pigs do not have to be sheared!"[31]

---

[30] Rudolf Schnackenburg, *The Gospel According to St. John*, trans. Kevin Smyth (New York: Crossroad, 1987), 1:298–99; F. F. Bruce, *The Gospel of John* (Grand Rapids: Eerdmans, 1983), 52–53. Among other possible Old Testament antecedents for John's language are the lamb to be provided for Abraham (Gen. 22:8) and the Passover lamb. However, "Abraham spoke of a lamb for a burnt offering, not a sin offering, and the Passover lamb was not prescribed as a sin offering.... In the levitical law, indeed, a lamb is not the characteristic animal for a sin offering; but behind John's language may be discerned the Servant of the Lord who suffered 'like a lamb that is led to the slaughter' and gave himself as 'an offering for sin' (Isa. 53:7, 10)" (Bruce, *The Gospel of John*, 52–53). While Isaiah's prophecy is probably the primary source of John's words, there can be no question that the NT picks up allusions to Christ as the lamb from a variety of sources, including Abraham's lamb and the Passover lamb (cf. 1 Cor. 5:7). Delitzsch wrote, "All the references in the New Testament to the Lamb of God (with which the corresponding allusions to the Passover are interwoven) spring from this passage in the Book of Isaiah (*Biblical Commentary on the Prophecies of Isaiah*, 2:323). See also: C. K. Barrett, *The Gospel According to St. John*, 2d ed. (Philadelphia: Westminster, 1978), 176; D. A. Carson, *The Gospel According to John*, PNTC (Grand Rapids: Eerdmans, 1991), 149–51.

[31] Culver, *The Sufferings and the Glory of The Lord's Righteous Servant*, 89–90.

It will be a heart-rending day when a restored and repentant Israel remembers all this and confesses the things we have read in Isaiah 53:1-9. Jesus fulfilled this prophecy perfectly. "He groaned, He called on God; but to Herod, Caiaphas, Pilate, and all the rest, He answered not one word of protest."[32]

THE VIOLENT DEATH OF THE MISTREATED SERVANT, VERSE 8

By oppression and judgment He was taken away;
And as for His generation, who considered
That He was cut off out of the land of the living
For the transgression of My people, to whom the stroke was due?

THE UNJUST TRIAL OF THE SERVANT

"By oppression (עֹצֶר, 'ōṣer) and judgment (מִשְׁפָּט, mišpāṭ) He was taken away" (NASB). Because of the highly emotional nature of this passage and the obscure meaning of certain words, every phrase of this verse is the subject of scholarly debate.[33] Most of the possible views

---

[32] Culver, *The Sufferings and the Glory of The Lord's Righteous Servant*, 90–91.

[33] Cf. North, *The Second Isaiah*, 240–41; Oswalt, *The Book of Isaiah, Chapters 40–66*, 392–93; Smith, *Isaiah 40–66*, 453; Lindsey, *The Servant Songs*, 126. The first problem has to do with the connotation of the preposition *from* (מִן, *min*) attached to *oppression* and *judgment*. There is a problem in that the meaning of עֹצֶר is debated, and the preposition מִן has a wide variety of meanings. (On the meanings of מִן, see *IBHS*, § 11.2.11 [212–14]). Waltke and O'Connor (*IBHS*) describe the spatial, temporal, ablatival, local, partitive, privative, and comparative senses. For other uses see GKC § 119v–y [382–83] and § 133 a–c [429–30] and WHSB, § 309–27 [120–25], and *HALOT*, s.v. "מִן," 1:597–99. Examples of the more common explanations are: (1) *Temporal sense*: "After arrest and trial he was taken away" (R. N. Whybray, *Isaiah 40–66*, NCB [Grand Rapids: Eerdmans, 1981], 177). (2) *Causal sense*: "Because of oppressive legal treatment he was taken away to his death" (Oswalt, *The Book of Isaiah, Chapters 40–66*, 393). Oswalt focuses on the injustice of the proceedings and treats "oppression and judgment" as a hendiadys. (3) *Privative sense*: "Without protection (of kin) and without due legal procedure," i.e., no one attempted to secure a fair trial for him (G. R. Driver, "Isaiah 52:13–53:12: the Servant of the Lord," *In Memoriam Paul Kahle*, eds. Matthew Black and Georg Fohrer [Berlin: Alfred Töpelmann, 1968], 90–105 [esp. 94]). Driver argues that the noun עֹצֶר does not mean "oppression" and questions whether it can be used in the concrete sense of "prison" or "imprisonment." However, the noun only occurs two other times in the OT (Prov. 30:16; Ps. 107:39), so it is unwise to state too dogmatically the nuances it might have had (*HALOT* [s.v. "עֹצֶר," 1:871] does offer *oppression* and *imprisonment* as two possible meanings for Isaiah 53:8). It should also be

suggest violent action against the Servant within the legal context of a court of law.[34] The preferred translation, it seems to me, is, "From imprisonment (custody) and from judgment (i.e., judicial proceedings) He was snatched or hurried away, i.e., to His death."[35] The thought is that of "hurried, forcible, violent treatment." It describes those early morning hours when Jesus was hurried from Gethsemane to trial and execution without any attempt to follow the just processes of law.[36]

Matthew puts the issue clearly: **"And they plotted together to seize Jesus by stealth and kill Him"** (Matt. 26:4). Among the illegalities perpetrated upon the Servant are the following: (1) they started his trial without first examining witnesses [John 18:20-21]; (2) they had the trial at night and physically abused him [Mark 14:65]; (3) they suborned perjury, i.e., they induced witnesses to give false testimony [Mark 14:56]; (4) they manufactured a false charge for Pilate.—their only charge was blasphemy, but that was meaningless to the Romans, so they accused him of perverting the nation, preventing the paying of tribute to Caesar, and saying that he was a king [Luke 23:2]. The third of these accusations impressed Pilate, for it was a charge of treason.

---

noted that the verb form עָצַר occurs frequently with the meaning of "shut up" or "imprison" (2 Kings 17:4; Jer. 33:1; 39:15; cf. *HALOT*, 1:870). (4) *Local sense.* "Out of oppression and judgment he was taken away, i.e., released by death or taken by God to Himself to escape the malice of his persecutors" (Delitzsch, *Biblical Commentary on the Prophecies of Isaiah*, 2:324; J. Skinner, *The Book of the Prophet Isaiah, Chapters 40–66*, CBSC [Cambridge: Cambridge University Press, 1956], 143; John Calvin, *Commentary on the Book of the Prophet Isaiah*, trans. William Pringle (1850; reprint ed., Grand Rapids: Baker, 1989], 3:120]. (5) *Spatial or ablatival sense*: "From imprisonment and trial he was hurried away to his death" (North, *The Second Isaiah*, 241; James Muilenburg, "Isaiah 40–66: Exegesis," in *The Interpreter's Bible*, ed. George Arthur Buttrick [Nashville: Abingdon, 1956], 5:626). The fifth view is advocated by the present writer.

[34] Lindsey, *The Servant Songs*, 125; Claus Westermann, *Isaiah 40–66*, OTL, trans. David M. G. Stalker (Philadelphia: Westminster, 1969), 265.

[35] Cf. North, *The Second Isaiah*, 241; Muilenburg, "Isaiah 40–66: Exegesis," 5:626.

[36] Culver, *The Sufferings and the Glory of The Lord's Righteous Servant*, 90–91. On the illegalities of Jesus' trials, see W. T. Dayton, "Trial of Jesus," *ZPEB*, 5:812–13. Powell wrote, "As we have seen, from the time Jesus raised Lazarus from the dead [John 11:45-53], the Rulers of the Jews conspired to put Jesus to death. It is abundantly clear from the Gospel narratives, that there was no question of holding a careful and judicial investigation into the claim of Jesus to be the Messiah. *The decision was to kill Jesus.* This fact cannot be over emphasized, for it dominates the events which took place after the arrest and fixes the true character of the so-called Jewish 'trials'" (Frank J. Powell, *The Trial of Jesus Christ* [Grand Rapids: Eerdmans, 1949], 54).

Yet after talking to Jesus, Pilate said, "I find no crime in Him" (John 18:38). Rather than handle a treason trial and call attention to his own failings from his superiors, Pilate acquiesced to the Jewish request for a hanging. "He was taken away,"[37] i.e., to his death.[38] The verb as used here, לְקַח (luqqāḥ), denotes a forcible taking away.[39] The Servant, deprived of a just trial, was hurried away to his death,[40] "the victim of a judicial murder."[41]

THE WICKED INDIFFERENCE OF HIS CONTEMPORARIES

"And as for His generation, who considered that He was cut off out of the land of the living?" The Hebrew word translated "generation" (דּוֹר, dôr) signifies "an age, or the men living in a particular age," i.e., "His contemporaries, or the men of His generation"[42] (so: KJV, Darby,

---

[37] Calvin concluded that this clause meant that he was taken into glory, i.e., that he was exalted to heaven. The verb לְקַח is used that way of Enoch, Gen. 5:24; cf. 2 Kings 2:3, 5 (John Calvin, *Commentary on the Book of the Prophet Isaiah*, trans. William Pringle [Edinburgh: Calvin Translation Society, 1850], 4:120). Most commentators, however, take it to mean that he was taken away to his death.

[38] R. N. Whybray attacks the idea that the Servant in this passage actually dies (*Thanksgiving for a Liberated Prophet: An Interpretation of Isaiah 53* [Sheffield: JSOT Press, 1978], 79–105). He denies the Messianic interpretation of the passage in favor of the view that the chapter refers to the maltreated and almost-killed "Deutero-Isaiah." After a brief (and adequate) rebuttal, Oswalt says of Isaiah 53, "The problem lies in the nature of the poem itself. It is too lofty, too convoluted, too atmospheric, and too mysterious to have sprung from such a mundane event as that (completely hypothetical) event would have been." [His hypothesis cannot] be found in this gloriously angular and unmanageable masterpiece, with its towering theologizing on sin and death, suffering and salvation. The person whom Whybray wants to put on this throne is simply too small to fit it" (*The Book of Isaiah, Chapters 40–66*, 393).

[39] The form used in Isaiah 53:8 is 3d msc. sg. pual [qal passive] perf. of לְקַח. See *HALOT*, s.v. "לְקַח," 1:535.

[40] Urwick, *The Servant of Jehovah*, 137.

[41] Allan A. MacRae, *The Gospel of Isaiah* (Chicago: Moody, 1977), 140.

[42] Delitzsch, *Biblical Commentary on the Prophecies of Isaiah*, 2:324; cf. Brevard S. Childs, *Isaiah*, OTL (Louisville: Westminster John Knox, 2001), 416; BDB, s.v. "דּוֹר," 190. Not all scholars have agreed with this interpretation. At least two other translations of the word דּוֹר have gained support: (1) "Plight" or "fate," i.e., "Who gave a thought to his fate?" [REB, TEV, HCSB]. This translation is based on Akkadian and Arabic cognates. See: Driver, "Isaiah 52:13–53:12: the Servant of the Lord," 90–105 [esp. 94–95]; North, *The Second Isaiah*, 230. *HALOT* [s.v. "דּוֹר," 1:218] suggests "fate," but with a question mark. (2) "Descendants" [NIV], i.e., "Who considered that the Servant was left without children in a culture where to die childless was to have lived an utterly futile

NASB, ESV, NET). **"Who considered"** (i.e., thoughtfully deliberated on the fact) that he was **"cut off"** (i.e., put to death) **"for the transgression of my people?"**[43] In their indifference or active wickedness, who cared? Who commiserated? Probably few in Israel had first-hand knowledge that it was even taking place.[44]

David Baron notes that the word translated "considered" (יְשׂוֹחֵחַ, *yᵉśôḥēaḥ*)[45] can be rendered "to complain" or "to lament."[46] He translates, "Who complained?" or "Who lamented?" or "Who declared it, or offered a plea in His behalf?" Baron points to the legal custom of the Jews of calling upon all who had anything to say in the accused's favor to come forward and declare it, or to complain on his behalf.

There is a passage in the Talmud based on this custom which tries to make the trial of Jesus look more legal. The Talmud reads:

> On the eve of the Passover Yeshu [i.e., Jesus] was hanged. For forty days before the execution took place, a herald went forth and cried, "He is going forth to be stoned because he has practiced sorcery and enticed Israel to apostasy. Any one who can say anything in his favor, let him come forward and plead on his behalf." But since nothing was brought forward in his favor he was hanged on the eve of the Passover!—Ulla retorted: "Do you suppose that he was one for whom a defense could be made? Was he not a *Mesith* [enticer], concerning whom Scripture says, *Neither shalt thou spare, neither shalt thou conceal*

---

life?" (Oswalt, *The Book of Isaiah, Chapters 40–66*, 395; Charles Cutler Torrey, *The Second Isaiah* [New York: Scribner's, 1928], 420; Muilenburg, "Isaiah: Introduction and Exegesis," 5:626). For a helpful, albeit brief, summary of the history of interpretation see John Goldingay and David Payne, *Isaiah 40–55*, ICC [London: T. & T. Clark, 2006], 2:313.

[43] Delitzsch, *Biblical Commentary on the Prophecies of Isaiah*, 2:325.

[44] North, *The Second Isaiah*, 240.

[45] The form יְשׂוֹחֵחַ is 3d pers. msc. sg. polel imperf. of שִׂיחַ.

[46] Baron, *The Servant of Jehovah*, 104. See Lowth's translation, "And his manner of life, who would declare?" (Lowth, *Isaiah: A New Translation*, 2:325–326). It should be noted that the standard lexicons do not give "lament" or "complain" as possible meanings of שִׂיחַ. Cf. BDB, s.v. "שִׂיחַ," 967; *HALOT*, s.v. "שִׂיחַ," 2:1321. They do give "lament" (*HALOT*) and "complaint" (BDB) for the identical noun form.

him? With Yeshu [Jesus] however it was different, for he was connected with the government [or royalty, i.e., influential]."[47]

However, the sense of the word יְשׁוֹחֵחַ (*yᵉsôḥēaḥ*) is probably to be understood as "considered" (NASB) or "pondered."[48] The NET Bible best captures the intent of the word here, "Who even cared?" However we understand the word יְשׁוֹחֵחַ, the end result was that **"He was cut off out of the land of the living."** The verb "cut off" (נִגְזַר, *nigzar*)[49] here means "to be cut off from life."[50] The term is never used "of a quiet, natural death...but always of a violent, premature death."[51] As Princeton Seminary professor Daniel Migliore put it, "Jesus did not die in bed."[52] Or, as German theologian Jürgen Moltmann wrote, Jesus "was crucified not between two candles on an altar, but between two thieves in the place of the skull, where the outcasts belong, outside the gates of the city."[53]

---

[47] *Sanhedrin* 43a, in *The Babylonian Talmud*, Seder Nezikin, ed. I. Epstein (1935; reprint ed., London: Soncino, n.d.), 3:281–82. This passage is remarkable for two reasons. First, it is apologetic in nature, i.e., it is an attempt to make a defence against Christian allegations in the Gospels that there were illegal aspects to the trials of Jesus. Second, contrary to modern Jewish historians who deny Jewish involvement in the death of Christ, the Jews here (in the Talmud) "fully accept responsibility for the trial and execution of Jesus" (David R. Catchpole, *The Trial of Jesus: A Study in the Gospels and Jewish Historiography from 1770 to the Present Day* [Leiden: Brill, 1971], 4–5).

[48] J. Alec Motyer, *The Prophecy of Isaiah* (Downers Grove: Inter Varsity Press, 1993), 434.

[49] The form used in Isaiah 53:8 is 3d pers. msc. sg. niphal perf. of גָּזַר.

[50] *HALOT*, s.v. "גָּזַר," 1:187.

[51] E. W. Hengstenberg, *Christology of the Old Testament*, trans. Theodore Meyer and James Martin (Edinburgh: T. & T. Clark, 1872–78; reprint ed., Grand Rapids: Kregel, 1956), 2:292. Cf. Urwick, *The Servant of Jehovah*, 139–40.

[52] This quotation is from a class lecture delivered at Princeton Theological Seminary. See "Reflections on the Cross," *Christianity Today* (April 23, 2001), 102.

[53] Jürgen Moltmann, *The Crucified God*, trans. R. A. Wilson and John Bowden (New York: Harper and Row, 1974), 40. For similar thoughts, see George F. MacLeod, *Only One Way Left*, 4th ed. (Glasgow: Iona Community, 1964), 38. "I simply argue that the Cross be raised again at the center of the market-place as well as on the steeple of the church. I am recovering the claim that Jesus was not crucified in a cathedral between two candles, but on a cross between two thieves; on the town garbage-heap; at a crossroad so cosmopolitan that they had to write his title in Hebrew and in Latin and in Greek; at the kind of place where cynics talk smut, and thieves curse, and soldiers gamble. Because that is where he died. And that is what he died about." MacLeod, a noted liberal scholar (1895–1991), was the founder of Scotland's famous Iona Community.

There is, from a purely human perspective, a true sadness in the poetic expression "**the land of the living.**" Like all the dead, the Servant was removed from the world of living people—from his family, his friends, and his nation.[54]

THE VICARIOUS NATURE OF HIS DEATH

The indifference of the Jewish people is underscored by the fact that it was for their transgressions that the Servant died. All of his suffering was "**for the transgression of my people, to whom the stroke was due.**" This colon or line may be translated "because of the rebellion of His own people He was struck" (cf. NET, HCSB). In the Hebrew text the line begins with the particle מִן (*min*) which here means "because."[55] It introduces the reason why the Servant was "struck." It was because of the transgression (פֶּשַׁע, *pêša‘*) or rebellious acts[56] of the people of Israel. These were "His own people"[57] who were guilty of sin.

---

[54] Cf. Motyer, *The Prophecy of Isaiah*, 434–35.

[55] Urwick, *The Servant of Jehovah*, 140; Delitzsch, *Biblical Commentary on the Prophecies of Isaiah*, 2:325. On the causal use of מִן see *HALOT*, s.v. "מִן," 1:598; Williams, *Williams' Hebrew Syntax* § 319 (121–22).

[56] A number of commentators argue that the word פֶּשַׁע speaks of something even more grievous than transgression, viz., the rebellious acts against the authority of God. See Smith, *Isaiah 40–66*, 450, n. 376; John Goldingay and David Payne, *Isaiah 40–55*, International Critical Commentary (London: T. & T. Clark, 2006), 2:314. Also: HCSB, NET.

[57] The MT has "my people" (עַמִּי), and the ancient versions agree as do most modern English translations. The first person singular ("my") seems odd in that it interrupts the report in vv. 1-9 by the group of end-time Israelites who consistently identify themselves by plural pronouns. Scholars explain the change in at least five ways: (1) Some say the singular pronoun identifies the speaker as God [e.g., Edward J. Young, *The Book of Isaiah*, NICOT (Grand Rapids: Eerdmans, 1972), 3:352]. However, in the poem Yahweh does not begin to speak again [cf. 52:13-15] until vv. 11-12, and in v. 10 he is twice named in the third person [North, *The Second Isaiah*, 230]. (2) Some say the speaker is Isaiah himself who offers "a momentary personal note" when he "observes the fact that it was his own people ["*my* people"] that were the beneficiaries of this strange transaction" [H. C. Leupold, *Exposition of Isaiah* (Grand Rapids: Baker, 1971), 2:230]. However, the prophet does not seem to interject himself until v. 10. (3) Others translate, "our people," citing 1 Samuel 5:10 and Zechariah 8:21 as examples that the singular form can be used by a plurality of speakers to mean "us" or "our" [Alexander, *Commentary on the Prophecies of Isaiah*, 2:300; cf. Hengstenberg, *Christology of the Old Testament*, 2:292]. (4) Another solution has been to point עַמֵּי [construct plural] instead of עַמִּי, which gives the translation "for the transgressions of peoples who deserved to be stricken," lit. "peoples of a striking to them" [North, *The Second Isaiah*, 230–31].

Although they were guilty and deserving of judgment, it was the Servant who was struck. There is no verb here, and the word translated "struck" is a noun (נֶגַע, *nega'*) meaning "blow,"[58] so the text literally reads, "a blow to him."[59] If a verb is added, the text reads, "the blow was His"[60] or "He was struck." The word (נֶגַע), says Delitzsch, "always signifies suffering as a calamity proceeding from God (e.g., Ex. 11:1; Ps. 39:11)." It can refer to plague, and especially leprosy (Lev. 13–14). Here it is a blow unto death, and the smiter is Yahweh.

The Jewish people did not see the true value of Jesus Christ during his lifetime. They were mistaken about him. Now that he no longer dwelled among the living, "they ought to see, as they looked back upon His actions and His sufferings, that it was not for His own wickedness, but for that of Israel, namely, to make atonement for it, that such a visitation from God had fallen upon Him."[61]

What we have in this line is "a restrained summary of the Servant's sufferings." In verse 7 his innocence is stressed. What stands out in verse 8 is "that He suffered for the sins of [people] who deserved to be stricken themselves."[62]

THE PARADOXICAL BURIAL OF THE MISTREATED SERVANT, V. 9

> His grave was assigned with wicked men,
> Yet He was with a rich man in His death,
> Because He had done no violence,
> Nor was there any deceit in His mouth.

---

(5) Others, following the best of the Isaiah manuscripts among the Dead Sea Scrolls [1QIsaᵃ has עמו], translate "his people." See *Discoveries in the Judaean Desert*, vol. 32: *Qumran Cave 1, II. The Isaiah Scrolls*, Part 1: *Plates and Transcriptions*, eds., Eugene Ulrich and Peter W. Flint [Oxford and New York: Oxford University Press, 2010], Column 44 [88–89]. Cf. NET; Joseph Blenkinsopp, *Isaiah 40–55*, AncB [New York: Doubleday, 2000, 345, 348, note w. What Goldingay and Payne say of the final two words of the verse applies here, "The expression is particularly allusive" [*Isaiah 40–55*, 2:315].

[58] *HALOT*, s.v. "נֶגַע," 1:669. The verb form (נֶגַע) in comparable contexts would mean "to touch violently, to strike" (idem., 1:668). In that one must supply a verb here, the translation, "He was struck" is not invalid.

[59] North, *The Second Isaiah*, 230.

[60] Oswalt, *The Book of Isaiah, Chapters 40–66*, 390.

[61] Delitzsch, *Biblical Commentary on the Prophecies of Isaiah*, 2:326.

[62] North, *The Second Isaiah*, 240.

THE BURIAL PLANS OF THE JEWISH RULERS

In verse 9 the redeemed Israelites of the end-time move on from their narration of the Servant's sufferings and death to a narration of the facts of his burial. [63] "His grave was assigned with wicked men" (רְשָׁעִים, r'šā'îm).[64] Commentators all speak of the difficulty in understanding the Hebrew text here. A recent commentator suggests, "The text of v. 9 is probably intentionally mysterious."[65] Happily we have the New Testament to guide us. Franz Delitzsch, one of the finest Hebrew scholars ever to write on Isaiah, confesses, "Without the commentary supplied by the fulfillment [i.e., in the New Testament] it would be impossible to understand verse 9a at all."[66]

The translation "His grave was assigned" (NASB) or "He was assigned a grave" (NIV) is defective, because the Hebrew text uses an active and not a passive verb (וַיִּתֵּן, wayittēn).[67] The translation "and they made his grave with the wicked" is much better (ESV, NRSV, HCSB).[68]

---

[63] As Westermann noted, there are echoes of the Apostles' Creed in Isaiah 53. Verse 2 ("a tender shoot...a root out of a parched ground") corresponds to the "was born" of the creed, and verses 7-9 correspond to "was crucified, dead, and buried" (Claus Westermann, *Isaiah 40–66*, trans. David M. G. Stalker, Old Testament Library [Philadelphia: Westminster, 1969], 264).

[64] The term "wicked" (רָשָׁע) can be used as a noun or adjective of one guilty of a crime or crimes and deserving of punishment, e.g. Ex. 2:13; 23:1; Deut. 25:2. It can also be used of a murderer or murderers who are punishable by death, e.g. 2 Sam. 4:11; Num 35:31. It is used as well of the counsel wicked people give (Ps. 1:1) or of groups or societies of sinners who scheme to do evil (Job 10:3; 21:16). In the present context it is an adjective suggesting guilty or wicked people in general (cf. 1 Sam. 2:9; Isa. 3:11; 11:4). See *BDB*, s.v. "רָשָׁע," 957; *HALOT*, s.v. "רָשָׁע," 2:1295. It is worth noting that Jesus was crucified between two criminals (Matt. 27:38; Luke 23:32-33).

[65] Klaus Baltzer, *Deutero-Isaiah: A Commentary on Isaiah 40–55*, Hermeneia, trans. Margaret Kohl (Minneapolis: Fortress, 2001), 417.

[66] Delitzsch, *Biblical Commentary on the Prophecies of Isaiah*, 2:327. Charles H. H. Wright concurred, "Our view of Isaiah 52–53 is that the prophecy was an enigma, which could not be fully understood in the days before Christ, but which has been solved by the sufferings, death, resurrection, and exaltation of Him who was both Son of Man and the Son of God" (*The Suffering Servant of Jehovah* [London: Francis Griffiths, 1905], 7).

[67] The form used in the text is וַיִּתֵּן (3d pers. msc. sg. qal imperf. of נָתַן with a waw consecutive prefix).

[68] Darby has, "And [men] appointed his grave with the wicked." In Hebrew the indefinite personal subject ("they," "one") is expressed by the 3d pers. msc. singular (*Gesenius' Hebrew Grammar* § 144d [460]). The Qumran manuscript 1QIsaᵃ makes the plural indefinite subject explicit by making the verb plural (ויתנו, ("they made"). See *The*

"It was usual for a man to be buried 'with his fathers,' and to be denied such burial was a calamity (1 Kings 13:22). For those who had no family grave there was the common public burial place (2 Kings 23:6; Jer. 26:23; cf. Matt. 27:7)."[69]

Josephus, the Jewish historian, comments on the laws of his people in the days of Jesus. He writes, "Let him that blasphemeth God be stoned, then hung for a day, and buried ignominiously and in obscurity."[70] What Josephus suggests is practiced by some governments even today. They give dishonorable burials to those who have committed capital crimes to perpetuate the indignity of the punishment even after death. This is for the general deterrence of like-minded individuals. The government does not give them decent burials, because their graves would become shrines for the wrong reasons. Many such criminals are buried in the penitentiary in a place known only to the warden. If the crimes are political, the authorities do not want the grave to be a rallying point for a "martyr." If they are murderous, they do not want them to be a rallying point for like-minded twisted people.[71]

Isaiah Scrolls, Part 1: *Plates and Transcriptions*, Column 44 [88–89]. Cf. Smith, *Isaiah 40–66*, 455.

[69] North, *The Second Isaiah*, 241. North adds, "Whether some part of this [common public burial place] was reserved for criminals we do not know, unless it may be inferred from this passage."

[70] Josephus, *Jewish Antiquities* 4.8.6 [4.202], trans. H. St. J. Thackeray, in *Josephus*, 10 vols., LCL (New York: Putnam's, 1930), 4:573. Thackeray notes that Josephus runs counter to the Mishnah by adding the phrase "for a day." The Mishnah says, "And if he [the hanged man] is left overnight, one transgresses a negative commandment on his account, as it is said, *His body shall not remain all night on the tree, but you will surely bury him on the same day, for he who is hanged is a curse against God* (Dt. 21:23)." See *Sanhedrin* 6.4, in The Fourth Division: The Order of Damages [*Nezikin*], in Jacob Neusner, *The Mishnah: A New Translation* (New Haven: Yale, 1988), 595.

[71] On June 4, 2011 the writer gave an address on this passage at the Fifty-Fifth Annual Men's Conference at the Guelph Conference Grounds in Ontario. Judge Ralph E. W. Carr of the Ontario Court of Justice was in the audience, and he made the above comments to me about modern day practices. He later noted that the ancients would not only not allow a "decent burial," but would often mutilate the bodies and publicly position them for public display (e.g., the treatment of King Saul after his death on Mt. Gilboa, 1 Sam. 31:8-10). During World War 2 the Japanese would shoot POWs who tried to escape and, rather than bury them, would publically hang the bodies as a deterrent to others. A good burial would be eschewed, as it might militate against the otherwise "general deterrence" message that the execution provided (email, Carr to MacLeod, June 8, 2011). Public desecration of one's enemies was illustrated in the Battle of Mogadishu ("Black Hawk Down," Oct. 3, 4, 1993) when the bodies of American soldiers were dragged through the streets and mangled. The burial of heinous criminals in

Culver writes, "Nothing would have given the cruel and venal men who caused our Lord to die greater pleasure than after having killed Him to bury Him in a public dump-ground among the graves of criminals, prostitutes, and the abandoned men of old Jerusalem's 'Skid Row.' Surely it would have brought pleasure to Satan, the arch-fiend of them all."[72] This would have been "the final insult in a life full of insults."[73]

THE BURIAL PLANS OF THE SOVEREIGN GOD

But the evil intentions of the Servant's enemies, evident in the gospel accounts (Matt. 27:62-66; 28:11-15), were not to be. Joseph of Arimathea, a member of the Sanhedrin (Mark 15:43), the highest governing body of Judaism, asked Pontius Pilate, the Roman governor, for the body of Jesus, and he gave it to him (Matt. 27:57-58). Joseph was until that time a secret disciple of Jesus (John 19:38). Matthew adds that he was "a rich man" who had recently had a tomb made ("his own new tomb") and that he laid Jesus' body in that tomb (Matt. 27:59–60).

The Israelites report, **"Yet He was with a rich man in His death."** The NET Bible has, "They intended to bury him with criminals, but he ended up in a rich man's tomb."[74] This line may be one of the most

---

unmarked graves was illustrated by the burial at sea on May 1, 2011 of Osama bin Laden, the mastermind behind the attack by the Al Qaeda terrorist group on the United States on Sept. 11, 2001, and the burial in the Libyan desert on October 25, 2011 of dictator Muammar Gaddafi. Explaining the secretive burial of Gaddafi, Libyan authorities said they were "anxious to avoid his grave site becoming a shrine for his supporters, or a target for his enemies." Gaddafi's body was mutilated and put on display for five days («http://www.theguardian.com/world/2011/oct/25/gaddafi-buried-in-unmarked-grave». Accessed Dec. 23, 2014).

[72] Culver, *The Sufferings and the Glory of The Lord's Righteous Servant*, 99.

[73] Oswalt, *The Book of Isaiah, Chapters 40–66*, 397.

[74] The Hebrew text reads בְּמֹתָיו ("in his deaths," plural), which makes no sense to most commentators. The ancient versions (LXX, Vulgate, and Targum) all read the singular, indicating one of three possibilities: (1) They may have been familiar with a Hebrew text that read in the singular. (2) They may have viewed the plural as a copyist's error and changed it. (3) They may have understood the plural to be intensive, meaning "in the condition of death" [Young, *The Book of Isaiah*, 3:353, n. 35]. Others argue that the original may have been בָּמָתוֹ ["his burial place"] or בּוֹמָתוֹ ["his burial mound"]. This suggestion is suspect in that בָּמָה ["high place"] is a technical term for Canaanite sanctuaries or other worship places forbidden to the people of Yahweh. Cf. James Muilenburg, "Isaiah 40–66: Introduction and Exegesis," in *IntB*, ed., George Arthur Buttrick (Nashville: Abingdon, 1956), 5:627; Baltzer, *Deutero-Isaiah*, 417. Cf. William

mysterious in the entire poem, and it has engendered a great deal of
debate and discussion. It has been pointed out that one might have
expected the colon to be parallel in thought to the first line (synonymous
parallelism). Some have even amended the text to read "He was assigned
a grave with the wicked, a burial-place among felons" (REB). The
Hebrew text does not say "felons," however; it says, "rich" (עָשִׁיר, 'āšîr).

Jesus' burial was not what one would have expected in light of his
ignominious death. That unexpectedness has led to the unexpected
structure of the two lines. Instead of synonymous parallelism, we are
given antithetical parallelism: **"they made His grave with the wicked—
but with the rich at His death!"** (NKJV).[75]

Foxwell Albright *Archeology and the Religion of Israel*, 5th ed. (Baltimore: Johns Hopkins,
1968), 105–107.

[75] Italics mine. Broadly speaking, the second colon or line of verse 9 has been interpreted
in two ways: First, it has been defined structurally as synonymous parallelism, with the
line emphasizing the same point made in the first line. The interpretation may be
paraphrased as follows, including line 3: "They made his grave with the wicked, and his
tomb was a burial-place among the wicked rich, although he had done no violence...." In
favor of this view the following arguments are made: (1) Line 2 begins with a *waw*
conjunctive ["and"], which indicates that the line is synonymous with the first colon
[NRSV, ESV]. (2) The second colon has no verb, so the verb in the first ["made,"
"assigned"] must govern both [cf. WHSB; Oswalt]. (3) "The last members in each colon
in Hebrew ['his grave' and 'in his death'] are synonymous. This leaves only the middle
terms, which one must assume are synonymous as well" [Oswalt]. (4) The consonants of
"wicked" [רשע] and "rich man" [עשר] are the same, though their order is reversed. Both
are preceded by the preposition אֶת ["with"]. This would make the reader link "wicked
man" and "rich man" as synonymous terms [Baltzer, following Gesenius]. The assonance
suggests "an association between wicked and rich" [Goldingay and Payne]. (5) The rich
are denounced by the prophets because of wealth they've gained dishonestly [Mic. 6:12;
Jer. 9:23; 17:11; cf. Prov. 11:16; 28:11; cf. De Boer, Muilenburg]. This has led some to
emend the text either by changing the Hebrew to עֹשֵׂי רָע ["evil doers," F. Böttcher, cited
by Delitzsch] or proposing that עָשִׁיר is cognate with Arabic *ġutr*ⁿⁿ ["rabble," "refuse of
mankind," Guillaume, cited by North]. (6) The conjunction עַל which begins the second
bicolon may have a concessive force and be translated "although." The thought would
then be, "Although he had done no violence, he was buried with the wicked and evil
doers" [Gesenius; REB, TEV]. See: WHSB § 591, 209; Oswalt, *The Book of Isaiah,
Chapters 40–66*, 397; Baltzer, *Deutero-Isaiah*, 417; Goldingay and Payne, *Isaiah 40–55*,
2:316; P. A. H. De Boer, *Second-Isaiah's Message*, in *OTS*, vol. 11 [Leiden: Brill, 1956],
114; Muilenburg, "Isaiah 40–66," 626–27; Delitzsch, *Biblical Commentary on the
Prophecies of Isaiah*, 2:327; A. Guillaume, "A Contribution to Hebrew Lexicography,"
SOAS Bulletin 16:1 (1954): 10; North, *The Second Isaiah*, 231; *GKC* § 160c [p. 499].

Second, the second line has been defined structurally as antithetical parallelism with
the second line suggesting a contrast between the intentions of the Servant's enemies
[humiliation, degradation] and the actual nature of the burial [honor (Delitzsch)]. This
interpretation may be paraphrased as follows including line 3: "They intended to make

As Robert Culver notes, the reason why Jesus Christ was saved from the ignominy and shame of a criminal's grave is that it was God's reward for a life lived in complete submission to his will. Culver writes, "Treatment of the corpse had nothing to do with atonement. His death accomplished that." He added, "After the soldier's spear was thrust into His side, wicked, violent men were not allowed to touch Him again. To the flood of Jewish spite and hate God said, 'No! Thus far and no farther.'"[76]

Old Testament scholar Bruce Waltke agreed. He pointed to the events of the cross just before Joseph of Arimathea entered the story

---

his grave with the wicked, but another buried him in a rich man's tomb." In favor of this view the following arguments may be made: (1) Line 2 begins with a waw adversative ["yet," "but," NASB, Lindsey, Unger], which indicates that line 2 introduces a contrast. (2) The word "rich" is found in the MT, the LXX, and the Targum. The various attempts to amend the text suggest that an alien interpretation is being forced upon it [Smith]. (3) The terms "wicked" and "rich" are not completely parallel in that the one ("wicked") is plural while the other ("rich") is singular [Goldingay and Payne]. (4) In OT usage the word "rich" is applied to the good as well as the bad [cf. Prov. 3:16; 8:18; 22:2]. The word itself "simply expresses an external condition. [In the word itself there is] "no intimation of character" [Urwick]. (5) The nuance "ungodly rich" would make no sense in this passage. The point of line 1 is that his enemies wished the Servant a dishonorable burial, but being buried in the grave/tomb of a rich man would be a decent and honorable burial, whether that rich man were godly or ungodly [Delitzsch]. (6) The most common translation of he conjunction עַל is "because," even though the majority of commentators prefer "although" for this verse. The concessive use ("although") is rare, although it does occur [Job 10:7; 16:17; 34:6; BDB, HALOT]. Taking the most common meaning ("because"), the thought would then be: "Because he had done no violence he was buried with the rich [as a reward]." So: Darby, KJV, NASB, NET. The other arguments for the first interpretation (2, 3, 4) would be true whether the parallelism was synonymous or antithetical. See: Delitzsch, Isaiah, 2:328; Lindsey, The Servant Songs, 129; Merrill F. Unger, Unger's Commentary on the Old Testament (Chicago: Moody, 1981; reprint ed., Chattanooga, TN: AMG Publishers, 2002), 1299; Smith, Isaiah 40–66, 455–56; Urwick, The Servant of Jehovah, 145; BDB, s.v. "עַל," 754, 758; HALOT, s.v. "עַל," 1:827.

Note: Commentators advocating a Messianic interpretation of Isaiah 53 do not consistently adopt each of the conclusions presented here as the second interpretation of v. 9a; nor do they necessarily reject each of the arguments given for the first interpretation. Interpreters of all schools acknowledge the difficulty in exegeting the passage. The principle of Delitzsch and Wright enunciated in the notes above of allowing the NT to guide the exegete in this difficult passage is a wise one.

[76] Culver, The Sufferings and the Glory of The Lord's Righteous Servant, 102. Unger agreed, "The reason for His honorable sepulcher, so different from what His foes had planned, was that after His redemptive work had been accomplished, the LORD allowed no more indignities to be perpetrated upon Him" (Unger's Commentary on the Old Testament, 1299).

(John 19:38). The Lord Jesus said, "'It is finished!' And He bowed His head and gave up His spirit" (v. 30). Soon thereafter, at the request of the Jews, the soldiers came and broke the legs of the men who were crucified with Jesus—an action called *crurifragium*, the breaking of the lower legs with hammers.[77] When they came to Jesus, however, they found that he was already dead, and they did not break his legs. Nevertheless, as a kind of *coup de grace*, "one of the soldiers pierced His side with a spear," and right away blood and water came out. John adds that this happened this way to fulfill two prophecies, that of Psalm 34:20, "Not a bone of Him shall be broken," and of Zechariah 12:10, "They shall look on Him whom they pierced" (John 19:32–36).

We know that the bones of the Passover lamb were not to be broken (Ex. 12:46), but John does not quote the Passover passage.[78] Instead he quotes Psalm 34:19-20, "Many are the afflictions of the righteous, but the LORD delivers him out of them all. He keeps all his bones, not one of them is broken." What is the point? "Once the wicked hands of men had accomplished God's purpose, they could touch the Son of God no further. Once Jesus had accomplished the work of offering his soul as a sacrifice for sin, God restrained the hands of men. He kept all his bones. In this way, then, God demonstrated that he was the One who offered up his Son upon the cross. [He was sovereign over the entire episode (Acts 2:23). Jesus, the Servant of the Lord, was] *God's* Passover lamb."[79]

THE GUILTLESS BEHAVIOR OF THE SUFFERING SERVANT

The reason why Yahweh's Servant received an honorable burial after his ignominious death is to be found in the concluding lines of verse 9: "Because He had done no violence, nor was there any deceit in His

---

[77] *Crurifragium* was not an integral part of crucifixion but was requested at this time in order to hasten the death of the three men that they might die quickly and be removed before the start of the Sabbath day (John 19:31). Cf. Raymond E. Brown, *The Death of the Messiah*, AncBRL (New York: Doubleday, 1994), 2:1175–76.

[78] That the Passover lamb is in the background of the events of the crucifixion there can be no doubt (cf. 1 Cor. 5:7), but the interpretation of the decision not to break Jesus' bones is to be found in the psalm.

[79] Bruce K. Waltke, "The Passover Ritual," Message 9 (Dallas: Dallas Theological Seminary, n.d.). In its original form, Waltke's essay was a radio sermon delivered on Dallas Seminary's radio program, "Heritage," in the 1960s.

mouth."[80] In short, the Servant was innocent of all the charges brought against him. False testimony was given at his trial—testimony that he was a violent terrorist who had predicted he would one day tear down the temple—but it was inconsistent and fabricated (Matt. 26:59-61; Mark 14:55-59). The Roman governor would confess, "**I find no guilt in Him**" (John 19:6; cf. Matt. 27:19). One of the criminals with whom he was crucified said, "**This man has done nothing wrong**" (Luke 23:41). Echoing this verse, the apostle Peter would later write, "**[He] committed no sin, nor was any deceit found in His mouth**" (1 Pet. 2:22). Both in what he did and what he said he was free from all sin.

CONCLUSION

In the fourth stanza the lamenting Israelites of the end-time report the final hours of the Servant's life. They report a number of events: (1) They note that he was treated violently by his oppressors, verse 7. (2) They observe that he was the victim of an unjust trial and an unwarranted execution, verse 8. (3) And they report that contrary to expectation, this convicted man was given an honorable burial, verse 9.

Additional details are provided that are important to their report. First, the Servant submitted in an uncomplaining way to the mistreatment he endured. Second, his contemporaries reacted with callous indifference to his plight. Third, the blow of judgment he endured was an act of substitution for the transgressions of his people. Fourth, his honorable burial was a vindication of his innocence. He was not guilty of the charges laid against him.

There are many lessons for Christians today in this passage, three of which I shall mention here. First, there is the testimony of fulfilled prophecy to the claims of Christ. As has been noted earlier in these chapters, the events described in Isaiah were prophecies of events that would take place seven hundred years later in the life of Jesus of Nazareth. Most naturalistic scholars deny this. For example, John L. McKenzie, a Jesuit Old Testament scholar, says of this writer's approach to prophecy, "In this form the opinion is defended by no one today except in a few fundamentalist circles. This type of predictive prophecy

---

[80] Oswalt draws attention to the "artistic mastery" of the prophet "as he brings the stanza to a close by circling it around to the point where it began—the mouth of the Servant" (*The Book of Isaiah, Chapters 40–66*, 396).

does not appear in the Old Testament."[81] In saying this, McKenzie dismisses the testimony of the writers of the New Testament.[82] Commenting on Isaiah 53:7, New Testament scholar S. Lewis Johnson wrote, "[Verse 7] is a true prophecy. It is so clearly a prophecy of Jesus Christ that the simplest student of Scripture can see it. It is only the modern...scholar who, assuming that prophecy is impossible, insists that the New Testament writers tailored their accounts to make them agree with the Old Testament prophecies."[83]

Second, the passage stresses the innocence of the Servant, who died for the transgressions of his people. This idea will be more fully developed in the New Testament where the writers stress that the one who died vicariously for others was a sinless victim. In fact, in the New Testament, substitution, redemption, propitiation, and sanctification depend on the sinlessness of Christ. "In virtue of his sinlessness, he can accomplish the purpose of the Incarnation."[84] In 2 Corinthians 5:21 Christ was able to become the sin bearer in our place because he himself **"knew no sin,"** i.e., had no experience of sin. Our redemption, says Peter, was accomplished **"with precious blood, as of a lamb unblemished and spotless, the blood of Christ"** (1 Pet. 1:19). Like the OT sacrificial animals, Christ had to be without blemish, i.e., without

---

[81] John L. McKenzie, *Second Isaiah*, AncB (Garden City, NY: Doubleday, 1968.), xlix.

[82] The quotations of and allusions to Isaiah 53 in the NT make it clear that the NT writers understood the OT prophecy to be predictive. See *The Greek New Testament*, 4th ed., eds. Barbara Aland, Kurt Aland, Johannes Karavidopoulos, Carlo M. Martini and Bruce Metzger (Stuttgart: United Bible Societies, 1993). The "Index of Quotations" (888) cites the following quotations (Old Testament order): Isa 52:15 LXX (Rom. 15:21); 53:1 LXX (John 12:38; Rom. 10:16); 53:4 (Matt. 8:17); 53:7-8 LXX (Acts 8:32-33); 53:9 (1 Pet. 2:22); 53:12 (Luke 22:37). The "Index of Allusions and Verbal Parallels" (897) cites the following allusions and parallels: Isa. 52:13 (Acts 3:13); 52:15 (1 Cor. 2:9); 53 (Luke 24:27, 46; 1 Pet. 1:11); 53:2 (Matt. 2:23); 53:3 (Mark 9:12); 53:4 (1 Pet. 2:24); 53:4-5 (Rom. 4:25); 53:5 (Matt. 26:67; 1 Pet. 2:24); 53:5-6 (Acts 10:43); 53:6 (1 Pet. 2:25); 53:6-7 (John 1:29); 53:7 (Matt. 26:63; 27:12, 14; Mark 14:60-61; 15:4-5; 1 Cor. 5:7; 1 Pet. 2:23; Rev. 5:6, 12; 13:8); 53:8-9 (1 Cor. 15:3); 53:9 (Matt. 26:24; 1 John 3:5; Rev. 14:5); 53:11 (Rom. 5:19); 53:12 (Matt. 27:38; Luke 23:33, 34; Heb. 9:28; 1 Pet. 2:24). See the commentary on these texts in G. K. Beale and D. A. Carson, *Commentary on the New Testament Use of the Old Testament* (Grand Rapids: Baker, 2007).

[83] S. Lewis Johnson, Jr., "The Submissive Messiah: An Exposition of Isaiah 53:7-9," *BBB* (Dallas: Believers Chapel, n.d.): 2.

[84] A. E. Brooke, *A Critical and Exegetical Commentary on the Johannine Epistles*, ICC (Edinburgh: T. & T. Clark, 1912), 86.

sin. Peter also says, "**Christ died for sins once for all, the just for the unjust**" (1 Pet. 3:18). John writes that it is "**Jesus Christ the righteous**" who is "**the propitiation for our sins**" (1 John 2:1-2), and that "**He appeared to take away sin, and in Him there is no sin**" (1 John 3:5).[85] That Christ was without sin is the consistent testimony of the NT (Matt. 3:14; John 8:46; Acts 2:27; 3:14; 4:30; 7:52; Heb. 4:15; 7:26; 1 Pet. 2:22; 1 John 3:3).

Finally, on a practical note, Jesus' refusal to defend himself even in the face of death is used by the apostle Peter as an example of how a Christian believer is to respond when attacked for his faith. "**For you have been called for this purpose, since Christ also suffered for you, leaving you an example for you to follow in His steps, 'who committed no sin, nor was any deceit found in His mouth;' and while being reviled, He did not revile in return; while suffering, He uttered no threats, but kept entrusting Himself to Him who judges righteously**" (1 Pet. 2:21-23). There's an old spiritual with this refrain, "He never said a mumblin' word."

> They led him to Pilate's bar
> Not a word, not a word, not a word
> They led him to Pilate's bar
> But he never said a mumblin' word.
>
> They all cried, "Crucify!"
> Not a word, not a word, not a word
> They all cried, "Crucify!"
> But he never said a mumblin' word.

---

85 Marshall writes, "It is significant that John uses the present tense [ἔστιν] to refer to the sinlessness of Christ; it is not simply his earthly life that is in mind but his eternal character as the Son of God" (I. Howard Marshall, *The Epistles of John*, NICNT [Grand Rapids: Eerdmans, 1978], 177, n. 10). Stott concurred, "The sinlessness of Christ does not belong only to his pre-existence, or to the days of his flesh, or to his present heavenly condition, but to his essential and eternal nature" (John Stott, *The Letters of John*, rev. ed., TNTC [Grand Rapids: Eerdmans, 1988], 127).

We nailed him on to a tree
Not a word, not a word, not a word
We nailed him on to a tree
But he never said a mumblin' word.[86]

How then are we to respond to suffering that happens when we have done nothing wrong? The apostle points to Jesus and says, "He did not retaliate." When people are insulted, they are inclined to return an insult for an insult. As Ray Pritchard says, there is a better way. When Jesus stood before Pilate and Herod, and when he faced the jeering mob, he uttered no insults and he made no threats. When they scourged him, he didn't retaliate (John 19:1). When the Sanhedrin and the soldiers spat at him, he didn't spit back (Matt. 26:67; 27:30; Mark 14:65; 15:19). When they slapped and punched him, he did not retaliate (Matt. 26:67; Mark 14:65). When the soldiers put a crown of thorns on his head, he didn't curse at them (John 19:2). When they drove the nails in his hands and feet, he didn't threaten them (Matt. 27:35; Mark 15:24; Luke 23:33; John 19:18). When people passing by joined the soldiers, priests, and robbers in mocking him, he said nothing (Matt. 27:39-44; Mark 15:29-32). When they reviled and humiliated him, he remained silent (Luke 22:65). "You find out what you really believe when others mistreat you. Sometimes the real test of your faith is what you don't do. Sometimes you'll be a better Christian by not saying anything at all .... *Sometimes you are known by what you don't say.*"[87]

---

[86] This American spiritual is variously called "And He Never Said a Mumblin' Word," "They Hung Him on a Cross," "Crucifixion," or "Easter." "The song narrates the crucifixion of Jesus Christ, detailing how he was nailed to the cross, 'whopped up the hill,' stabbed in the side, bowed his head and died, all the while keeping a dignified silence. Like all traditional music the lyrics vary from version to version but maintain the same story." The song probably predates the Civil War. "It is known to be a companion piece to and possibly holds the same author(s) as 'Were You There?' another spiritual." «"He Never Said a Mumblin' Word," from Wikipedia, accessed December 26, 2014». The version quoted here was downloaded from "The Welcome Wagon." «http://www.lyricsmania.com/he_never_said_a_mumblin_word_lyrics_welcome_wagon _the.html. Accessed December 26, 2014.

[87] Ray Pritchard, "The Silent Savior," Keep Believing Ministries, Elmhurst, Illinois. Email sermon received, April 9, 2014 (ray@keepbelieving.com). Ray Pritchard was for many years pastor of Calvary Memorial Church, Oak Park, Illinois. He continues to minister the Word as an itinerant Bible teacher, blogger, and conference speaker.

CHAPTER 5

THE RESURRECTION AND REWARD OF THE SERVANT OF THE LORD

ISAIAH 53:10-12

INTRODUCTION

In my early teen years my family would occasionally visit friends in Boston and attend the Brethren assembly there. One Sunday we were invited to the home of a cultured German family, and the distinguished father of the family (Mr. Ernest Hallbach) taught my brothers and me the rudiments of chess. I played off-and-on for a few years but never became very good. Yet I did learn the unspoken premise of the game of chess: "Protect the King!" As in the real world, when the king falls, the kingdom is lost. Most kingdoms do anything they can to protect their king. He must be protected at all costs.[1]

A notable example of this comes from the Allied invasion of Normandy on D-Day, June 6, 1944. The English Prime Minister, Winston Churchill, insisted that he go along and watch the progress of the invasion from the bridge of a battleship. General Dwight Eisenhower said that as Supreme Commander of Allied Forces he was ordering Churchill not to go. Churchill pulled rank on the general and said that he had no authority over the British government. It was a foolhardy idea, because a strike on Churchill's ship would force four or five other ships to come to his aid and not proceed with their primary responsibilities. Churchill would not back down. Someone got word to King George VI, and the king said that if Churchill was going, then he too would ship out at the head of his troops and participate in the invasion. The ploy

---

[1] Cf. Philip Ryken, "Long Live the King," *Preaching Today.com* (accessed Aug. 11, 2008).

worked; Churchill immediately backed down, because he knew that at all costs he must "protect the king."[2]

The unspoken premise, "protect the king" was abandoned when God sent his Son, **"the Lord of glory"** (1 Cor. 2:8), into this world. He came as a lowly bondservant and gave his body to be crucified. He died for all of the wrongs that we have ever done and paid the debt that we owed. No one stepped in to protect him from the violence of men; no one cared about the injustice, cruelty, and lies. That is why the apostle could say, **"For I determined to know nothing among you except Jesus Christ, and Him crucified"** (1 Cor. 2:2). It is why we revere the cross— it is the place where heaven's prince died. Isaac Watts wrote,

> When I survey the wondrous cross
>   Where the young Prince of Glory died,
> My richest gain I count but loss,
>   And pour contempt on all my pride.
>
> See from his head, his hands, his feet,
>   Sorrow and love flow mingled down!
> Did e'er such love and sorrow meet,
>   Or thorns compose so rich a crown?
>
> His dying crimson, like a robe,
>   Spreads o'er his body on the tree;
> Then I am dead to all the globe
>   And all the globe is dead to me.[3]

The passage under consideration in this chapter is the fifth and final strophe of Isaiah's great Servant Song. The song began in chapter 52 (vv. 13-15) with a divine oracle in which Yahweh announced the exaltation of his Servant. This was followed in chapter 53, verses 1-9 with a lament

---

[2] Stephen E. Ambrose, *The Supreme Commander: The War Years of Dwight D. Eisenhower* (New York: Doubleday, 1970; reprint ed., Jackson: University Press of Mississippi, 1999), 407–408.

[3] Isaac Watts, "Crucified to the World through the Cross of Christ," quoted by Stephen R. Holmes, *The Wondrous Cross: Atonement and Penal Substitution in the Bible and History* (Colorado Springs, CO: Paternoster, 2007), ix. In the second edition of his hymnbook (1709) Watts changed the second line to "On which the prince of Glory died."

by believing Israelites in the end-time, who will mourn over the terrible treatment received by the Servant when he walked this earth.

In verses 10-12 the prophet Isaiah and Yahweh will both speak. First, in verse 10, Isaiah declares that the will of Yahweh was accomplished through the sacrificial death and exaltation of the Servant.[4] Then, in verses 11-12, there is a concluding oracle in which Yahweh promises that the Servant will justify many (v. 11) and that he will have victorious dominion because he died bearing the sins of many.[5]

THE SERVANT ADVANCES THE PLAN OF YAHWEH, VERSE 10

> But the LORD was pleased
> To crush Him, putting Him to grief;
> If He would render Himself as a guilt offering,
> He will see His offspring,
> He will prolong His days,
> And the good pleasure of the LORD will prosper in His hand.

HE SUFFERED AND DIED AS A GUILT (RESTITUTION) OFFERING

Verse 10 begins with a Hebrew particle that expresses a contrast.[6] Perhaps some might think that the Servant's death was an accident of history, a good person in the wrong place at the wrong time. "Not at all," says the prophet, "God wanted this to happen! It is no accident—it [was] his will!"[7] **"But the LORD was pleased to crush Him, putting Him to grief; if He would render Himself as a guilt offering."**

We are inclined to attribute the death of Jesus to Judas, the Jews, and the Romans. Isaiah reminds us he died according to the will and plan of God. In the New Testament, Peter concurs. **"This man [was] delivered over by the predetermined plan and foreknowledge of God"**

---

[4] Delitzsch was of the opinion that repentant Israel spoke from verse 1 through verse 10. Franz Delitzsch, *Biblical Commentary on the Prophecies of Isaiah*, trans. James Martin (Edinburgh: T. & T. Clark, 1877; reprint ed., Grand Rapids: Eerdmans, 1965), 2:330–31.

[5] F. Duane Lindsey, *The Servant Songs: A Study in Isaiah* (Chicago: Moody, 1985), 131.

[6] The verse begins with a disjunctive *waw* (ו) Cf. *IBHS*, § 39.2.3 (650–52).

[7] John N. Oswalt, *The Book of Isaiah, Chapters 40–66*, NICOT (Grand Rapids: Eerdmans, 1998), 400.

(Acts 2:23a).[8] It is true, as Isaiah says, that he was **"pierced," "crushed," "scourged," "oppressed," "afflicted," "slaughtered,"** and **"cut off"** at the hands of wicked men (vv. 5-8). Peter agreed with that too, as he said to his Jewish listeners in Jerusalem: **"You nailed [him] to a cross by the hands of godless men and put him to death"** (Acts 2:23b).

Yet God was directly involved in the death of his Son and Servant. He was the *causa efficiens* ("efficient cause") of the death of Christ.[9] Human sentimentality says this is a terrible thing to say of God. "God wanted to crush this man? God wanted to visit terrible pain on him? Surely not! The faithful God of the Bible would not visit such bad things on [an innocent person], would he? Yes he would if some greater good would be served."[10]

One evening Martin Luther and his wife and children gathered for family devotions. He read the story in Genesis 22 of God's command to Abraham to take his son Isaac and offer him as a sacrifice. Luther drew the parallel to God the Father and Christ. He sacrificed his Son who, like Isaac, submitted in complete obedience. When he had finished, his wife Katie spoke up, "I do not believe it. God would not have treated his son like that." "But Katie," Luther answered, "he did."[11]

People will often reject this or that doctrine of Scripture with remarks such as, "My God wouldn't do that," or "I couldn't believe in a God like that." Such remarks tell us nothing of what God is like. As Luther said to his wife, "But Katie, he did it." If we want to know what God is like, we have to consider what he does. And the Bible says that he planned to deliver Jesus over to the cross.

All of this goes back to eternity past when God the Father, God the Son, and God the Holy Spirit agreed on a plan to redeem fallen mankind. Some theologians call this plan "the covenant of

---

[8] This text strongly emphasizes God's sovereign determination of the delivering over of Christ. "The most likely option is that the πρόγνωσις ["foreknowledge"] is grounded in the ὡρισμένη βουλή ["predetermined plan"] (thus "foreknowledge" is a part of the "predetermined plan"), for one part of the foci of the chapter is on the divine *plan* in relation to the Messiah's death and resurrection. Thus, God's decrees are not based on him simply foreknowing what human beings will do; rather, humanity's actions are based on God's foreknowledge and predetermined plan" (Daniel B. Wallace, *Greek Grammar Beyond the Basics* [Grand Rapids: Zondervan, 1996], 288).

[9] Delitzsch, *Biblical Commentary on the Prophecies of Isaiah*, 2:330.

[10] Oswalt, *The Book of Isaiah, Chapters 40–66*, 400.

[11] Roland H. Bainton, *Here I Stand: A Life of Martin Luther* (Nashville: Abingdon, 1950), 369–70.

redemption."[12] Whether we call it that or not, the Father determined to send his Son, the Son agreed to go and die for sinners, and the Holy Spirit agreed to apply the benefits of that death to all who believe (John 17:4-5; cf. 16:7-11; Eph. 1:4, 7, 13).[13]

Isaiah says, **"But Yahweh was pleased to crush Him."** The Hebrew verb translated "pleased" (חָפֵץ, *ḥāpēṣ*) means "to delight in" or "take pleasure in,"[14] and this is how it is rendered in a number of versions (e.g., Darby, KJV, NASB, HCSB). Others balk at this rendering and translate, **"It was the LORD's will to crush him"** (NIV, and variations in ESV, NRSV, TEV).[15]

Commentators caution that we should not think of God as a sadist who enjoyed watching his Servant suffer. One writes, "The cup must have been as bitter for the Father as for the Son."[16] There is no question that Yahweh willed the Servant's atoning death (Acts 2:23), yet the verb used here implies that and more. The translation **"was pleased to crush Him"** is the correct one. He who takes **"no pleasure in the death of the wicked"** (Ezek. 33:11), **"was pleased to crush"** his Servant.[17] The question is, what does this mean? It certainly does not mean that God enjoyed watching his Servant suffer, much as a boxing fan would enjoy watching a fighter be pummeled by his opponent. Rather, God took

---

[12] Charles Hodge, *Systematic Theology* (New York: Scribner, 1872; reprint ed., Grand Rapids: Eerdmans, 1975), 2:359–61. Cf. Lewis Sperry Chafer, *Systematic Theology, vol. 1: Prolegomena–Bibliology–Theology Proper* (Dallas: Dallas Seminary Press, 1947), 42.

[13] Cf. R. C. Sproul, "Precious Blood," in Richard D. Phillips, ed., *Precious Blood: The Atoning Work of Christ* (Wheaton: Crossway, 2009), 102.

[14] The form used here is חָפֵץ (3rd pers. msc. sg. qal perf.). Cf. *HALOT*, s.v. "חָפֵץ," 1:340; BDB, s.v. "חָפֵץ," 343.

[15] The LXX reads, καὶ κύριος βούλεται καθαρίσαι αὐτόν. Gottlob Schrenk understands the use of βούλομαι in Isaiah 53:10 to speak of "the divine resolve and will" (*TDNT*, s.v. "βούλομαι," 1:631, n. 19).

[16] Robert D. Culver, *The Sufferings and the Glory of the Lord's Righteous Servant* (Moline, IL: Christian Service Foundation, 1958), 107–108.

[17] At least five times the Scriptures speak of God's pleasure in his Son: (1) At the baptism the Father expressed his pleasure at the Son's obedience during the "hidden years," Matt. 3:17; Mark 1:11. (2) At the transfiguration of Jesus, the Father expressed his pleasure in the Son's public ministry, Matt. 17:5. (3) At Golgotha, the Father, silently behind the closed doors of the darkened heavens, took pleasure in the obedience of his Son in enduring the cross, Isa. 53:10. (4) At his exaltation, God's actions, although the word "pleasure" is unexpressed, indicate his delight in his Servant, Isa. 52:13; Phil. 2:9-10. (5) At the beginning of the millennial age although again—the word "pleasure" is unexpressed—God's words indicate his full satisfaction in his Son, Ps. 2:6-12.

pleasure in contemplating the obedient, heroic, and self-sacrificing love of Christ.

Christian believers take pleasure in contemplating the cross and what it means to them to know of Christ's love and God's forgiveness. They have a similar attitude when reading of the martyrs of the church. They do not dwell on the physical torture they endured; rather, it ceases to be a horror in their eyes, and becomes a glory. We read of their sufferings with joyful hearts, amazed at the grace God gave them and the courage and obedience to God they displayed.[18]

We are always impressed and encouraged when we read of men like Ridley and Latimer. On October 16, 1555 Dr. Nicholas Ridley, Bishop of London, and Mr. Hugh Latimer, sometime Bishop of Worcester, were burned in one fire in Oxford for their evangelical views. When they lay a burning bundle of sticks at Ridley's feet, Mr. Latimer encouraged him, "Be of good comfort, Mr. Ridley, and play the man! We shall this day light such a candle, by God's grace, in England, as I trust never shall be put out."[19] In my own lifetime, on January 8, 1956, Jim Elliott, Pete Fleming, Nate Saint, Ed McCully, and Roger Youderian were killed by members of the Auca (Waorani) tribe in Ecuador—tribesmen to whom the young missionaries had come to proclaim the gospel of Christ. William Barclay, the Scottish New Testament scholar said later, after reading their story, "It ought to read as a tragedy, humanly speaking, and somehow it reads as a triumph." Christians everywhere agreed. Yes, believers sorrowed over their deaths, but they took great pride in the unfailing brilliance of lives given in the service of the Lord. We read their story with delight! And so God viewed the death of his Servant.[20]

The word "**crush Him**" (דַּכְּאוֹ, *dakkᵉʾô*)[21] is followed by the expression "**putting Him to grief**" (הֶחֱלִי, *heḥĕlî*)[22] meaning, "he made him sick." Together the two words literally mean "to crush him with

---

[18] David Baron, *The Servant of Jehovah* (New York: George H. Doran, 1921), 119.

[19] Mark Water, compiler, *The New Encyclopedia of Christian Martyrs* (Grand Rapids: Baker, 2001), 706–15 (esp. 715).

[20] William Barclay is quoted on the back cover of the paperback edition of Elisabeth Elliott, *Through Gates of Splendor* (New York: Harper & Row, 1965).

[21] The form used here (דַּכְּא) is a piel (intensive) infinitive of דָּכָא. Cf. *HALOT*, s.v. "דכא," 1:221.

[22] The form used here (הֶחֱלִי) is 3d pers. msc. sg. hiphil (causative active) perfect of חָלָה. Cf. *HALOT*, s.v. "חלה," 1:316–17 (esp. 317).

sickness."[23] In some OT contexts, including this one, the verb חָלָה (ḥālāh, "to be sick") is used of sickness caused by violence or wounds. For example when Ahab, king of Israel, was struck by an arrow, he said, "I am severely wounded" (1 Kings 22:34). It is this same verb (חָלָה). He was made sick, i.e., by his wound. Ahab's son Joram was also wounded, and Ahaziah visited him "because he was sick," i.e., from his wounds (2 Kings 8:29). [24] So it was with God's Servant. He was **"crushed severely"** (HCSB); he was "broken by suffering." Hebrew scholar Christopher North implies there aren't words to describe the physical and emotional destruction of the Servant. He says, "Language breaks down under the strain imposed upon it."[25]

In the remaining part of the verse Isaiah explains what God wants to come out of the Servant's sufferings. His goal is one of monumental proportions. He wants "'a full and sufficient sacrifice'[26] [for his people] satisfying all the unpaid debts of their behavior, debts they could never hope to pay, but debts that if left unpaid would stand forever between them and a just God."[27]

The perspective changes somewhat at this point. In verses 1-9 the end-time Israelites are looking at Christ's sufferings in the past. Now, however, Isaiah looks at those sufferings from his own perspective (between 740–680 BC) and speaks of those sufferings as if they are future—which they were in his day. In the remaining lines of verse 10 he looks to the Servant's death and makes three statements: First, he states "the condition that will need to be met if God's purpose is to be realized." The condition is that the Servant be offered as a guilt offering. Second, he "expresses the results of that condition having being met." The result will be the joyous resurrection of the Servant. Third, he affirms that God's purpose will then have been realized.[28]

Isaiah first states the condition that needs to be met. "If (אִם, 'im) He **would render** (תָּשִׂים, tāśîm) **Himself** (נַפְשׁוֹ, napšô) **as a guilt offering**

---

[23] Young construes the two verbs together as a hendiadys (Edward J. Young, *The Book of Isaiah*, NICOT [Grand Rapids: Eerdmans, 1972], 3:354, n. 37).

[24] Christopher R. North, *The Second Isaiah* (Oxford: Oxford University Press, 1964), 242.

[25] North, *The Second Isaiah*, 242.

[26] This wording is from the *Book of Common Prayer*, "Ritual for Communion."

[27] Oswalt, *The Book of Isaiah, Chapters 40–66*, 400.

[28] Oswalt, *The Book of Isaiah, Chapters 40–66*, 401.

(אָשָׁם, 'āšām) (NASB). This line is difficult, and I offer the following translation with due deference to other interpreters: "When (אִם, 'im)[29] his soul (נַפְשׁוֹ, napšô), i.e., he,[30] shall make (תָּשִׂים, tāśîm)[31] a guilt offering."[32]

---

[29] The particle אִם occurs 1,060 times in the OT, most often to express contingency ("if"). Cf. *IBHS*, § 31.6.1, n. 31 (510). It is used with a variety of nuances as is suggested by translations of this verse: "though" (concessive use, cf. *GKC* §160a [498]), as well as "when" (KJV, ESV, HCSB), "once" (NET), "whether," "not" (Jack B. Scott, "אִם," in *TWOT*, 1:48–49), "because," "since" (Culver, *The Sufferings and the Glory of the Lord's Righteous Servant*, 109). Waltke and O'Connor say concerning the many unpredictable usages, "[We] confess that the calculus of the particles is beyond our specification" (§ 40.2.2a [679]). In the present context the translation "when" is probably best (KJV, Darby, NRSV, ESV, HCSB). The particle is so translated in Genesis 38:9; Numbers 36:4; Judges 6:3; Psalm 78:34; Isaiah 4:4; 24:13; 28:25; Amos 7:4. The translation "if" would be misleading here for two reasons: (1) The particle אִם need not convey the idea of doubt as "if" does in English. (2) The previous context (vv. 1-9) make it clear that the Servant's offering was never in doubt but was the result of the will of God. Cf. Allan A. MacRae, *The Gospel of Isaiah* (Chicago: Moody, 1977), 145.

[30] The form in the text is the feminine singular noun (נֶפֶשׁ, "soul" or "life") with the 3rd pers. msc. sg. pronominal suffix ("his soul"). The word נֶפֶשׁ has a number of nuances in the Old Testament ("throat," "neck," "breath," "living being," referring to animals, "people," "personality," "life," "soul," as the center and transmitter of feelings and perceptions, and "soul," as the animating principle of the body [*HALOT*, s.v. "נֶפֶשׁ," 1:712–13]). There continues to be debate over the exact translation in specific contexts and whether the translation "soul" in the metaphysical, theological sense is ever appropriate. The generally accepted opinion today is summarized by Westermann: "The *nepeš* is not set apart as a distinct aspect of the human." He later quotes another with approval, "The LXX never goes in the direction in which 'soul' would be understood as opposite to 'body' (as in Platonic dualism)." For summaries of contemporary discussion, cf. Bruce K. Waltke, "נֶפֶשׁ," *TWOT*, 2:587–91; H. Seebass, "נֶפֶשׁ," *TDOT*, 9:497–519 (esp. 514); C. Westermann, "נֶפֶשׁ," in *TLOT*, 2: 743–59 (esp. 755, 759). For an older but still valuable discussion, see Robert Baker Girdlestone, *Synonyms of the Old Testament*, 2d ed. (1897; reprint ed., Grand Rapids: Eerdmans, n.d.), 56–59. Girdlestone assumes the nuance "soul" as the "animating principle of the body" and draws attention to Leviticus 17:11, 14. In this passage "blood is (i.e., represents) 'the soul.'" If the one flows out from the body, the other passes away too." The identification of "the blood and the life is of great interest as bearing upon the atoning work of Christ. We are told that He poured out his soul unto death [Isa. 53:12], and that He shed his blood for the remission of sins [Matt. 26:28, KJV]. Evidently the shedding of the blood was the outward and visible sign of the severance of the soul from the body in death." Cf. also Culver, *The Sufferings and the Glory of the Lord's Righteous Servant*, 109–112 (discussion in footnote). The present writer sees a progressive development in the anthropology of the Bible. While in Genesis 2:7 man is portrayed as psychosomatic unity, in later Scripture a duality in man is recognized (e.g., Dan. 7:15). Cf. John Laidlaw, *The Biblical Doctrine of Man*, Cunningham Lectures, rev. ed. (Edinburgh: T. & T. Clark, 1895), 64, 96–98, 258. The soul (נֶפֶשׁ, ψυχή) of man may be defined as "the whole inner life of

The offering he makes is called "a guilt offering" (NASB, NIV, ESV).[33] The Hebrew noun (אָשָׁם) is related to the verb (אָשַׁם, 'āšam) meaning "to be guilty" (Lev. 4:3, 13, 22, 27) and in some texts "to pay, suffer for one's guilt" (Isa. 24:6; Zech. 11:5; Ps. 34:22-23).[34] Although the noun is often translated "guilt offering," it should be rendered as in the KJV, "trespass offering," [35] or (even better) "reparation offering."[36] I say "even better" because it is more helpful to name the offering after its purpose, which was to make reparation or restitution.[37]

The reparation offering is described in Leviticus 5:14–6:7 [MT = 5:14-26]. It is interesting that the same word describes the wrong (why

---

man with his powers of will, reason, and emotion" (G. Harder, "Soul," *NIDNTT*, 3:684). H. D. McDonald defined the soul of man as his "essential being, the seat of the individual's personal identity" (*The Christian View of Man* [Westchester, IL: Crossway, 1981], 78).

[31] The form תָּשִׂים is rendered here as a 3d pers. fem. sg. qal imperfect of שִׂים. The subject of the verb is "his soul," the feminine noun נֶפֶשׁ taking the feminine verb. Some take the verb to be 2d. pers. msc. sg. ("you"), and it is usually applied to Yahweh (KJV, Darby, NRSV, HCSB; cf. NIV). This view is preferred by Oswalt and Kelley in that they take the novel ("unique") view that the reader is being addressed, i.e., "If you make his life a guilt offering." If the reader takes the broken self the Servant offers him, and in turn offers it back to God as his substitute, then the Servant's sacrifice will atone for him. Kelley writes, "It is the worshiper who must appropriate the servant's sacrifice and make it the means of his own approach to God" (Oswalt, *The Book of Isaiah, Chapters 40–66*, 401; Page H. Kelley, "Isaiah," in *The Broadman Bible Commentary*, ed. Clifton J. Allen [Nashville: Broadman, 1971], 5:344). Motyer mentions this view and does not rule it out (J. Alec Motyer, *The Prophecy of Isaiah* [Downers Grove: IVP, 1993], 440). Delitzsch asks however, "Is it really [the reader who] makes the soul of the Servant an אָשָׁם and not the Servant Himself?" See *Biblical Commentary on the Prophecies of Isaiah*, 2:331.

[32] Christopher R. North, *The Second Isaiah* (Oxford: Oxford University Press, 1964), 232.

[33] North, *The Second Isaiah*, 243.

[34] *HALOT*, s.v. "אשם," 1:95.

[35] *BDB*, s.v. "אָשָׁם," 79. Cf. Delitzsch, *Biblical Commentary on the Prophecies of Isaiah*, 2:331–35; Gustav Friedrich Oehler, *Theology of the Old Testament*, trans. George E. Day (New York: Funk and Wagnalls, 1883), § 137 (300–304); T. Ernest Wilson, *Blood Sacrifices of the Old Testament* (Port Colborne, ON: Gospel Folio Press, 2009), 52–55.

[36] S. C. Gayford, *Sacrifice and Priesthood*, 2d ed. (London: Methuen, 1953), 44–46; Roland De Vaux, *Studies in Old Testament Sacrifice* (Cardiff, University of Wales Press, 1964), 98–102; Allen P. Ross, *Holiness to the Lord* (Grand Rapids: Baker, 2002), 146–54. The HCSB has "restitution offering," which is equally good.

[37] Some commentators argue that אָשָׁם is used here generically to speak of the sacrificial system as a whole (e.g., MacRae, *The Gospel of Isaiah*, 144–45; Young, *The Book of Isaiah*, 3:354–55). The use of the term, however, suggests that Isaiah had the reparation offering in mind.

the person was guilty) and the remedy (what he had to do about it). The Leviticus passage describes the remedy. If an Israelite sinned inadvertently against the Lord's "holy things" (5:14)[38] or if he sinned blatantly against the Lord's holy name by defrauding a neighbor financially and then lying about it, he was to do the following things: he was to return what was taken or repay the full value of it plus a surcharge of 20 percent, and he was to bring a reparation offering of a ram to the priest, who would make atonement for him. He would then be forgiven. That God would forgive the person, even when he sinned blatantly, indicates that he had remorse (felt the guilt), paid restitution (Lev. 6:4), and confessed his sin (cf. Num. 5:6-8).[39]

The various OT sacrifices all find a counterpart in the one sacrifice of Jesus Christ (cf. Heb. 10:1).[40] In his sacrifice on the cross, Jesus

---

[38] Leviticus 5:15 describes one who "acts unfaithfully" (מָעַל) "against the LORD's holy things" (מִקָּדְשֵׁי יְהוָה). The Lord's holy things included that which is called "holy" (קֹדֶשׁ) and "most holy" (קֹדֶשׁ הַקֳּדָשִׁים). This includes all the sacred property of the Lord, including the tabernacle, its furnishings, things belonging to the priests, and anything dedicated to the Lord. For a full discussion, see Jacob Milgrom, *Leviticus 1–16*, AncB (New Haven: Yale, 2009), 322–26. Examples of such sacrilege include Achan's taking booty from defeated Jericho when the people had been forbidden to do so (Josh. 6:17-19; 7:1, 19-26), King Uzziah's usurping the priestly prerogative of offering incense in the temple (2 Chron. 26:16-18), and King Ahaz's altering the true worship of Yahweh at the Jerusalem temple and encouraging idolatry throughout the land (2 Chron. 28:19-25; 29:19). See John E. Hartley, *Leviticus*, WBC (Dallas: Word, 1992), 80.

[39] The reparation, or restitution, offering is a paradox according to Milgrom. In Numbers 15:24-29 the Lord instructed Moses that unintentional sins could be atoned for by sacrifice. Willful, defiant sins, however, would result in the person being cut off from the people. In Leviticus 6:2-4 (MT = 5:22-23), however, Moses says that even when a person deliberately sins and then lies about it and swears an oath that he is innocent, he may be forgiven when he brings a restitution offering (Lev. 6:5-7 [MT = 5:24-26]). Milgrom provided a solution to this apparent paradox by his novel translation of the verb אָשֵׁם ("becomes guilty," NASB) in Leviticus 6:4 [MT = 5:23]. The verb, he argues, has a wider semantic range and here has the psychological nuance "to feel guilty," i.e., to repent. Whenever a guilty person genuinely repented, he lowered his sin to the level of unintentional guilt and gained the possibility of forgiveness by presenting a restitution offering (Jacob Milgrom, *Cult and Conscience: The ASHAM and the Priestly Doctrine of Repentance* (Leiden: Brill, 1976), 9, 84–85, 117 and passim; idem., *Leviticus 1–16*, 319–78 (esp. 373).

[40] On the significance of the various sacrifices, see Delitzsch, *Biblical Commentary on the Prophecies of Isaiah*, 333–34; G. J. Wenham, *The Book of Leviticus*, NICOT (Grand Rapids: Eerdmans, 1979), 111–12; S. H. Kellogg, *The Book of Leviticus*, 3d ed. (New York: A. C. Armstrong, 1899; reprint ed., Minneapolis, MN: Klock & Klock, 1978), 169.

covered the guilt of his people—guilt in the sense of a debt owed to God. He satisfied the demands of the justice of God. In fact, he paid a penalty plus 20 percent, i.e., his sacrifice outweighed the guilt of sinners.[41] **"Where sin increased, grace abounded all the more"** (Rom. 5:20). In a passive sense he met the demands of justice against the sinner as a rebel under the sentence of death. In an active sense his death was the supreme act of obedience to the will of God whereby he discharged to the last penny the debt we owed.[42] Here again in poetic form we see the idea of vicarious sacrifice. In the words of Ellis J. Crum's hymn,

> He paid a debt He did not owe;
>> I owed a debt I could not pay;
> I needed someone to wash my sins away.
>> And now, I sing a brand new song, "Amazing Grace."
> Christ Jesus paid a debt that I could never pay.

HE RISES FROM DEATH TO ENJOYMENT OF "FAMILY" AND PROSPERITY

There are positive consequences of the Servant's sacrifice for his people. Four things will happen: three relate to the Servant, and one relates to the larger purposes of God.[43] Of the three consequences for the Servant, two are spoken and one is assumed. First, **"He will see His offspring"** (זֶרַע, zera', lit. "his seed"). "The Hebrews regarded the presence of children in the family as a mark of divine favor and greatly to be desired (Gen. 15:2; 30:1; 1 Sam. 1:11, 20; Ps. 127:3; Luke 1:7, 28)."[44] The Servant died without children, an additional calamity in the eyes of his countrymen.

Yet, Isaiah says, **"He will see His offspring."** In the OT the word "seed" generally refers to literal children. Here, however, the prophet is looking on to the future and speaking of the Servant's spiritual

---

[41] Delitzsch, *Biblical Commentary on the Prophecies of Isaiah*, 2:334.

[42] Kellogg, *The Book of Leviticus*, 173.

[43] Oswalt, *The Book of Isaiah, Chapters 40–66*, 402.

[44] W. N. Stearns, "Child," *ISBE* rev, (1979): 1:645. "Long life and numerous descendants are regarded by the Hebrews as the highest prosperity, as a theocratic blessing and a reward of piety" (E. W. Hengstenberg, *Christology of the Old Testament*, trans. Reuel Keith, abridged by Thomas Kerchever Arnold [London: Rivington, 1847; reprint ed., Grand Rapids: Kregel, 1970], 240).

children—the justified ones in verse 11, the many that Yahweh will give him in verse 12, and the sprinkled ones of chapter 52 (v. 15).[45] The Servant will have a large family of descendants.

Second, **"He will prolong His days."**[46] In chapter 65 (vv. 20-23) Yahweh promises that in the future kingdom, long life will be the rule.[47] Isaiah could not have imagined that the Servant would actually live forever, yet eternal life is the Servant's lot in the fulfillment of this prophecy (cf. Heb. 7:16-22; Rev. 1:18).

Third, Isaiah assumes that the Servant will rise from the dead. He does not specifically mention resurrection here (he does in 26:19), but he does assume that something very dramatic will happen—the Servant will return from the world of the dead.[48]

Sigmund Mowinckel, the noted Norwegian scholar, wrote:

> For a great miracle will take place, whereby the others will realize that the Servant was in the right, and that he suffered for their sakes. Kings and nations will be amazed when they hear of and see the miracle. Yahweh will raise the dead man from the grave; his greatness and his honor will be restored; he will see his seed (…his spiritual children), prolong his days, see his work crowned with success, and reap all the glory that an eastern poet could possibly describe.[49]

In light of the above accomplishments it can be rightly said "that the Servant successfully completed his task."[50] **"And the good pleasure of the LORD will prosper in His hand."** Some versions have "the will of the LORD will prosper" (NIV, NRSV, ESV), and others have "the LORD's

---

[45] H. D. Preuss simply ignores the text and writes, "There is no suggestion of spiritual descendants, the devout. He seems to imply there will be no "seed" whatsoever, literal or spiritual (s.v. "זרע," TDOT, 4:161). Oswalt, surprisingly, adopts a similar view (*The Book of Isaiah, Chapters 40–66*, 403).

[46] Some have joined the two lines: ""He shall have seed and in them prolong his days" (Preuss, "זרע," 161); "He shall see seed which shall lengthen days" (North, *The Second Isaiah*, 243)

[47] Cf. North, *The Second Isaiah*, 243.

[48] North, *The Second Isaiah*, 243; Gary V. Smith, *Isaiah 40–66*, NAC (Nashville: B & H, 2009), 460.

[49] Sigmund Mowinckel, *He That Cometh: The Messiah Concept in the Old Testament and Later Judaism*, trans. G. W. Anderson (Nashville: Abingdon, 1954), 204–5.

[50] Smith, *Isaiah 40–66*, 460.

purpose will prosper" (NET, REB, TEV). However, "the good pleasure of the LORD will prosper" is to be preferred (Darby, KJV, NASB, HCSB). Isaiah uses the noun form here (חֵפֶץ, *ḥēpeṣ*) of the verb he uses in the first line of the verse (חָפֵץ, *ḥāpēṣ*), which is there rendered "was pleased." The noun means "delight, pleasure" and here has the nuance, "that in which one takes delight."[51] As Smith observes, "This success connects the end of the Servant's ministry with the prophecy in 52:13 that foretold that the Servant would prosper and be exalted."[52] He goes on to note that pain, piercing, beating, suffering, and bearing guilt may not sound like success to the pleasure-seeking consumer of the modern world. But the Servant was successful in God's eyes, and that "does not relate to the money, praise, position, status, or worldly success that a person gains for himself."[53] One evaluates a servant by asking, did he do the task he was assigned to do? It is clear that Yahweh judged his Servant to be a good servant. He did the "job"[54] he was asked to do.

The verb (יִצְלַח, *yiṣlaḥ*)[55] is correctly rendered as a future ("will prosper" or "will be successful"). As Johnson notes, the divine purpose goes beyond the sacrifice of the Servant to a glorious future and the successful conclusion of his work.[56] As well known pastor Tony Evans remarked, "Jesus didn't say, 'I am finished.' He said, 'It is finished.' He was just getting started."[57] Delitzsch wrote:

> His self sacrifice, therefore, merely lays the foundation for a progressively self-realizing "pleasure of the LORD," i.e. (cf. ch. 44:28) for the realization of the purpose of God according to his determinate counsel, the fuller description of which we had in ch. 42 and 49, where it was stated the he should be the mediator of a new covenant, and the restorer of Israel, the light of the

---

[51] BDB, s.v. "חֵפֶץ," 343.

[52] Smith, *Isaiah 40–66*, 460.

[53] Smith, *Isaiah 40–66*, 460.

[54] Instead of "good pleasure" or "delight," *HALOT* prefers the translation, "business" (s.v. "חֵפֶץ," 1:340). "The business of the Lord will prosper."

[55] The verb יִצְלַח is 3d pers. sg. qal imperfect of צָלַח, "to succeed, be successful" (*HALOT*, s.v. "צלח," 2:1026).

[56] S. Lewis Johnson, Jr., "The Righteous Servant, Bruised but Exalted (Isaiah 53:10-12)," *BBB* (Dallas: Believers Chapel, n.d.): 1–7 (esp. 3).

[57] Tony Evans, "facebook"™ posting, Feb. 6, 2014.

Gentiles and salvation of Jehovah even to the ends of the earth.[58]

THE SERVANT ACCOMPLISHES THE JUSTIFICATION OF HIS PEOPLE, VERSE 11

As a result of the anguish of His soul,
He will see it and be satisfied;
By His knowledge the Righteous One,
My Servant, will justify the many,
As He will bear their iniquities.

HE IS SATISFIED IN THE KNOWLEDGE OF HIS ACCOMPLISHMENTS

In verses 11 and 12 the poem moves from Isaiah's retrospective acknowledgment of the Servant's work (verses 1-9) to God's acknowledgement of the Servant as his own.[59] The Lord states the results of the Servant's sacrifice, first in terms of the Servant, and then in terms of the people.[60] It should be repeated that the stanza continues to use the future tense because Isaiah was writing not from the perspective of the end-time Israelites for whom these things will be in the past, but from his own perspective as one for whom the work of Christ was yet future.

Because of his accomplishments, the Servant will be satisfied. The NASB reads: "**As a result of the anguish of His soul, He will see it and be satisfied.**" The sentence begins with a preposition (מִן, *min*), which has here a causal sense, i.e., "**because of the anguish of his soul,**" or "**as a result of the anguish of his soul.**"[61] The noun "**anguish**" (עָמָל, *'āmāl*]

---

[58] Delitzsch, *Biblical Commentary on the Prophecies of Isaiah*, 2:335.

[59] Delitzsch, *Biblical Commentary on the Prophecies of Isaiah*, 2:335.

[60] Oswalt, *The Book of Isaiah, Chapters 40–66*, 403.

[61] The preposition מִן has been taken in three ways in this context: (1) the spatial or locational sense, i.e., "out of his anguish" or "from his anguish" [NRSV, ESV, HCSB; Oswalt, *The Book of Isaiah, Chapters 40–66*, 399]. (2) the temporal sense, i.e., "after his anguish" or "from the time of his anguish" [NIV, REB, TEV, NET; North, *The Second Isaiah*, 244; William Urwick, *The Servant of Jehovah: A Commentary, Grammatical and Critical Upon Isaiah LII.13 to LIII.12* (Edinburgh: T. & T. Clark, 1877), 154; Klas Baltzer, *Deutero-Isaiah: A Commentary on Isaiah 40–55*, Hermeneia, trans. Margaret Kohl (Minneapolis: Fortress, 2001), 424. (3) the causal sense, i.e., "because of his anguish," or "as a result of his anguish [NASB; Delitzsch, *Biblical Commentary on the Prophecies of*

NASB, NRSV, ESV, HCSB) is rendered by some as "suffering" (NIV, REB, NET) or "trouble."[62] Yahweh speaks of **"the anguish of his soul,"** i.e., of his innermost being.

Delitzsch noted that the "anguish" or "trouble" Christ experienced at the cross was "not only in His body, but [in] the inmost recesses of His soul."[63] This is an important observation in that there has often been a tendency to overly emphasize the bodily sufferings of Christ at the expense of his deeper spiritual sufferings. He did not only suffer the physical assaults of his executioners; he also suffered the penalty for our sins, a penalty inflicted by God himself.

John Calvin, the great reformer, wrote, "If Christ had died only a bodily death, it would have been ineffectual. No—it was expedient at the same time for him to undergo the severity of God's vengeance, to appease his wrath and satisfy his just judgment. For this reason, he must also grapple hand to hand with the armies of hell and the dread of everlasting death...." While in the sight of man he suffered in his body, in the sight of God "he paid a greater and more excellent price in suffering in his soul the terrible torments of a condemned and forsaken man."[64]

The result of his anguish is seen in the next line: **"He will see it and be satisfied."** There are two difficulties with this translation, and they need to be clarified. First, where does the second line end? Some translations end it with the word "satisfied" (KJV, NASB, NIV, ESV). Others, however, end the line with "knowledge" (NRSV, REB, HCSB). **"Because of the anguish of his soul, he will see it and be satisfied by his knowledge."** The second approach divides the verse more evenly into two equal halves and is therefore preferable.[65]

Isaiah, 2:335;]. Cf. *IBHS*, § 11.2.11 [pp. 212–14]; *WHSB*, § 315, 316, 319 [pp. 120–22].

[62] *HALOT*, s.v. "עָמָל‎," 1:845.

[63] Delitzsch, *Biblical Commentary on the Prophecies of Isaiah*, 2:336.

[64] John Calvin, *Institutes of the Christian Religion*, trans. Ford Lewis Battles (Philadelphia: Westminster, 1960), 2.16.10 (1:515–16).

[65] North, *The Second Isaiah*, 233; H. Wheeler Robinson, *The Cross in the Old Testament* (Philadelphia: Westminster, 1955), 64; Culver, *The Lord's Righteous Servant*, 105; Smith, *Isaiah 40–66*, 460; Oswalt, *The Book of Isaiah, Chapters 40–66*, 399, n. 44. As Oswalt notes, this punctuation departs from that of the MT, the traditional Jewish understanding of the text, but it follows that proposed by BHS (*Biblia Hebraica Stuttgartensia*, ed. K. Ellinger and W. Rudolph [1983]), the standard scholarly edition of the Hebrew Bible. Goldingay and Payne, as well as Gelston, follow the punctuation of

Second, what is the object of the verb "will see" (יִרְאֶה, *yir^e' eh*)?[66] There is no object for the verb in the Masoretic Text, the traditional edition of the Hebrew Bible. Commentators and translators will often add an object to complete the thought, e.g. "it" (NASB, HCSB), "his work" (NET), or "seed," i.e., his spiritual "offspring" mentioned in verse 10.[67] Help is provided at this point by the Dead Sea Scrolls. A number of the Isaiah scrolls (1QIsaᵃ, 1QIsaᵇ, 4QIsaᵈ) supply an object, viz., the word "light" (אוֹר, '*ôr*).[68] Because these manuscripts antedate the MT by a thousand years or so,[69] and because the Septuagint also has the object "light" (φῶς, *phōs*), the translation, "he will see light" is now widely

---

the MT. See John Goldingay and David Payne, *A Critical and Exegetical Commentary on Isaiah 40–55*, ICC (London: T. & T. Clark, 2006), 2:323–24; A. Gelston, "Some Notes on Second Isaiah," *VT*, 21 (Dec., 1971): 517–27 (esp. 524–27).

[66] The form in the text (יִרְאֶה) is 3ʳᵈ pers. msc. sg. qal imperf. of רָאָה. Cf. *HALOT*, s.v. "ראה," 2:1159.

[67] Oswalt, *The Book of Isaiah, Chapters 40–66*, 399; Goldingay and Payne, *Isaiah 40–55*, 2:323. Darby agreed with this view. He translated, "He shall see of [the fruit of] the travail of his soul." Likewise Hengstenberg has, "[He shall see] the fruits and rewards of his sufferings" (*Christology of the Old Testament*, 2:304). Unger wrote, "He shall see a glorious spiritual progeny, Old Testament and Tribulation saints, the New Testament church (latent, but unrevealed in the Old Testament), and Israel restored in Kingdom blessing" (*Unger's Commentary on the Old Testament*, 1300).

[68] With Masoretic pointing the word would read אוֹר. For the "Great Isaiah Scroll" (1QIsaᵃ), see *Discoveries in the Judaean Desert*, vol. 32: Qumran Cave 1, II. *The Isaiah Scrolls*, Part 1: *Plates and Transcriptions*, eds., Eugene Ulrich and Peter W. Flint (Oxford and New York: Oxford University Press, 2010), Column 44 (pp. 88–89 [1QIsaᵃ]) and Column 23, Plate 69 (pp. 140–41 [1QIsaᵇ]). Ulrich and Flint note that אור also occurs in 4QIsaᵈ but without the letter ר (idem., Part 2: *Introductions, Commentary, and Textual Variants*, 176).

[69] The Masoretic (or Rabbinic) text of the Hebrew Bible is the text in back of all English translations of the Old Testament. The modern English translations are, in fact, based on a single manuscript, the Leningrad Codex, which was copied in AD 1008 and is the earliest complete copy of the Masoretic text. The Hebrew University in Jerusalem is currently producing a new edition of the Hebrew Bible, which is based on the Aleppo Codex of the Masoretic Text (AD 925). In that the Aleppo Codex is incomplete, the Hebrew University project will have to rely in part upon the Leningrad Codex and other manuscripts. The Dead Sea Scrolls, discovered between 1947 and 1956, are dated between 250 BC and AD 68. Twenty-one Isaiah manuscripts were found at Qumran; the best known and best preserved (virtually in its entirety) is the *Great Isaiah Scroll* (1QIsaᵃ). See Martin Abegg, Jr., Peter Flint, and Eugene Ulrich, trans. *The Dead Sea Scrolls Bible* (San Francisco: Harper, 1999), x, xiv, 267. This manuscript has been dated by F. M. Cross to "c. 125–100 BCE" (*The Isaiah Scrolls*, Part 2: *Introductions, Commentary, and Textual Variants*, 61).

accepted as the reading of the original text (NIV, NRSV, REB).[70] The translation of the line would then be **"Because of the anguish of his soul, he will see light and be satisfied by his knowledge."**

This raises another question: What is the light that the Servant sees? A clue is provided by the NIV rendering, "He will see the light [of life]." As Duane Lindsey wrote, "Death does not spell defeat for the Servant." He will enjoy a "postmortem" resurrection existence in which He has great satisfaction.[71]

In the Old Testament, seeing light is contrasted with death.[72] For example, Job speaks of miscarried children as **"infants that never saw light"** (Job 3:16). Of the unbelieving wicked the psalmist wrote, **"They will never see the light"** (Ps. 49:19 [MT, v. 20]), i.e., this life is the end for them. In Job 33:30 God delights to rescue a person from the pit, the brink of the grave, with the result that **"he may be enlightened with the light of life"** (cf. Ezek. 33:11).[73] Here the "light of life" is contrasted with "the pit," i.e., death from which the Lord delivers him.

"He will see the light of life and be satisfied by his knowledge." The translation "satisfied" is probably too weak here. The word "satisfied" only means that the Servant will be content. The verb (שָׂבַע, śāba') is used to mean "to eat one's fill," "to satiate oneself."[74] North prefers a translation such as "He will have fullness of knowledge" or "He will be sated with his knowledge." [75] Were we to paraphrase, following

---

[70] Among those who accept the reading "light" as genuine are: North, *The Second Isaiah*, 244; Smith, *Isaiah 40–66*, 460, n. 416; Joseph Blenkinsopp, *Isaiah 40–55*, AncB (New York: Doubleday, 2002), 346, 348; Baltzer, *Deutero-Isaiah*, 423; Islwyn Blythin, "A Consideration of Difficulties in the Hebrew Text of Isaiah 53:11," *BT* 17 (Jan., 1966): 27–31 (esp. 28–29); Gelston, "Some Notes on Second Isaiah," 526. Among those rejecting the reading are: Oswalt, *The Book of Isaiah, Chapters 40–66*, 399; Brevard S. Childs, *Isaiah*, OTL (Louisville: Westminster John Knox, 2001), 419; Goldingay and Payne, *Isaiah 40–55*, 2:324.

[71] Cf. Lindsey, *The Servant Songs*, 134.

[72] See the discussion in North, *The Second Isaiah*, 244.

[73] Édouard Dhorme, *A Commentary on the Book of Job*, trans. Harold Knight (Nashville: Nelson, 1984), 506.

[74] *HALOT*, s.v. "שבע," 1302–03. The form used in the text is יִשְׂבָּע (3rd pers. msc. sg. qal imperf.).

[75] North, *The Second Isaiah*, 244.

this author, we might say, "Because of the anguish of his soul, 'he will be saturated/drenched with light.'"[76]

In this passage it seems that the Servant's fullness of knowledge comes instantaneously as he sees the light.[77] This may very well be linked with the Servant's ascension into heaven. Baltzer wrote, "If he can see the 'light,' he has been judged worthy to enter into the immediate presence of God; he has been received into the company of the heavenly beings."[78] He cites a passage from the pseudepigraphal book of 1 Enoch (92:3-4):

> And the righteous one shall arise from sleep,
> [Shall rise] and walk in the paths of righteousness,
> And all his path and conversation shall be in eternal goodness and grace.
>
> He will be gracious to the righteous and give him eternal uprightness,
> And He will give him power so that he shall be (endowed) with goodness and righteousness,
> And he *shall walk in eternal light.*[79]

What will this fullness of knowledge include?[80] North wrote, "On the content of the Servant's 'knowledge' we are free to meditate, of

---

[76] North, *The Second Isaiah*, 233–34. He acknowledged that such a paraphrase may be good English, but it has no parallel in the Hebrew Old Testament.

[77] North, *The Second Isaiah*, 244.

[78] Baltzer, *Deutero-Isaiah*, 423–24.

[79] Book of Enoch 92:3-4, in R. H. Charles, ed. *The Apocrypha and Pseudepigrapha of the Old Testament*, vol. 2: *Pseudepigrapha* (Oxford: Oxford University Press, 1913), 261.

[80] Brief mention should be made of some alternate interpretations of דַּעַת ("knowledge," NASB). Reicke understood it to mean "obedience": "Through his obedience my servant proves to be truly righteous." Thomas suggested there is a second root ידע meaning in the qal "to become still, quiet, at ease," and thence "to be submissive, humiliated." He offered this translation: "When he shall have drunk deep of his anguish, when the righteous one shall have received his full measure of humiliation." Gelston has, "By his humiliation/chastisement shall my servant justify the many, and he shall bear their iniquities/guilt/penalties." Williamson accepted Thomas's proposal of the second root ידע, but took it in its primary sense, "rest." He translated, "After his deep suffering, he will see light (i.e., live), he will be satisfied with his rest; my Servant will justify many, and he will bear their iniquities." Noting parallels in Isaiah 53:3 and Daniel 12:4, Day defended Gelston against Williamson. He has, "By his humiliation my Servant will make

course within the bounds of the OT connotation of the word."[81] He adds it may be taken for granted that it includes the knowledge of God (Isa. 11:2; 58:2; Job 21:14; Jer. 22:16). In the book of Proverbs, knowledge is an ethical concept associated with wisdom (חָכְמָה, ḥokmāh], Prov. 14:6) and understanding or discernment (תְּבוּנָה, tᵉbûnāh], Prov. 17:27; cf. Isa. 44:19). Even when Proverbs is addressing the most practical of issues, knowledge is never divorced from the **"fear of the LORD"** (Prov. 1:7).[82]

In the presence of the Lord the Servant will be drenched with light and will have a fullness of knowledge—knowledge of God, to be sure, but knowledge of how successful he was in atoning for the sins of his people. As our high priest, the one who **"sprinkled the nations"** (52:15), he will have full knowledge of all the needs of his people and all he has done to meet them.[83]

---

many righteous." For full discussion of the issues involved see: Bo Reicke, "The Knowledge of the Suffering Servant," in *Das Ferne und nahe Wort*, Festschrift Leonhard Rost (Berlin: Alfred Töpelmann, 1967), 186–92; D. Winton Thomas, "A Consideration of Isaiah LIII in the Light of Recent Textual and Philological Study," *ETL* 44 (1968): 79–86; A. Gelston, "Some Notes on Second Isaiah," *VT* 21 (1971): 517–27; H. G. M. Williamson, "*DAʿAT* in Isaiah LIII," *VT* 28 (1978): 118–122. John Day, "*DAʿAT* 'Humiliation' in Isaiah LIII 11 in the Light of Isaiah LIII 3 and Daniel XII 4, and the Oldest Known Interpretation of the Suffering Servant," *VT* 30 (1980): 97–103.

[81] North, *The Second Isaiah*, 244. *HALOT* (s.v. "דַּעַת," 1:229) says it refers to the knowledge of God, while BDB says it speaks of discernment, understanding, and wisdom (s.v. "דַּעַת," 395).

[82] North, *The Second Isaiah*, 244.

[83] Smith (*Isaiah 40–66*, 461) wrote, "It appears that his knowledge that led to his satisfaction must be connected to the Servant 'seeing the light' in the first line. If this 'seeing the light' refers to his perception of how his travail and suffering led to 'light, salvation' for others, one could understand that he would be 'satisfied with his knowledge' of this wonderful benefit for others. His travail and suffering were not wasted; he satisfactorily accomplished what he was sent to do for the sake of others." Delitzsch speaks at length on the "knowledge" of the Servant. He notes that in Isaiah 11:2 "the spirit of knowledge" is one of the seven spirits that descends upon the sprout of Jesse "so that 'knowledge' (דַּעַת) is represented as equally the qualification for the priestly, the prophetic, and the regal calling." He also quotes Matthew 11:27, "No one knows the Son except the Father; nor does anyone know the Father except the Son, and anyone to whom the Son wills to reveal Him." "Let us remember also," he says, "that the Servant of [Yahweh], whose priestly mediatorial work is unfolded before us here in ch. 53, upon the ground of which He rises to more than regal glory (ch 52:15; cp. 53:12), is no other than He to whom his God has given the tongue of the learned, 'to know how to speak a word in season to him that is weary, i.e., to raise up the weary and heavy laden' (ch. 50:4). He knows God, with whom He stands in loving fellowship; He knows the counsels of his

HE IS SUCCESSFUL IN THE JUSTIFICATION OF A MULTITUDE

Having described the results of the Servant's sacrifice in terms of the
Servant, Yahweh now describes the results of the Servant's sacrifice in
terms of the people. The two concluding parallel lines of verse 11 explain
what the Servant did for others. First, "the Righteous One, My Servant,
will justify the many." The title, "the Righteous One," is most
significant in this chapter. Earlier in the poem his people treated the
Servant shamefully—as a wicked person who deserved to be struck,
beaten, and humiliated by God. He was scourged, crushed, and crucified
like the worst of criminals. Now Yahweh says that this man will make
many righteous. How can this be? Yahweh proved the Servant's
innocence by raising him from the dead[84] and asserts his innocence by
the title "the Righteous One" (צַדִּיק, ṣadadîq). The word "righteous"
originally meant "to be straight." The word connoted conformity to an
ethical or moral standard or norm. In the Old Testament the righteous
man is the one who serves God (Mal. 3:18). His life is conformed to the
standard of the will of God. He is just and lawful in his behavior.[85]

The righteous Servant "will justify many." The word "justify" (צָדֵק,
ṣādēq) is the verb form of the adjective "righteous." The form of the
verb used here[86] (יַצְדִּיק, yaṣdîq), like its synonym in the Greek New
Testament (δικαιόω, dikaioō) means "to declare as in the right," [87] "to
declare righteous" (cf. Deut. 25:1), "to acquit."[88] As the translation "to
acquit" indicates, the word has a forensic (Lat. *forum* = "courtroom")
sense in this Servant song. This is evident because the context deals with
guilt, punishment, and court proceedings (53:5, 8, 10).

---

love and the will of his grace, in the fulfillment of which his own life ascends, after having
gone down into death and come forth from death; and by virtue of this knowledge,
which rests upon his own truest and most direct experience, He, the righteous One, will
help 'the many,' i.e., the great mass,...hence all his own nation, and beyond that, all
mankind (so far as they were susceptible of salvation; = τοῖς πολλοῖς, Rom. 5:19, cf.
πολλῶν, Matt. 26:28)" (*Biblical Commentary on the Prophecies of Isaiah*, 2:337).

[84] Cf. the discussion of the clause, "was vindicated by the Spirit" in David J. MacLeod,
"Christology in Six Lines: An Exposition of 1 Timothy 3:16," *BibSac* 159 (2002): 334–
48 (esp. 340–42).

[85] Harold G. Stigers, "צָדֵק," *TWOT*, 2:752–53.

[86] In the simple active stem (qal) the verb means "to be just, righteous." The form used
in the text is in the hiphil (causative) stem (יַצְדִּיק, 3d pers. msc. sg. hiphil imperfect).

[87] *HALOT*, s.v. "צדק," 2:1004.

[88] North, *The Second Isaiah*, 244.

The verb ("to justify," "declare righteous," "acquit") assumes that people stand guilty before a holy God as he sits upon his judgment bench. In light of the actions of the "Righteous One," the Servant, God can acquit sinners and declare them to be "not guilty!" How can a holy and just God declare sinners—"many" sinners, at that—to be "not guilty"? The answer is in the next line: **"He will bear their iniquities."** Here the verb "will bear" (יִסְבֹּל, *yisbōl*) has the sense "to bear a heavy load," namely a load of guilt or punishment.[89] He took "the sum total of their guilt" upon himself and bore the condemnation for it.[90] He acted as the substitute for the "many." This act of the Servant explains how the holy God of heaven can be righteous and at the same time declare sinners righteous. The just penalty for their sins has been inflicted upon the sinless Servant of the Lord (Rom. 3:26).

Hugh Martin, highly respected minister of Greyfriars Free Church in Edinburgh, was speaking one day with William Cunningham (1805–61), principal of New College in the same city.[91] The conversation turned to justification, and Cunningham offered this "priceless gem," to quote Martin. He said, "The righteousness of God is the righteousness which God's righteousness requires him to require."[92]

---

[89] The form used in verse 12 (יִסְבֹּל) is 3d pers. sg. qal imperfect of סָבַל. The verb is used twice in Isaiah 53; in verse 4 it speaks of the Servant's bearing a load of pain, and in verse 11 of his carrying a load of guilt [or punishment]. See BDB, s.v. "סָבַל," 687.

[90] North, *The Second Isaiah*, 245.

[91] New College opened in 1846 to train men for ministry in the Free Church of Scotland. Since the 1930s it has been the School of Divinity (formerly Faculty of Divinity) of the University of Edinburgh.

[92] Hugh Martin, *The Atonement: In Its Relationship to the Covenant, the Priesthood, the Intercession of Our Lord* (Edinburgh: James Gemmell, 1882; reprint ed., Edinburgh: John Knox, 1976), 203, footnote.

THE SERVANT IS EXALTED FOR THE FULFILLMENT OF HIS MISSION, VERSE 12

Therefore, I will allot Him a portion with the great,
And He will divide the booty with the strong;
Because He poured out Himself to death,
And was numbered with the transgressors;
Yet He Himself bore the sin of many,
And interceded for the transgressors.

HE IS REWARDED WITH UNIVERSAL DOMINION

The Servant Song ends where it began in Isaiah 52:13-15 with the exaltation of the Servant. **"Therefore, I will give him a portion among the great,[93] and he will divide the spoils with the strong"** (NIV). The imagery is military, alerting the reader that Isaiah is returning to the

---

[93] Scholars have debated the precise meaning of בָּרַבִּים in verse 12. There are two views. (1) Some translate the word בָּרַבִּים as "many" and argue that "the many" are given to the Servant as a portion. ("Therefore I will give him the many as a portion, and he will receive the mighty as spoil" HCSB). They note that in several OT passages "the many" and "the strong" are "a standard pair of terms" (Exod. 1:9 ["many more and stronger"]; 7:1 ["more numerous and stronger"]; Deut. 26:5 ["a great, mighty, and numerous nation"]; Isaiah 8:7 ["the strong and numerous waters"]). Furthermore, since the word רַבִּים is translated "many" in Isaiah 52:14, 15; 53:11; 53:12e, it should also be translated "many" in verse 12a. (On the five-fold use of רַבִּים in Isaiah 52:13–53:12, see J. Jeremias, "πολλοί," *TDNT*, 6:537–38). The following versions have "many": ESV, HCSB, NET ["multitudes"]. See John Goldingay, *The Message of Isaiah 40–55: A Literary-Theological Commentary* (London: T. & T. Clark, 2005), 517; cf. Smith, *Isaiah 40–66*, 462; Jan Ridderbos, *Isaiah*, Bible Student's Commentary, trans. John Vriend (Grand Rapids: Zondervan, 1985), 487, n. 33. Olley concluded that the two expressions בָּרַבִּים and עֲצוּמִים refer to people in general and not to the great or powerful. He translates, "[with] the many" and "with numerous people" (John W. Olley, "'The Many': How is Isa 53:12a To Be Understood?" *Bib* 68 [1987]: 330–356). (2) The NASB and other English versions translate בָּרַבִּים as "with or among the great" (Darby, KJV, NIV, NRSV, REB; also: BDB, s.v. "רַב," 913). The parallelism with "the strong" in line two favors that translation. Delitzsch also notes that to have a portion in the spoils of victory is to have a portion among those who are great (*Biblical Commentary on the Prophecies of Isaiah*, 2:339; cf. Edward J. Kissane, *The Book of Isaiah* [Dublin: Browne and Nolan, 1943], 2:191). Ernst Jenni and Claus Westermann say that the use of רַב in Isaiah 53:12a follows Aramaic usage when rendered "great" (Gen. 25:23; Josh. 11:8; 19:28; 2 Sam. 23:20). See *TLOT*, 3:1198.

kingly imagery of 52:13-15.[94] The word "therefore" (לָכֵן, *lākēn*) brings to mind Paul's great hymn in Philippians 2:9, "**Therefore** (διό, *dio*) **God has highly exalted Him.**" In obedience to Yahweh the Servant has descended to the lowest depths, and now God will exalt him to the highest heights.[95]

The picture is a military one with the "Servant, of all people, marching in the role of conqueror, bringing home the spoils of conquest."[96] In the words of an old hymn, "The strife is o'er, the battle done."[97] When Christ reigns, foreign enemies and weapons of warfare will no longer be a danger for Zion/Jerusalem. "**And they will hammer their swords into plowshares and their spears into pruning hooks. Nation will not lift up sword against nation, and never again will they learn war**" (Isa. 2:4).[98]

The first two lines are similar in that the same imperfect verb (חָלַק, *ḥālaq*, line 1 = "allot" or "give"; line 2 = "divide") is used in both.[99] They differ however in that line one explains what Yahweh will do for the Servant, and line two explains what the Servant will do himself.[100]

---

[94] Goldingay and Payne, *Isaiah 40–55*, 2:328.

[95] Oswalt, *The Book of Isaiah, Chapters 40–66*, 405.

[96] Oswalt, *The Book of Isaiah, Chapters 40–66*, 405. Baltzer (*Deutero-Isaiah*, 426) argues against military imagery. "The Servant is not warlike at all"). Yet such a juxtaposition of images (servant—conqueror) is not out of place in apocalyptic/prophetic literature. One thinks, for example, of the lion who is a lamb in Revelation 5:5-6. Baltzer does concede that "spoil" or "booty" [שָׁלָל, *šālāl*] "clearly belongs to the language of war."

[97] Francis Pott, trans., "The Strife is O'er," Hymn 170, *Hymns of Truth and Praise* (Fort Dodge, IA: Gospel Perpetuating Publishers, 1971).

[98] Cf. Baltzer, *Deutero-Isaiah*, 426. Some commentators see the military imagery as purely metaphorical. They argue that the victories of Christ are spiritual and have nothing to do with outward worldly power. It is the sprinkling of the nations that leads them to believing reverence (cf. Hengstenberg, *Christology of the old Testament*, 2:308). However, this and other Scriptures are clear that the return of Jesus Christ will lead to outward worldly dominion in the millennial kingdom. The humiliation and atoning death are certainly "the basis and the boast of Christianity." Yet it is "an inexcusable error to confine it to us who are now called from Gentiles as well as from Jews. The day hastens when the fullness shall have come in; and so Israel shall be saved. Then will this vision (Isa. 52:13–53:12) be fulfilled, and not as a whole till then" (William Kelly, *An Exposition of the Book of Isaiah*, 4th ed. [London: C. A. Hammond, 1947; reprint ed., Oak Park, IL: Bible Truth Publishers, 1975], 346–47).

[99] The form used in the first line of Isaiah 53:12 is אֲחַלֶּק, 1st pers. sg., piel imperfect (future). The second use is יְחַלֵּק, 3d pers. msc. sg. piel imperfect (future).

[100] Smith, *Isaiah 40–66*, 462. The commentators differ over the interpretation of the two lines. The first two lines of verse 12 have been interpreted in two ways: (1)

First, Yahweh explains what he will do to reward the Servant. **"Therefore I will give him a portion among the great"** (NIV). The primary meaning of the word חָלַק (ḥālaq) is "to give or receive the portion coming to one by law and custom." The Servant will be given his place among the great ones, i.e., the kings of 52:15. Elsewhere we are told that he will have primacy over the rulers of the earth. During the millennial age he will be **"KING OF KINGS, AND LORD OF LORDS"** (Rev. 19:16). The great ones of the earth will submit to him and render him homage.[101]

All of this was prophesied by David. **"Ask of Me, and I will surely give the nations as Your inheritance, and the very ends of the earth as Your possession"** (Ps. 2:8). **"May he also rule from sea to sea and from the River to the ends of the earth. Let the nomads of the desert bow before him, and his enemies lick the dust. Let the kings of Tarshish and the islands bring presents; the kings of Sheba and Seba offer gifts. And let all kings bow down before him, all nations serve him"** (Ps. 72:8-11).[102]

"Therefore I will give Him the many as a portion, and He will receive the mighty as spoil" [NET; cf. also: North, *The Second Isaiah*, 245; Muilenburg, "Isaiah 40–66," 5:630–31; J. Ridderbos, *Isaiah*, BSC, trans. John Vriend (Grand Rapids: Zondervan, 1985), 487; Smith, *Isaiah 40–66*, 463; J. Alec Motyer, *The Prophecy of Isaiah: An Introduction and Commentary* (Downers Grove: Inter Varsity, 1993), 442]. Proponents of this first view argue that the בְּ prefix before "the many" functions to introduce the object of a transitive verb [Smith, 463, n. 424; GKC § 119k (379)]. The אֵת prefix before "the powerful" is the mark of the direct object [Goldingay and Payne, *Isaiah 40–55, Volume II*, 329]. (2) "Therefore I will give him a portion among the great [or 'many'], and he will divide the spoils with the strong [or 'numerous']" [NIV; cf. also Darby, KJV, NASB, NRSV, REB, ESV, NET; Delitzsch, *The Prophecies of Isaiah*, 2:338–39; Oswalt, *The Book of Isaiah, Chapters 40–66*, 405–6]. Proponents of this second view take the prefix of "great" or "many" [בָּרַבִּים (prefix = בְּ)] and the particle before "strong" or "numerous" [עֲצוּמִים (prefix = אֵת)] as prepositions [בְּ and אֵת]. Following the traditional language of battle, Yahweh gives his Servant a share of the spoils of victory. Once despised, the Servant will now be at the forefront dividing the spoils with the victors, viz., those who went with him to battle against the hostile powers of the world [Rev. 19:14]; these will participate in the spoils of his victory [Delitzsch, 339].

[101] Unger, *Unger's Commentary on the Old Testament*, 1300–1301.

[102] Not all commentators agree with the interpretation of line one that is adopted here. The interpretation of line one presented above, says J. Alec Motyer, leaves the reader with "a sense of anticlimax!" (*The Prophecy of Isaiah*, 442). After all he has done, the Servant only gets a share with other "great ones" or "with many." "This [interpretation] hardly suits the astonishment of the kings at the glory of the servant (52:15), and the general context leads us to expect something more than that he will share the power of other potentates" (Muilenburg, "Isaiah 40–66," 5:630–31). These commentators prefer a

In the second line Yahweh says what the Servant will himself do. **"And he shall divide the spoil with the strong"** (ESV). Here the verb "allot" or "divide" ((חָלַק, *ḥālaq*) refers to the division of the spoils of war.[103] When the Israelites conquered a large section of Canaan, Joshua oversaw a division of it among the twelve tribes. The same word is used for the division that is used here (חָלַק): **"He shall divide the spoil with the strong"** (Josh. 13:7; 14:4, 5; 15:13; 18:2-10, etc.). David used the same word in referring to the division of spoil among his men after their victory over the Amalekites (1 Sam. 30:24).[104]

Who are the strong with whom he divides the spoil? They are the people, says Delitzsch, "who surround him and fight along with him."[105] They are described in Psalm 110:3, **"Your people will volunteer freely in the day of Your power."**[106] They are the people who go with him "to battle, and join with him in the conquest of the hostile powers of the world" (Rev. 19:14):"[107] **"And the armies which are in heaven, clothed in fine linen, white and clean, were following Him on white horses."** "They participate with him "in the enjoyment of the spoils of his victory."[108]

---

translation such as that of the HCSB, which reads in the first line, "Therefore I will give him the many as a portion." The "many" are the same group as in verse 11, namely those the Servant has justified. The Septuagint reads, "He will inherit many" (κληρονομήσει πολλοὺς). The scene is eschatological, and the Servant receives his reward. His redeemed people are part of that reward. They are his inheritance.

103 M. Tsevat, "חָלַק II," *TDOT*, 4:447–51 (esp. 449); *HALOT*, s.v. "חלק," 1:323.

104 Culver, *The Sufferings and the Glory of the Lord's Righteous Servant*, 119.

105 Delitzsch, *Biblical Commentary on the Prophecies of Isaiah*, 2:339.

106 Klaus Baltzer, a leading contemporary commentator on Isaiah, expressed puzzlement at verse 12: "How can the Servant give a share if, being dead, he is in the heavenly sphere? (*Deutero-Isaiah*, 425). The puzzle disappears if one identifies the Servant as Jesus Christ, if one accepts the implication of the text that the Servant would rise from the dead and ascend to heaven, and if one accepts the teaching of these and other texts that the great ones of the earth will one day recognize Christ as King of kings.

107 Delitzsch, *Biblical Commentary on the Prophecies of Isaiah*, 2:339.

108 Delitzsch, *Biblical Commentary on the Prophecies of Isaiah*, 2:339. Again, the commentators do not all agree with the interpretation of line two that is given above. They argue that the more traditional translation adopted here, "And he shall divide the spoil with the strong" (ESV), misses the point. The thought is not one of the Servant dividing or sharing the spoils of war with others. Preferable is a translation like that of the HCSB, "And he will receive the mighty as spoil." Others have, "He will share out the powerful as spoil" (Goldingay and Payne, *Isaiah 40–55*, 2:328.), or "He will possess the mighty as spoil" (Jan L. Koole, *Isaiah III*, HCOT, trans. Anthony P. Runia [Leuven, Belgium: Peeters, 1998], 2:339), or "He will distribute the mighty as spoil" (North, *The*

Motyer argues that this interpretation of the first two lines of verse 12 leaves the reader with "a sense of anticlimax!" After all he has done, the Servant only gets a share with other "great ones" or "with many."[109]

In response it must be said that the Servant will be a different kind of king than the world has ever known. He will be a Servant-King.[110] With the "great ones" and the "many" he "condescends to share his triumph and to divide the spoil taken from the enemy by making them partners with himself in his kingdom and glory, even as they were sharers in his sufferings."[111]

HE IS REWARDED BECAUSE OF HIS REDEMPTIVE WORK

His Death was Voluntary

The Song closes with four reasons for the Servant's exalted position.[112] First, he willingly paid the "the ultimate penalty of suffering and death."[113] **"He poured out Himself** (lit. 'his soul') **to death."** The verb הֶעֱרָה (heʿĕrāh) is from a root meaning "to bare" or "become naked."[114] In Psalm 141:8 it is translated "do not leave me defenseless" (NASB, NRSV, NET). The LXX has "do not take away my life," which

---

Second Isaiah, 245). The "mighty" or the "strong" are to be contrasted with the redeemed kings of chapter 52 (verse 15). The setting is the future when Christ defeats the hostile powers of the world at his second coming (Rev. 19:14). The kings and other great ones of the earth will be brought to do homage to him or to be subdued by him. In the end the Servant will be "the arbiter of the spoils accruing from His victory" (North, *The Second Isaiah*, 246).

[109] Motyer, (*The Prophecy of Isaiah*, (Downers Grove: InterVarsity Press, 1993), 442). For further discussion of this view, see the footnotes above on the first two lines of verse 12.

[110] Baltzer greatly overstates the case when he writes, "Perhaps it is just here that the 'offence' of the text is to be found—that the Servant is not warlike at all" (*Deutero-Isaiah*, 426). It is more accurate to say that the Servant is unlike all other warriors in his victory.

[111] Baron, *The Servant of Jehovah*, 137.

[112] Motyer, *The Prophecy of Isaiah*, 443; Smith, *Isaiah 40–66*, 463.

[113] Smith, *Isaiah 40–66*, 463.

[114] BDB, s.v. "עָרָה," 788. North translates, "He laid bare his soul" (*The Second Isaiah*, 246). The form used in Isaiah 53:12 (הֶעֱרָה) is 3d msc. sg. hiph. perf. In the OT the hiphil stem of עָרָה is used both literally ("to uncover" [Lev. 20:18-19] or "lay bare" [Zeph. 2:14]) and metaphorically, as here, "to tip out" or "throw away one's life to death" (*HALOT*, s.v. "ערה," 1:882).

Anderson says is "a reasonable interpretation" of the Hebrew text.[115]
The Servant denied all of his natural instincts for survival and allowed his
life, his most precious possession, to be taken away. As Motyer notes,
"The Servant was both the agent and the substance of this
outpouring.[116] No one took his life away from him, he laid it down of
his own accord (John 10:18; Phil. 2:7)." [117] In short, despite all
appearances, his was a voluntary death.[118]

His Death was Unjust

The second reason for his exaltation is expressed in the next line, "**And
was numbered with the transgressors.**" The verb "to number" (מָנָה,
mānāh) here has the sense "to be counted among, grouped among,
assigned a place among."[119] The form of the verb used here (נִמְנָה,
nimnāh)[120] has a tolerative or voluntative sense, i.e., he allowed or
permitted himself to be numbered with the transgressors.[121]

The word "transgressors" or "rebels" (פֹּשְׁעִים, *pōšeʿîm*) is a participle
and may be rendered "those in a state of rebellion."[122] It is "God's
strongest word of condemnation for his people (cf. 1:2; 46:8; 48:8; 57:4;
59:12-13; 66:24)."[123] Those who saw him crucified considered him to
be a rebel (cf. v. 4b). Delitzsch wrote, "He has [allowed] himself to be
reckoned with transgressors, i.e., numbered among them, namely in the
judgment of his countrymen, and in the unjust judgment by which he
was delivered up to death as a wicked apostate and transgressor of the

---

[115] A. A. Anderson, *The Book of Psalms*, NCB (Grand Rapids: Eerdmans, 1972), 2:921.
See also: NIV, HCSB.

[116] This looks on to the epistle to the Hebrews, where Jesus is both priest and victim.

[117] Motyer, *The Prophecy of Isaiah*, 443.

[118] "Since the suffering and death of the Servant is absolutely once for all in its
character, the same holds true of the expiatory sacrifice which he offered—because it is a
once for all act, it takes the place of the recurrent expiatory sacrifice, and so abolishes this,
Here, of course, this is not carried to its logical conclusion. But the ἐφάπαξ of the epistle
to the Hebrews [7:27; 9:12; 10:10] and its logical conclusions are already implicit here"
(Claus Westermann, *Isaiah 40–66*, trans. David M. G. Stalker, OTL [Philadelphia:
Westminster, 1969], 268).

[119] BDB, s.v. "מָנָה," 584.

[120] The form used here (נִמְנָה) is 3d msc. sg. niph. perf. of מָנָה.

[121] On the tolerative niphal, see *IBHS*, § 23.4f–g (389). Oswalt uses the term
"voluntative niphal" (*The Book of Isaiah, Chapters 40–66*, 406, n. 62).

[122] The participle פֹּשְׁעִים is a qal ptc. msc. pl. absolute of פָּשַׁע.

[123] Oswalt, *The Book of Isaiah, Chapters 40–66*, 406.

law."[124] "He was content to suffer loss, not only of his life, but also of his good name."[125] That his death was unjust was demonstrated by his exaltation to God's right hand (Heb. 1:3; Phil. 2:9-10), and it will be demonstrated when he reigns in regal splendor.

His Death was Substitutionary

The third reason for his exaltation is that he acted as a substitute for sinners. As Oswalt noted, "He did not merely die *with* the rebels. As the final bicolon explains, he died *for* the rebels, and that is all the difference. He did not die for his own sin or for his own rebellion; he was carrying the sin and rebellion of many."[126]

"Yet He Himself bore the sins of many."[127] This line has been understood in two ways:[128] Some have suggested that it means he "took away" the sins of many.[129] It is more probable, however, that the verb is used here in the sense of vicarious satisfaction for sins. [130] As Delitzsch notes, when connected with sin the verb "to bear" (נָשָׂא, *nāśā'*)[131] can

---

[124] Delitzsch, *Biblical Commentary on the Prophecies of Isaiah*, 2:339.

[125] Motyer, *The Prophecy of Isaiah*, 443.

[126] Oswalt, *The Book of Isaiah, Chapters 40–66*, 406.

[127] The MT has the msc. sg. construct חֵטְא ("sin"), but the Qumran mss. (1QIsaᵃ, 1QIsaᵇ, 4QIsaᵈ) have the plural חטאי, as do the LXX (ἁμαρτίας), the Targum, and the Syriac. The MT may have overlooked the final *yod* due to its smallness (Oswalt, *The Book of Isaiah, Chapters 40–66*, 399, n. 48; cf. Payne and Goldingay, *Isaiah 40–55*, 2:331). See *The Isaiah Scrolls*, Part 1: *Plates and Transcriptions*, eds., Ulrich and Flint, Column 44 (pp. 88–89 [1QIsaᵃ]) and Column 23, Plate 69 (pp. 140–41 [1QIsaᵇ]). On 4QIsaᵈ see Ulrich and Flint, idem., Part 2: *Introductions, Commentary, and Textual Variants*, 176.

[128] Delitzsch, *Biblical Commentary on the Prophecies of Isaiah*, 2:316.

[129] Oswalt, *The Book of Isaiah, Chapters 40–66*, 406, n. 63.

[130] Mention should be made of scholars who deny the messianic interpretation of Isaiah 53. Such contemporary scholarship is opposed to the idea of vicarious atonement. Harry M. Orlinsky says the idea of vicarious suffering is "a theological and scholarly fiction." The concept "is not to be found either here or anywhere else in the Bible" ("The So-Called 'Servant of the Lord' and 'Suffering Servant' in Second Isaiah," in *Studies on the Second Part of the Book of Isaiah*, by Harry M. Orlinsky and Norman H. Snaith (Leiden: Brill, 1967), 51, 54). Also see: R. N. Whybray (*Isaiah 40–66*, NCB [Grand Rapids: Eerdmans, 1981], 175, 183) who argues that verse 11 [and vv. 4 and 6] speak of the Servant's "identification with them in their suffering: there is nothing to suggest that he suffered in their place." He adds, "The Servant shared with others a penalty which was appropriate for them but not for him."

[131] The verb "to bear" (נָשָׂא, *nāśā'*) is used about two hundred times with the meaning "to lift up" and about one hundred times with the meaning "to bear" or "to carry." The verb occurs over 650 times (597 times in the qal stem) in the Old Testament. See D. N.

have two nuances: (1) It can signify the taking the debt of sin upon one's self and feeling it as one's own (Lev. 5:1, 17). In such a case the guilty person feels the full weight of sin and its consequences, i.e., the punishment for that sin (Lev. 17:16; 20:19-20; 24:15). (2) It can also signify the bearing of punishment for sin in the place of another, the atoning for sin. In the OT sacrificial system the sin offering was a substitute for the guilty person (Lev. 10:17). The second of these nuances is intended here. It must be understood, of course, that the person bearing the sin is not himself the guilty person; rather he bears the sin in a mediatorial capacity for the purpose of making atonement for it (Lev. 10:17). [132]

Throughout the Servant Song there is the assumption that all people are sinners and in need of atonement (cf. vv. 4-6, 8, 11). This is reinforced in the New Testament, where it is affirmed that all are sinners and incapable of earning God's favor by their own efforts (Rom. 2:9-19; 3:23; Eph. 2:8-9). Many people think they can earn their way into heaven and bypass the need for cleansing of sin. In an interview with the *New York Time,s* former New York mayor, Michael Bloomberg, spoke with pride of his work on gun safety, obesity, and smoking cessation. He said, "I am telling you if there is a God, when I get to heaven I'm not stopping to be interviewed. I am heading straight in. I have earned my place in heaven. It's not even close."[133] As well-known preacher, Ray Pritchard, observed, "Bloomberg is wrong. The only way to heaven is to admit you don't deserve to go there, and to confess that because of your sin you deserve hell, and to cast yourself on the mercy of Jesus who loved you and died for you and paid the price for your sin when he died on the cross."[134]

Freedman, B. E. Willoughby, Heinz-Josef Fabry, and Helmer Ringgren, "נָשָׂא," in TDOT, 10:24–40 (esp. 27); cf. *HALOT*, s.v. "נשׂא," 1:724. Of those one hundred, about thirty have reference to the bearing of guilt, and six have reference to the vicarious bearing of guilt, one of them being Isaiah 53:12 (BDB, s.v. "נָשָׂא," 669–72 [esp. 671]; *HALOT*, s.v. "נשׂא," 1:726. The other occurrences are in Leviticus 10:17; 16:22; Ezekiel 4:4, 5, 6. Ezekiel 18:19-20 speaks of wrongful bearing of another's punishment.

[132] Delitzsch, *Biblical Commentary on the Prophecies of Isaiah*, 2:316.

[133] Paige Lavendar, "Michael Bloomberg Is Sure He Has a Spot in Heaven," *The Huffington Post* (April 16, 2014). (huffingtonpost.com). Accessed 2/22/15. Lavendar says that Bloomberg was introspective in the interview due to how many of his college classmates had been appearing in the "in memoriam" pages of his college newsletter.

[134] Ray Pritchard, "The Conquering Christ," *Keep Believing Ministries* (April 20, 2014): 1–8 (esp. 4). (www.keepbelieving.com/sermon/the-conquering-christ). Accessed 1/24/15.

His Death was Foundational (i.e., the Basis of His Post-Cross Work)
The fourth reason for his exaltation is his intercessory work. **"He will intercede for the transgressors** [or: for their transgressions]."[135] The verb "intercede" (פָּגַע, *pāgaʿ*) has the general sense "to meet," "encounter," or "reach."[136] In the present context the hiphil stem is used, which, with this verb, conveys two distinct meanings:[137] First, it can be causative, "cause to strike." It is used this way in verse 6, where Yahweh causes the punishment for the iniquity (עָוֹן) of Israel to strike against (בְּ), the servant of God.[138] Second, it can be transitive in the sense of the qal: "entreat passionately (on behalf of someone)," i.e., intercede for someone. This second sense appears here in verse 12, where the servant intercedes for (לְ) the transgressors.[139] Delitzsch agrees; he says that the hiphil has here the intensive force of the qal, "to press forward with entreaty, hence to intercede."[140]

It is significant that the verb יַפְגִּיעַ (*yapgiaʿ*)[141] is in the imperfect tense ("he will intercede").[142] This is a change from the perfect verbs (past completed action) in the previous lines ("poured out," "numbered,"

---

[135] The MT has וְלַפֹּשְׁעִים ("and for the transgressors/rebels") and is supported by Aquila, Theodotion, Symmachus, Vulgate, Syriac, and the Targum. The Qumran manuscripts have ולפשעיהם ("for their transgressions/rebellions"). The LXX (διὰ τὰς ἁμαρτίας αὐτῶν) supports the Qumran copies. See *The Isaiah Scrolls*, Part 1: *Plates and Transcriptions*, eds., Ulrich and Flint, Column 44 (pp. 88–89 [1QIsaᵃ]) and Column 23, Plate 69 (pp. 140–41 [1QIsaᵇ]). On 4QIsaᵈ see Ulrich and Flint, idem., Part 2: *Introductions, Commentary, and Textual Variants*, 176. Commentators who prefer the Qumran reading include: Oswalt, *The Book of Isaiah, Chapters 40–66*, 399; Goldingay and Payne, *Isaiah 40–55*, 2:331; Joseph Blenkinsopp, *Isaiah 40–55*, AncB (New York: Doubleday, 2002), 349, n. ff. A decision between the MT reading and the Qumran copies makes little difference in the point being made by the prophet.

[136] BDB, s.v. "פָּגַע," 803.

[137] P. Maiberger, "פָּגַע," *TDOT*, 11:470–76 (esp. 474).

[138] Maiberger, "פָּגַע," 474. When the verb denotes a hostile action it is often accompanied, as here, by the preposition בְּ ("against"). See Goldingay and Payne, *Isaiah 40–55*, 2:308. Cf. *HALOT*, s.v. "פגע," 2:910.

[139] The lāmed used here (לְ) is a compound of the preposition and the article ("for the"). It can be rendered "on behalf of" the transgressors or "for" the transgressors. See *HALOT*, s.v. "פגע," 2:910. Cf. GKC, § 119r–u (381).

[140] Delitzsch, *Biblical Commentary on the Prophecies of Isaiah*, 2:340.

[141] The form in the text (יַפְגִּיעַ) is 3d pers. msc. sig. hiphil imperf. of פָּגַע.

[142] The verb is commonly translated as a perfect ("he interceded"). See KJV, Darby, NASB, NIV, NRSV, REB, HCSB.

"bore"). The imperfect tense and the fact that the verb is placed at the end of the message suggests "that it refers to something done after" the Servant's exaltation.[143] The line may therefore translated, **"He will intercede for the transgressors."**[144] It may be further inferred from the

---

[143] Smith, *Isaiah 40–66*, 464.

[144] Commentators do not agree on the correct translation/interpretation of the concluding line of the poem. There are at least seven views: (1) "He interceded for the transgressors." The imperfect verb [יַפְגִּיעַ] is to be taken as a perfect because it is closely connected (by the ו) with the perfects that immediately precede it. This conclusion is supported by the word "because" [תַּחַת] earlier in the verse. The "because" introduces the ground upon which the reward in v. 12a is based. The acts of the Servant ["poured out," "was numbered," "bore," and "interceded"] are acts that preceded his exaltation and rewarding. The intercession is not that of the glorified One but of the suffering One on behalf of his foes. The prophecy finds fulfillment in the prayer of Jesus, "Father, forgive them; for they do not know what they are doing" (Luke 23:34). The Servant prayed that the sins of those who crucified him would be forgiven. Delitzsch wrote, "Every word stands here as if written beneath the cross on Golgotha" [*Biblical Commentary on the Prophecies of Isaiah*, 3:340; cf. Urwick, *The Servant of Jehovah*, 162]. (2) "He interceded for the transgressors." The second view is a modification of the first. Ignorance of the law is no excuse; therefore Jesus is not praying for their eternal salvation on the basis of their ignorance. Rather, Jesus was praying for a suspension of the judgment for a period of time so that men may have opportunity to reverse their rebellious hostility through the knowledge of God's revelation of the Servant's redeeming sacrifice. The Greek word translated "forgive" in Luke 23:34 is ἀφίημι which can be rendered "let them go," or "release them" [Matt. 15:14; Mark 14:6; Luke 13:8; John 11:48; 12:7; cf. BDAG, s.v. "ἀφίημι," 156]. "So Jesus prayed for the continuation of general history in order that the special history of salvation [might] continue and flourish" [S. Lewis Johnson, Jr., "The Righteous Servant, Bruised but Exalted," *BBB* (Dallas: Believers Chapel, n.d.), 1–7 (esp. 5, 7]. (3) "He interceded for the transgressors." The third view is a Reformed modification of the first. "He performed the office of an advocate, and interceded for all who embraced this sacrifice by faith; as is evident from that prayer which he left to us, written by the hand of John, 'I pray not for these only, but for all who shall believe on me through their word' (John 17:20)." See John Calvin, *Commentary on the Book of the Prophet Isaiah*, trans. William Pringle [Edinburgh: Calvin Translation Society, 1850; reprint ed., Grand Rapids: Baker, 1989], 4:131–32. (4) "He intervened for the transgressors." As in views 1–3, this view takes the imperfect verb as a perfect. However, noting the usage of the verb in Isaiah 59:16, the verb is translated "intervene," and is taken to mean that the Servant intervened for the transgressors by dying for them. "With his life, his suffering and his death, he took their place and underwent their punishment in their stead" [NET; Westermann, *Isaiah 40–66*, 269]. However, as P. Mailberger notes ["פָּגַע," *TDOT*, 11:470–76 (esp. 474)], in Isaiah 59:16 "the context suggests that the participle מַפְגִּיעַ [msc. sg. hiph.] refers to intervention with deeds rather than words." The NIV has "no one to intervene" [also: NRSV; cf. REB, NET]. (5) "He intervened for their transgressions/rebellions." This view differs from the fourth view only in that it follows the Qumran copies in replacing "transgressors" with "transgressions." See Oswalt, *The Book of Isaiah, Chapters 40–66*, 399, 407; Blenkinsopp, *Isaiah 40–55*, 346, 349, n. ff.

usage of the verb (פָּגַע) that this intercession will be with words.[145] Calvin wrote:

> He expressly mentions "transgressors," that we may know that we ought to betake ourselves with assured confidence to the cross of Christ, when we are horror-struck by the dread of sin. Yea, for this reason he is held out as our intercessor and advocate; for without his intercession our sins would deter us from approaching.[146]

NT fulfillment of the final colon is found in Hebrews 7:25: **"Therefore He is able also to save completely those who draw near to God through Him, since He always lives to make intercession for them."**[147] Intercession may be defined as "the sympathetic appeals and

---

(6) "He will intervene for the transgressors." This view differs from the fourth in allowing the imperfect verb to stand as a future and in understanding intervention as something other than the Servant's death. The intercession spoken of by the prophet must not be understood "in the restricted sense of prayer for others, but in the wider one of meritorious and prevailing intervention, which is ascribed to Christ in the New Testament, not as a work already finished, like that of atonement, but as one still going on [Rom. 8:34; Heb. 9:24; 1 John 2:1]" [Alexander, *Commentary on the Prophecies of Isaiah*, 2:307]. "The base meaning is 'to cause to reach' and hence to 'cause someone's plea to reach someone's ears' [to intercede] or to 'introduce someone into someone's presence' [to mediate]. The Servant is thus a go-between, interposing between two parties, not as a barrier but as a bridge.... Here the Servant comes voluntarily to stand with us so that when he had borne our sin he might bring us to God" [Motyer, *The Prophecy of Isaiah*, 443]. (7) "He will intercede for the transgressors," i.e., those for whom he has died and who embrace this sacrifice by faith. This view accepts the imperfect [future] tense as it stands, and interprets the verb as "intercession," i.e., as prayers to God by the Servant on behalf of others, specifically transgressors who believe. It combines elements of views 3 and 6. See Smith, *Isaiah 40–66*, 464.

[145] Mailberger, "פָּגַע," 474; *HALOT*, s.v. "פגע," 2:910.

[146] Calvin, *Commentary on the Book of the Prophet Isaiah*, 4:132.

[147] Historically the work of intercession has been understood in a variety of ways: (1) The Arians suggested that intercession proved Christ's inferiority to the Father. The church fathers responded that it proved his love, not his inferiority. (2) The Eastern church regarded the statements about intercession as symbolical representations of Christ's love. (3) The Western church developed the concept of the perpetual offering of the finished sacrifice and identified the intercession with the offering. The churches of the Reformation argued that Christ's offering was completed at the cross, and therefore they distinguished his intercession from his offering. (4) The Lutherans argued that intercession was the offering of literal, vocal (*vocalis et realis*) petitions. (5) The Reformed (Calvinistic) churches interpreted Christ's intercession as real but not oral and as

petitions of the ascended, incarnate Son of God to God the Father (on the basis of a finished sacrifice) for the preservation, forgiveness, renovation, and bringing to glory of his people."[148]

"Christ is to his church," says Calvert, "a perfect redeemer.... There are those that would join with him other intercessors, Mary and the saints. We need but One in the court of heaven; no more are mentioned in the word of God."[149] Thomas Manton added, "Jesus Christ is, and is alone, the Intercessor for poor sinners.... It is the business of his endless life ['who liveth forever, to make intercession for us,' Heb. 7:25]."[150]

CONCLUSION

In the closing strophe of Isaiah's great Servant Song the prophet sets forth answers to the question "Why did the Servant (Jesus Christ) die? Isaiah explains the origin, results, and benefits of the Servant's sufferings.

---

consisting in Christ's presence in heaven (representation) and not in articulate supplications. (6) The English Reformers allied themselves with the Lutheran view, but in the mid-19th century they shifted to the continental Reformed view. See: Arthur J. Tait, *The Heavenly Session of Our Lord* (London: Robert South, 1912), 149–76; R. S. Wallace, "Intercession of Christ," *ISBE* rev (1982): 2:859–60; David J. MacLeod, "The Present Work of Christ in Hebrews," *BibSac* 148 (April, 1991): 193, n. 46.

[148] MacLeod, "The Present Work of Christ in Hebrews," 197. As the title of the quoted article suggests, the definition offered here applies particularly to the Epistle to the Hebrews. Baltzer offers an interesting comment on the intercession of the Servant, "I believe that this final saying in the Servant text may also contain an implicit stage direction. In order to fulfill his function, the Servant goes into the innermost domain 'before Yahweh,' who for the spectators is not visible. He must be imagined as an *orans* [Lat., 'praying,' or 'one praying'], a man with arms raised in prayer. As has been mentioned, פָּגַע also has a spatial component, in the sense of 'meet, encounter.' Here we should remember in addition that it was Moses—not Aaron—who was allowed to enter 'the tent of meeting' (אֹהֶל מוֹעֵד, '*ōhel mô'ēd*, Num. 1:1; 7:89; 12:1-16). On his final exit, does the Servant enter a tent that in the drama represents the (heavenly) 'tent of meeting.'" Baltzer, however, does not view Isaiah 53 as a direct prophecy of Jesus Christ; rather, "the portrait of the Servant is molded by the Moses tradition." Nevertheless, he suggests, it is "clear why the suffering Servant became in typology a foreshadowing of Jesus Christ" (p. 429). The writers of the NT, however, saw in Isaiah 53 a direct prophecy of Jesus Christ.

[149] Thomas Calvert, *Mel Cæli, Medulla Evangelii; or, The Prophet Isaiah's Crucifix, Being An Exposition of the Fifty third Chapter of the Prophecie of Isaiah* (London: Tho. Pierrepont, 1657), 346, 348.

[150] Thomas Manton, *A Practical Exposition Upon the Fifty-Third Chapter of Isaiah*, in *The Complete Works of Thomas Manton* (London: James Nisbet, 1871; reprint ed., Edinburgh: Banner of Truth, 1993), 3:492.

The origin of his sufferings was the good pleasure/will of God. "The premature and violent death of the Servant portrayed in the preceding verses might have tempted [readers] to think that God had left his Servant in the lurch."[151] George Adam Smith wrote, "The innocent Servant was put to a violent and premature death. Public apathy closed over him and the [intended] unmarked earth of a felon's grave. It is so utter a perversion of justice, so signal a triumph of wrong over right, so final a disappearance into oblivion of the fairest life that ever lived, that men might be tempted to say, God has forsaken his own."[152] Lewis Johnson remarks:

> Overlooking the guilt of both Herod and Pontius Pilate, as well as the malice of Caiaphas, the Jewish high priest, the prophet traces the death to the determinate counsel of God. He was the ultimate *causa efficians. Deus vult!*[153] (cf. v. 6; Acts 2:23). Pilate, Herod, and Caiaphas were responsible and guilty, but God determined that he die for sinners (cf. Eph. 1:11). It is the mystery of God's sovereignty and man's responsibility at its clearest.[154]

Looking on to the future the prophet sees that the Servant will die for sinners as a restitution or reparation offering.

As a result, there will be a number of consequences for the Servant. First, he will see his offspring, i.e., his spiritual children. Second, his days will be prolonged—death will not be the end of his story; he will be resurrected. In spite of the rejection by his people, the Servant will be deemed a success in the eyes of God, and blessings will continue to accrue because of his sacrifice (v. 10). Following his death and resurrection the Servant will ascend to heaven, be drenched with the light of God's presence, and have full knowledge of his success in atoning for the sins of his people. Furthermore, he will justify many on the basis of his atoning work.

---

[151] Johnson, "The Righteous Servant, Bruised but Exalted," 2.

[152] George Adam Smith, *The Book of Isaiah*, ExpB (New York: A. C. Armstrong, 1903), 2:362.

[153] God was the efficient or effective cause. He wills it!

[154] Johnson, "The Righteous Servant, Bruised but Exalted," 2.

In the closing lines (v. 12) Yahweh speaks of the reward of the Servant (victory and exaltation) and the basis of that reward, the Servant's voluntary, unjust, and substitutionary death for sinners.[155] The final line speaks of his future intercessory work for the forgiven transgressors.

DOCTRINAL NOTES

At the conclusion of his exposition of Isaiah 53, Franz Delitzsch briefly speaks of the doctrinal contribution of the Servant Song to our understanding of Messiah and his work. He makes the following observations:

First, he summarizes the doctrine of the Servant's relationship to Israel. Delitzsch uses the figure of a three-story pyramid to illustrate Isaiah's idea of "the Servant of Yahweh." The base or first level of the pyramid is the elect nation of Israel as a whole (41:8, 9; 42:19 [twice], 43:10; 44:1, 2, 44:21 [twice]; 45:4; 48:20). The central section or second level is "that Israel which was not merely Israel according to the flesh, but according to the spirit," i.e., the believing remnant within the nation, especially the prophets (44:26; 54:17; cf. 65:8-9, 13, 14, 15; 66:14). At the apex or third level is "the person of the Mediator of salvation springing out of Israel," viz., the servant who suffers vicariously for his people (42:1, 3; 49:5, 6, 7; 50:10; 52:13; 53:11).[156]

In an earlier work Delitzsch used the figure of a pyramid, but he added a second figure, the conception of "two concentric circles with a common center. The wider circle is the whole of Israel, the narrower Jeshurun (Isa. 44:2),[157] the center Christ."[158] He is "(1) the center of

---

[155] As Delitzsch notes, Isaiah returns again and again in this chapter to the vicarious suffering, the sacrifice for sin. He is "never tired of repeating it" (*Biblical Commentary on the Prophecies of Isaiah*, 341).

[156] Delitzsch, *Biblical Commentary on the Prophecies of Isaiah*, 174, 260–61, 340.

[157] The Hebrew יְשֻׁרוּן (*yᵉšurûn*) occurs four times in the OT (Deut. 32:15; 33:5, 26; Isa. 44:2). It is generally understood to be built on the root יָשַׁר ("be upright"), and because of its suffix (-ûn) it is taken as a diminutive. Because it is paired with Jacob it is understood to refer to Israel. The LXX translates ὁ ἠγαπημένος (*ho ēgapēmenos*, "the beloved") and adds the explanatory Ἰσραήλ. The Hebrew word is a proper name, "a diminutive with 'benevolent overtones.'" Israel's new name is intended to be in contrast with "Jacob" with its notions of trickery and dishonesty (M. J. Mulder, "יְשֻׁרוּן," *TDOT*, 6:). Baltzer (*Deutero-Isaiah*, 185) says it is "a honorific and a pet name." He renders it "the upright one" or "the dependable one."

the circle of the promised kingdom—the *second David*;[159] (2) the center of the circle of the people of salvation—the *second Israel*; (3) the center of the circle of the human race—the *second [man, or last Adam]*."[160]

Delitzsch concludes that in the Servant of the LORD "we see Israel itself in personal self-manifestation: the idea of Israel is fully realized, and the true nature of Israel shines forth in all its brilliancy."[161] In the second Servant song (Isaiah 49:1-13 [esp. v. 3]), the LORD calls his Servant "Israel." "But Israel was from the very first the God-given name of an individual. Just as the name Israel was first of all given to a man, and then after that to a nation, so the name which sprang from a personal root has also a personal crown."[162] He adds, "The Servant of Jehovah in these prophecies is regarded as the kernel of the kernel of Israel, as Israel's inmost center, as Israel's highest head."[163]

Second, the Servant Song enriches Isaiah's treatment of the *munus triplex*, i.e, the threefold offices of Christ (prophet, priest, and king). Early in the book, Messiah stands forth as a king (9:6-7; 11:1-5). Later, the Servant of the Lord is portrayed as a prophet who instructs the nation, calls Israel back to God, mediates a new covenant, and is a light to the nations (chs. 42, 49, 50). At the close of his work he is exalted and receives the homage of kings (52:13, 15; 53:12). In between his prophetic work and his exaltation lies his self-sacrifice, which is the ground of his priesthood (52:14; 53:4-9).

---

[158] Franz Delitzsch, supplementary note to M. Drechsler, *Der Prophet Jesaja übersetzt und erklärt. Dritter Theil nach dem Tode Dreshslers fortgesetzt und vollendet von F. Delitzsch und A. Hahn* (Berlin, 1857), 306. The English translation is found in Christopher R. North, *The Suffering Servant in Deutero-Isaiah*, 2d ed. (London: Oxford University Press, 1956), 44.

[159] As North observes, Isaiah 53 does not explicitly say that the Servant is the Davidic Messiah of chapters 9 and 11. He does concede, however, "there are undoubtedly kingly features in the Servant" (*The Suffering Servant in Deutero-Isaiah*, 218).

[160] Delitzsch, *Biblical Commentary on the Prophecies of Isaiah*, 2:174.

[161] Delitzsch, *Biblical Commentary on the Prophecies of Isaiah*, 2:340.

[162] Delitzsch, *Biblical Commentary on the Prophecies of Isaiah*, 2:260.

[163] Delitzsch, *Biblical Commentary on the Prophecies of Isaiah*, 2:261. H. S. Nyberg regards the name "Israel" as a title of honor, inasmuch as 'a nation's ancestor, living on in his descendants, can be especially associated with the leader or king as the current head and 'father'" (cf. 2 Sam. 19:44). Cited by John H. Eaton, *Festal Drama in Deutero-Isaiah* (London: SPCK, 1979), 63–64. See F. Duane Lindsay, *The Servant Songs: A Study in Isaiah* (Chicago: Moody, 1985), 66, n. 23.

Third, Isaiah contributes to our understanding of the *status duplex*, i.e. the two states of Christ (humiliation and exaltation).[164] David, says Delitzsch, is a type of the twofold state of Christ. But where, he asks, in any direct prophecy before Isaiah 53 does the suffering path of Messiah lead to the grave? "But the Servant of Jehovah goes through shame to glory, and through death to life. He conquers when he falls; he rules after being enslaved; he lives after he has died; he completes his work after he himself has been apparently cut off."[165]

Fourth, the prophet makes very clear the nature of the sufferings of the Servant. "These sufferings are not those of a confessor or martyr.... They are "vicarious atoning suffering, a sacrifice for sin. To this the chapter before us returns again and again, being never tired of repeating it."[166]

Fifth, the typical significance of the animal sacrifices, commanded but unexplained by Moses, grows in clarity in Isaiah 53. "The banner of the cross is here set up. The curtain of the most holy is lifted higher and higher. The blood of the typical sacrifice, which has been hitherto dumb, begins to speak. Faith, which penetrates to the true meaning of the prophecy, hopes on not only for the Lion of the tribe of Judah, but also for the Lamb of God, which beareth the sin of the world."[167]

Sixth, Zechariah parallels Isaiah 53 in his treatment of Messiah's reception by the nation of Israel in three ways: (1) He portrays Messiah as both a king ruling upon his throne and a priest sitting upon his throne [Zech. 6:13]. (2) He predicts that Messiah will be rejected by his people [Zech. 12:10a]. (3) He portrays that same people longing for Messiah in lamentation and weeping [Zech. 12:10b-14]. The penitential and believing confession to be made in the end-time by Israel is expressed in the words of Isaiah 53:1-9, "mourning in bitter sorrow the lateness of its love."[168]

---

[164] In the New Testament there is the fuller revelation of a three-stage Christology (preexistence, humiliation, exaltation). See Philippians 2:6-11.

[165] Delitzsch, *Biblical Commentary on the Prophecies of Isaiah*, 2:341.

[166] Delitzsch, *Biblical Commentary on the Prophecies of Isaiah*, 2:341.

[167] Delitzsch, *Biblical Commentary on the Prophecies of Isaiah*, 2:341.

[168] Delitzsch, *Biblical Commentary on the Prophecies of Isaiah*, 2:341.

AN EVANGELISTIC NOTE

Robert Chisholm has written that Isaiah's fourth Servant Song "is a rags-to-riches story."[169] It begins with the startling announcement that the Servant of the LORD, who was so battered and disfigured that he did not look like a human being, will be **"high and lifted up and greatly exalted"** (Isa. 52:13). The One who was despised and accounted as nothing by his contemporaries will one day be elevated to a royal throne and be treated with reverential awe by the kings of the earth (Isa. 52:15).

As Chisholm notes, there is another rags-to-riches story imbedded within the Servant's story. It is the story "about wandering sheep, hardened rebels against God, diseased and destined for destruction, who because of the Servant's suffering, end up being healed and transformed."[170]

A variety of terms are used to express salvation[171] and forgiveness[172] in Isaiah 52:13–53:12. (1) Many nations will be "besprinkled." People from around the world will be cleansed, i.e., they will have their sins expiated, blotted out, or wiped away [52:15]. (2) Because of his sufferings people have "peace with God," which includes reconciliation

---

[169] Robert B. Chisholm, Jr., "Forgiveness and Salvation in Isaiah 53," in *The Gospel According to Isaiah 53*, eds. Darrell L. Bock and Mitch Glaser (Grand Rapids: Kregel, 2012), 191–210 (esp. 191).

[170] Chisholm, "Forgiveness and Salvation in Isaiah 53," 193.

[171] As Chisholm notes, the standard words for salvation in the Hebrew Bible are not found in Isaiah 53 ("Forgiveness and Salvation in Isaiah 53," 193, n. 4). The standard terms include: גָּאַל ("redeem," Ps. 103:4, BDB, 145); יָשַׁע ("deliver, save," Ezek. 36:29, BDB, 446); נָצַל ("deliver from [sin and guilt]," Ps. 39:8 [MT=39:9]; 51:16 [MT=51:14] BDB, 665); מָלַט ("deliver," Ps. 22:5 [MT=22:6]; Job 22:30, BDB, 572); and פָּדָה ("set free," "ransom," Ps. 102:20 [MT=102:21], Isa. 58:6, Jer. 40:4, BDB, 804).

[172] Chisholm also notes that one does not find in the Servant song the standard Hebrew terms or idioms for forgiveness ("Forgiveness and Salvation in Isaiah 53," 193, n. 3). The standard terminology for forgiveness includes: טָהֵר ("to cleanse," "to purify," Lev. 16:30; Ps. 51:2, 7 [MT=51:4, 9]; Ezek. 36:25, BDB, 372); כָּבַס ("to wash," Ps. 51:2 [MT=51:4]; Jer. 4:14, BDB, 460); כָּפַר ("to cover," "make propitiation," Exod. 30:10; 32:30; Lev. 7:7; BDB, 497); מָחָה ("blot out" = "obliterate from the memory," Ps. 51:9 [MT=51:11]; BDB, 562); נָשָׂא ("take away guilt, iniquity, transgression, i.e., forgive" Gen. 50:17; Ex. 32:32; Mic. 7:18, BDB, 671); סָלַח ("forgive," "pardon," Ex. 34:9; Ps. 103:3; Isa. 55:7, BDB, 699); עָבַר ("pass over" = "overlook," "forgive," Mic. 7:18; Prov. 19:11; Amos 7:8; 8:2, BDB, 717). As Chisholm notes, when the verb נָשָׂא is used of forgiveness, it takes עָוֹן ("iniquity," "guilt"), חַטָּאת ("sin"), or פֶּשַׁע ("transgression") as its object. In Isaiah 53:12 it takes חֵטְא and means "to bear guilt, to experience punishment." Nowhere in the O.T. does נָשָׂא חֵטְא mean "to lift up sin" in the sense of forgiveness.

with God, the forgiveness of sins, and the annulment of all punishment [53:5]. (3) Because the Righteous One bore their sufferings, many will be justified, i.e., acquitted, declared righteous or not guilty [53:11].

How may these benefits be appropriated? It is clear from other passages in Isaiah that Yahweh promises forgiveness to sinful rebels. **"Though your sins are as scarlet, they will be as white as snow; thought they are red like crimson, they will be like wool"** (1:18). Shortly following the Servant song the Lord invites those who are spiritually thirsty and hungry to come and he will freely bless them. **"Ho! Every one who thirsts, come to the waters; and you who have no money come, buy and eat. Come, buy wine and milk without money and without cost"** (55:1).

The New Testament clearly identifies the Servant as the Lord Jesus Christ. He is the one who has offered Himself as an atoning sacrifice for sin. He is the one through whom salvation (Eph. 2:8), cleansing (Heb. 1:3; 9:22-24), forgiveness (Col. 1:14), justification (Rom. 3:26; 4:5), and peace with God (Rom. 5:1) are given to the sinner. The condition of salvation is faith in Christ and his finished work. The New Testament writers make it clear that the sinner is to confess his sins and believe in Christ, i.e., he is to put his trust in Christ (John 1:7, 12; 3:16; Acts 2:38, 44; 16:31; 20:21). The testimony of Isaiah 53 is true. The Servant of the LORD, Jesus Christ, died a substitutionary death; he has been punished in our place. We are to take God at his word concerning the atoning work of his Servant. Those who believe in Christ will be saved. The story of every believer in Jesus Christ is indeed a rags-to-riches story.

APPENDIX 1

THE SUFFERING SERVANT OF ISAIAH 53

IN THE JEWISH INTERPRETERS[1]

In a lecture at Oxford University (March 4, 1888), Semitic scholar Charles H. H. Wright remarked, "Our view of Isaiah lii, liii is that the prophecy was an enigma, which could not be fully understood in the days before Christ, but which has been solved by the sufferings, death, resurrection, and exaltation of Him who was both Son of Man and the Son of God."[2] Reflecting on this observation, David Baron, in his classic defense of the Messianic interpretation of Isaiah 53, wrote, "It is therefore not surprising to find that in the Talmud and Rabbinic Midrashim there is much confusion and contradiction in the various interpretations advanced by the Rabbis."[3] The following extracts will be of interest to students of Isaiah 52:13–53:12.

---

[1] A. McCaul, *The Doctrine and Interpretation of the Fifty-Third Chapter of Isaiah* (London: London Society's House, 1888), 18–40; idem., *Proofs That the LIII Chapter of Isaiah Refers to Messiah, and was Fulfilled in Jesus of Nazareth* (London: James Duncan, 1832); Charles H. H. Wright, *The Suffering Servant of Jehovah Depicted in Isaiah LII and LIII* (London: Francis Griffiths, 1905); David Baron, *The Servant of Jehovah: The Sufferings of the Messiah and the Glory that Should Follow* (New York: Doran, 1921), 143–58; Frederick A. Aston, "The Servant of the Lord in Isaiah LIII," *EvQ* 11 (July 15, 1939), 193–206; Christopher R. North, *The Suffering Servant in Deutero-Isaiah*, 2d ed. (London: Oxford University Press, 1956), 11–17; J. Jeremias, "παῖς θεοῦ," in *TDNT*, 5 (1967): 677–717; Ad. Neubauer and S. R. Driver, *The Fifty-Third Chapter of Isaiah According to the Jewish Interpreters*, vol. 2: *Translations* (1877; reprint ed., New York: KTAV, 1969); Emil Schürer, *The History of the Jewish People in the Age of Jesus Christ*, rev. and ed., Geza Vermes, Fergus Millar, and Matthew Black (Edinburgh: T. & T. Clark, 1979), 2:547–49; J. F. Stenning, trans., *The Targum of Isaiah* (Oxford: Oxford University Press, 1949); I. Epstein, *The Babylonian Talmud*, 18 vols. (London: Soncino, 1935–52 [Quincentenary Edition, 1978]); Rav Shimon bar Yochai [traditional authorship], *The Zohar*, 23 vols., rev. ed., Rabbi Michael Berg (New York: Kabbalah Center, 2003).

[2] Wright, *The Suffering Servant*, 7.

[3] Baron, *The Servant of Jehovah*, 10.

THE TARGUM OF ISAIAH[4]

The Targum is a paraphrase which reads as follows:

> "[52:13]Behold my servant, the Messiah, will have success, will become very high, great and strong. [14]As the house of Israel hoped for him many days when their appearance was darkened in the midst of the peoples and their glory less than that of men, [15]so he will scatter many peoples; for his sake kings will be silent, will lay their hand on their mouth; for what they have not been told they see, and what they have never heard of they perceive. [53:1]Who believed this our message, and to whom was the strength of the arm of Yahweh thus revealed? [2]And the righteous shall be great before him, lo, as sprouting branches and as a tree which sends out its roots to brooks of water, so shall the holy generations increase in the land which needed him (the Messiah). His appearance is not like that of a profane thing, and the fear which he inspires in not an ordinary fear, but his radiance will be a holy radiance so that whoever sees him will gaze (fascinated) upon him. [3]Then he will be despised and will (cause to) cease the glory of all kingdoms. They will be weak and pitiable—lo, as a man of sorrows and as one destined for sicknesses, as when the *shekinah* turns its face from us, the despised and unesteemed. [4]Then he will make intercession for our transgressions, and for his sake our iniquities will be forgiven, though we were accounted stricken, smitten by Yahweh and afflicted. [5]But he will build up the sanctuary which was desecrated because of our transgressions and delivered up

---

[4] See Stenning, *The Targum of Isaiah*, 178–81. This targum (Aramaic paraphrase) received its final form in Babylon in the fifth century AD, but it originated in Palestine in the first century (Stenning, vii). Gesenius dated the final form in the third century AD (cited by McCaul, *The Doctrine and Interpretation of the Fifty-Third Chapter of Isaiah*, 19). It has been attributed by tradition to Jonathan ben Uzziel, a disciple of Hillel (The Babylonian Talmud, *Seder Mo'ed*, vol. 4: *Megillah* 3a, trans. Maurice Simon [London: Soncino, 1978], 9, n. 6). Jeremias ("παῖς θεοῦ," 692) argued that the oral tradition which culminated in the Targum goes back to the pre-Christian period. The translation given here is that of Jeremias ["παῖς θεοῦ," 693–94; English translation, G. W. Bromiley]. See also the translation (and original text) in Stenning, *The Targum*, 178–81; Bruce D. Chilton, *The Isaiah Targum*, Aramaic Bible, vol. 11 (Wilmington: Michael Glazier, 1987), 103–105.

because of our sins, and through his teaching his peace will be richly upon us, and when we gather around his words our transgressions will be forgiven. [6]We were all scattered as sheep, every one went his own way into exile; but it was Yahweh's will to forgive the iniquities of us all for his sake. [7]When he prays, he receives an answer and he hardly opens his mouth before he finds a hearing. He will hand over the strong of the peoples to be slaughtered like a lamb, and as a ewe that is dumb before its shearers, and no one will (dare to) open his mouth and put in a word (sc. of advocacy). [8]He will bring back our exiles out of suffering and chastisement. Who can recount the wonders which will come upon us in his days? For he will remove the dominion of the peoples from the land of Israel; he will lay on them the transgressions of which my people was guilty. [9]And he will deliver up the ungodly to hell, and those who have enriched themselves by robbery to (eternal) destruction, so that those who commit sin may not be preserved and may not (any longer) speak deceitfully with their mouth. [10]And it pleased Yahweh to refine and purify the remnant of his people, to cleanse their soul from iniquities. They will see the royal dominion of their Messiah; they will have many sons and daughters; they will live long, and those who keep the law of Yahweh will by his good pleasure prosper. [11]He will cause their soul to escape from the bondage of the nations; they will see the chastisement of those that hate them, and will be satisfied with the plunder of their kings. By this wisdom he will pardon the innocent, to make many servants of the law. And for their transgressions he will make intercession. [12]Hereafter I will apportion to him of the spoil of many people, and he will divide the possession of strong towns as booty, because he gave up his soul to death, and subjugated gainsayers to the law. And he will make intercession for many transgressions and gainsayers will be forgiven for his sake.

The Targum depicts the future glorious establishment of Messiah's rule over Israel. However, it radically eliminates the sufferings of the Servant, and at only two places do traces remain (Tg. 53:3, "he will be despised;" 53:12, "he gave up his soul to death"). It also consistently reinterprets verses that apply to Messiah and applies them to Israel (e.g., Tg. 52:14, "their glory less than that of men," 53:2, "the sprouting branches," "the tree," "the roots," 53:3, "man of sorrows," "the despised and unesteemed," 53:4, "we were accounted stricken, smitten by Yahweh and afflicted," 53:10, "they will have many sons and daughters"). The Targum speaks of the cleansing of Israel (Tg. 53:10), but attributes it not to the Servant's vicarious sufferings, but to his intercession (Tg. 53:4) and his transference of Israel's sins to its oppressors (53:8).

Jeremias draws two important conclusions. First, by the time the Targum was written, the messianic interpretation was so firmly established that it could not be changed. Second, the only possible explanation for "this violent wrestling of" Isaiah's original meaning is that "we have here an instance of anti-Christian polemic. By the time the Targum reached its present form, Judaism was seeking "in various ways to rescue Isa. 53 from its use by Christians as a Christological proof from Scripture."[5]

JUSTIN MARTYR, DIALOGUE WITH TRYPHO

Justin Martyr (c. AD 100–165) was the most outstanding of the early Christian apologists. He was born of pagan parents in Flavia Neapolis ("Nablus"), the ancient Shechem in Samaria. After a long search for truth in pagan philosophies, he embraced Christianity (c. 130).[6] For some time he taught in Ephesus,[7] and it was there that he engaged in a discussion over a two-day period with a Jew named Trypho in which he used numerous quotations from the Old Testament to prove that Jesus was the Messiah promised in the Prophets.[8] Significantly, Trypho, a

---

[5] Jeremias ("παῖς θεοῦ," 694–95). Jeremias asserts, "The description of the Messiah as the servant of God occurs only in the pre-Rabbinical stratum of later Jewish literature" (693).

[6] Cf. *ODCC*, s.v. "Justin Martyr, St.," 770.

[7] Eusebius, *The Ecclesiastical History* 4.18.5-6, trans. Kirsopp Lake, LCL (Cambridge: Harvard, 1926), 1:370–71. Recent scholarship has proposed "Caesarea as a more likely venue." Cf. Thomas B. Halton, "Introduction" to St. Justin Martyr, *Dialogue with Trypho*, trans. Thomas B. Falls, rev. Thomas P. Halton (Washington: Catholic University of America, 2003), xii. Quotations from *Dialogue with Trypho* in this appendix are taken from the translation of Falls and Halton.

[8] Trypho introduced himself to Justin as "a Hebrew of the circumcision, a refugee from the recent war, and a present a resident of Greece, mostly in Corinth" (*Dialogue* 1.3 [4]). Henceforth references to *Dialogue* will be to chapters and paragraphs. Page numbers in

second-century Jew, agreed that these prophecies spoke of the Messiah who would suffer for his people. For the purposes of this study I shall concentrate on his quotations of Isaiah 52:13–53:12.[9]

Justin's *Dialogue* "makes the greatest use of Isaiah 53 of any Christian work of the first two centuries."[10] Miroslav Marcovich has

---

Falls and Halton will be enclosed in square brackets. Trypho's introduction helps in dating his encounter with Justin. The war in question was "the revolutionary war instigated by Bar Kochba in Palestine. It lasted from CE 132–135, during which time Hadrian captured Jerusalem and slew thousands of Jews" [4, n. 5]. Did this debate actually occur? In my opinion it did, and the historical references (e.g., "the recent war") point in that direction as do the vivid descriptions of the emotions of Justin and Trypho. "We gain a clear impression of the character and outlook of Trypho and his friends— which is essentially liberal and tolerant—in contrast to the fierce hatred of the Palestinian Jews against Christians which the war had inflamed. These personal references seem to rule out the view that the historical setting of the *Dialogue* is fictitious and that Trypho is a 'straw man' who is merely a tool in Justin's hands. On the other hand it is unlikely that Justin remembered nearly thirty years later, all that was said in the debate. But probably some repetitions did occur in view of the addition of further friends of Trypho on the second day [of the dialogue]. Discussions such as these must have been frequently held, as Christians sought to commend their faith openly, although not all may have been so amiable as this one. The best solution to the literary problem of the *Dialogue* is to postulate an original, historical debate with Trypho which occurred soon after AD 132, which Justin subsequently elaborated (c. AD 160), drawing on oral and written testimony material, which was known and used in the Church of his day. Nevertheless, to describe the *Dialogue* as 'a collection of all possible arguments rather than a report of a discussion in which each argument was actually brought up as recorded' seems unduly skeptical" (L. W. Barnard, *Justin Martyr: His Life and Thought* [Cambridge: Cambridge University Press, 1967], 23–24).One further note: Justin did promise Trypho that he would put their debate in a book to confirm all that had been said. He made this promise when Trypho seemed doubtful about Justin's assertion that Christians believed Messiah would return and reign in a rebuilt Jerusalem in which Christians as well as the OT saints would live joyfully together. Justin said, "However, you may be assured that I am not making this admission only in your presence. I promised to write up our whole debate as best I can, and there I will inscribe the admission I just made to you, for I do not desire *to be a follower of men and their teachings, but of God and his doctrines....* Whereas I, and all other wholeheartedly orthodox Christians, feel certain that there will be a resurrection of the flesh, *followed by a thousand years in the rebuilt, embellished, and enlarged city of Jerusalem,* as was announced by the prophets Ezekiel, Isaiah, and the others" [Ezek. 37:12-14; Isaiah 65:17-25]. (*Dialogue* 80.3, 5 [125, 126]). Justin defends his chiliastic/premillennial views in *Dialogue* 80 and 81 [125–27].

[9] In several of the quoted passages I substitute [Messiah] for the word "Christ" in Justin's text. These are passages where the OT prophecies of a coming Messiah are found. When describing the historical Jesus I have not changed the text but left the word "Christ" as is.

[10] Daniel P. Bailey, "'Our Suffering and Crucified Messiah;' Justin Martyr's Allusions to Isaiah 53 in his Dialogue with Trypho with Special Reference to the New Edition of M. Marcovich," in *The Suffering Servant: Isaiah 53 in Jewish and Christian Sources*, eds.

calculated that Justin refers to Isaiah 53 in thirty-six passages, while Bailey concluded that there may be as many as forty-two.[11] The quotations begin in *Dialogue* 13, where Justin quotes Isaiah 52:10–54:6.[12] In addition, the following sentences and phrases appear:

(1) "And Isaiah speaks as though in the person of the apostles (when they relate to Christ that the people were convinced, not by their words, but by the power of him who sent them), and says, 'Lord, who has believed our report, and to whom is the arm of the Lord revealed? We have preached before him as a little child, as if a root in a thirsty ground'" [Isa. 53:1-2].[13]

(2) "Isaiah already stated that man cannot describe it, when he exclaimed, 'Who shall declare his generation? Because his life is cut off from the earth; for the wickedness of my people he was led to death' [Isa. 53:8]. The prophetic Spirit thus declared that the birth of him who was to die in order to save us sinners 'by his stripes' was inexpressible" [Isa. 53:5].[14]

(3) "The Jews planned to crucify Christ himself and to slay him...as was likewise prophesied by Isaiah, 'as led like a

Bernd Janowski and Peter Stuhlmacher, trans. Daniel P. Bailey (Grand Rapids: Eerdmans, 2004), 324–417 (esp. 324).

[11] Bailey, "Our Suffering and Crucified Messiah," 324, 334, 345; cf. M. Marcovich, *Iustini Martyris Dialogus cum Tryphone*, PTS 47 (Berlin/New York: de Gruyter, 1997), 125, 130, 136, 138, 150, 155, 189, 192, 197, 202, 216, 225, 240, 241, 258, 260, 287. The lists of Bailey and Marcovich have a number of passages that do not directly quote Isaiah 53. They also include as allusions passages that include the word παθητός (*pathetos*, "passible" or "susceptible to suffering"). They argued that implicit in Justin's thought is the view that παθητός is Isaianic almost every time it is used—even though the word does not appear in Isaiah 53 (LXX). The term occurs nineteen times in seventeen paragraphs of the Dialogue. Eleven of the seventeen refer to Isaiah 53:8d ("he was led to death"). The chapters with παθητός are: *Dialogue* 34.2 [52]; 36.1 [twice, 52]; 39.7 [61]; 41.1 [62–63]; 49.2 [74]; 52.1 [twice, 78]; 68.9 [107]; 70.4 [110]; 74.1 [114]; 76.6 [119]; 85.2 [132], Bailey's corrected text reads, "who was born of a virgin and became a passible [παθητοῦ] man;" 89.2 [139]; 99.2 [150]; 100.2 [151]; 110.2 [164]; 111.2 [166]; 126.1 [189].

[12] *Dialogue* 13.2-9 [23–24]; cf. *Dialogue* 63.1-2 [97].

[13] *Dialogue* 42.2 [64].

[14] *Dialogue* 43.3 [65]. Justin here mistakenly applied the expression "his generation" to Christ's birth. Cf. *Dialogue* 63.1-2 [97]; 68.4 [105–106]; 76.2 [118].

lamb to slaughter' [Isa. 53:7], and in accordance with this passage he is marked as an 'innocent lamb.'"[15]

(4) "And does not the statement of Isaiah, 'Who shall declare his generation?' [Isa. 53:8] show that his origin is indescribable?"[16]

(5) "The following words…were spoken…solely of this Christ of ours, 'who appeared without beauty or honor' [Isa. 53:2-3] as Isaiah, David, and all the Scriptures testify."[17]

(6) "And the same Isaiah also predicted his resurrection: 'His burial has been taken out of the midst,' and 'I will give the rich for his death' [Isa. 53:9].[18]

(7) "For Isaiah said that he did not sin, even by word, 'for he has done no iniquity, neither was there deceit in his mouth" [Isa. 53:9].[19] "The Passover, indeed, was [Messiah] who was later sacrificed, as Isaiah foretold when he said, 'He was led as a sheep to the slaughter'" [Isa. 53:7].[20]

(8) "I have also shown that the prophecy of Isaiah, 'his burial has been taken away from the midst' [Isa. 53:8], referred to Christ, who was to be buried and to rise again."[21]

(9) "Isaiah, in wonderment at this, said, 'And kings shall shut their mouth; for they to whom it was not told of him, shall see; and they that heard not, shall understand. Lord, who has heard our report? And to whom is the arm of the Lord revealed?'" [Isa. 52:15; 53:1].[22]

(10)   "But Trypho," I continued, "if you had known who he is who at one time is called 'angel of great counsel,' and 'Man' by Ezekiel, and 'the Son of Man' by Daniel, and 'child' by Isaiah, and '[Messiah]' and 'Stone' by many prophets, and 'Wisdom' by Solomon and 'Joseph' and 'Judah' and a 'Star' by Moses, and 'Dawn' by Zechariah,

---

[15] *Dialogue* 72.3 [112].

[16] *Dialogue* 76.2 [118].

[17] *Dialogue* 85.1 [131].

[18] *Dialogue* 97.2 [148].

[19] *Dialogue* 102.7 [155].

[20] *Dialogue* 111.3 [166].

[21] *Dialogue* 118.1 [176].

[22] *Dialogue* 118.4 [177].

and the 'the Suffering One' and 'Judah' and 'Israel' again by
Isaiah [Isa. Isa. 53:8; cf. 42:1], and a 'Rod' and 'Flower' and
'Cornerstone' and 'Son of God' you would not have
blasphemed him who has come, and assumed human
nature, and suffered, and ascended into heaven."[23]

(11)   "My brothers, do not speak anything evil against the
crucified one, nor scoff at his wounds, by which every one
may be healed, as we have been healed" [Isa. 53:5].[24]

What is significant about Justin's work are the concessions by
Trypho that he and his teachers accepted the idea of the παθητὸς
Χριστός (*pathētos Christos* ["suffering Messiah"], cf. Acts 26:23).
Although Trypho and his friends conceded the point, they rejected the
idea that Jesus fulfilled the OT passages. "Trypho then said, 'It may also
be admitted that this is exactly as you say, and that the prophets
predicted that [Messiah] was to suffer, that he was to be called a Stone,
that his first coming in which he was proclaimed to appear in suffering
would be followed by another in glory, and that he would thenceforth be
the Judge of all men and the Eternal King and Priest. But prove to us
that Jesus Christ is the one about whom these prophecies were
spoken.'"[25] Later, Justin remarked, "Under pressure, [your teachers] are
forced to agree that some of the passages we cited—passages already
quoted to you which clearly prove that [Messiah] was to suffer, to be
worshipped, and to be called God—were indeed spoken of [Messiah].
They dare to deny that he whom we worship is the [Messiah], yet they
confess that [another] will come and suffer and rule and be
worshipped."[26]

The authenticity of this *Dialogue* is demonstrated by the fact that
Justin made no claim that Trypho in the end became a Christian.[27]
Trypho's reasons were two-fold: First, he did not agree with Justin that a

---

[23] *Dialogue* 126.1 [189].

[24] *Dialogue* 137.1 [206]. Other quotations from Isaiah 53 will be cited in the next two
paragraphs and accompanying footnotes.

[25] *Dialogue* 36.1 [56].

[26] *Dialogue* 68.9 [107].

[27] *Dialogue* 142.1-3 [212].

suffering Messiah had already come.[28] He noted that Elijah was to appear as Messiah's forerunner, and Elijah had not yet appeared. "Prove to us," interrupted Trypho, "that this man who you claim was crucified and ascended into heaven is the [Messiah] of God. It has indeed been proved sufficiently by your Scriptural quotations that it was predicted in the Scriptures that Christ should suffer, and that he should come again in glory to accept the eternal kingdom over all nations, and that every kingdom should be made subject to him. But what we want you to prove is that Jesus is the Messiah spoke of in the Scriptures."[29] He elsewhere said, "We [Jews] all expect that [Messiah] will be a man of human origin, and that Elijah will come to anoint him. If this man appears to be the [Messiah], he must be considered to be a man of human origin, yet, from the fact that Elijah has not yet come, I must declare that this man is not the [Messiah]."[30]

Second, he argued that while Messiah might suffer, he could not die of crucifixion, in light of the Torah's curse upon hanging (Deut. 21:23).[31] "When I finished, Trypho objected, 'Sir, your quotations from Scripture prove that we must look forward to that glorious and great Messiah who, as the Son of Man, receives the everlasting kingdom from the Ancient of days. But, the one whom you call Christ was without glory and honor to such an extent that he incurred the last curse of God's law, namely, he was crucified."[32] "But we doubt whether the [Messiah] should be so shamefully crucified, for the Law declares that he who is crucified is to be accursed. Consequently, you will find it very difficult to convince me on this point. It is indeed evident that the Scriptures state that Messiah was to suffer, but you will have to show us, if you can,

---

[28] Justin responded that Isaiah spoke as if Messiah had already suffered. "When the Holy Spirit says through Isaiah, 'He was led as a sheep to the slaughter, and as a lamb before the shearer [Isa. 53:7], he speaks as though the Passion had already taken place. And again, when he says, 'I have stretched out my hands to a disobedient and contradicting people' [Isa. 65:2], and, 'Lord who has believed our report' [Isa. 53:1], he likewise speaks of events as though they had already happened" [Isa. 53:1]. See *Dialogue* 114.2 [170].

[29] *Dialogue* 39.7 [60-61].

[30] *Dialogue* 49.1 [74]. Justin's response, having gotten Trypho to admit there will be two advents of Messiah, was that Elijah will be Messiah's forerunner at the second advent. Furthermore, he quoted Jesus' response to those in his day who advanced the same argument as Trypho that Elijah had come in spirit as Christ's forerunner at the first advent in the person of John the Baptist (*Dialogue* 49.2-7 [74-76]; cf. Matt. 17:10-13).

[31] Jeremias ("παῖς θεοῦ," 5:696); Bailey, "Our Suffering and Crucified Messiah," 324.

[32] *Dialogue* 32.1 [49].

whether it was to be the form of suffering cursed by the Law."[33] "We are indeed aware that he was to endure suffering, and to be led as a sheep to the slaughter [Isa. 53:7]. But what we want you to prove to us is that he was to be crucified and subjected to so disgraceful and shameful a death (which even in the Law is cursed). We find it impossible to think that this could be so."[34]

EARLY RABBIS[35]

Some of the early rabbis quoted Isaiah 53 in reference to the Messiah.

Rabbi Jochanan († 279)[36] comments on Ruth 2:14 to show that it speaks of the king, the Messiah. "At mealtime Boaz said to

---

[33] *Dialogue* 89.1-2 [139]. Trypho's request is for Justin to show him Messiah's suffering should take the form cursed by the law, namely crucifixion. Justin's indirect response is "his most impressive combined quotation…of unmistakable phrases from Isaiah 53: "'If indeed, Christ was not to suffer,' I answered him, 'and if the prophets did not predict that because of the sins of the people [Isa. 53:8] he would be put to death [53:8] and be dishonored [53:3-4] and scourged [Isa. 53:5], and be numbered among sinners [53:12], and be led as a sheep to the slaughter [Isa. 53:7], whose birth the prophet declares no one can describe [53:8], your feelings of astonishment would be justified" (*Dialogue* 89.3 [139]). Elsewhere Justin links the birth of Messiah to Isaiah's "Who shall declare his generation?" (*Dialogue* 43:3 [65]). Cf. Bailey, "Our Suffering and Crucified Messiah," 379.

[34] *Dialogue* 90.1 [140]. Justin does address the notion of the cross as a curse in three ways: (1) He speaks of the cross as "this apparent curse of Christ" (*Dialogue* 90.3 [140]). (2) He asserts "our suffering and crucified Christ was not cursed by the Law (111.2 [166]), i.e., "nothing of the sort could touch Christ, the Son of God, the Holy One; in reference to Himself, this was only in appearance (90.3)." (3) The curse Christ bore was vicarious, i.e., he was crucified in the place of sinful men. Justin said, "If, then, the Father of the Universe will that his [Messiah] should shoulder the curses of the whole human race, fully realizing that he would raise him up again after his crucifixion and death, why do you accuse him, who endured such suffering in accordance with the Father's will, of being a cursed person, instead of rather bewailing your own iniquity?" (*Dialogue* 95.2 [146]). See A. Lukyn Williams, *Justin Martyr, The Dialogue with Trypho* (London: SPCK, 1930), 201, n.1.

[35] According to Jeremias ("παῖς θεοῦ," 5:697), it was the school of Rabbi Akiba (c. AD 50–135) that preserved the tradition of a messianic interpretation of the passion sayings in Isaiah 53.

[36] Rabbi Jochanan, i.e., Johanan ben Nappaha (c. 180–c. 279) was "a Palestinian *amora* whose teachings comprise a major portion of the Jerusalem Talmud" ("Johanan ben Nappaḥa," *EncJud*, 10:144–147). The Jerusalem Talmud was compiled by succeeding generations of his disciples ("Talmud, Jerusalem," *EncJud*, 15:772–79 [esp. 772–73]).

her, 'Come here, that you may eat of the bread and dip your piece of bread in the vinegar.' 'Come here,' that means come here to the authority to rule as king; 'Eat of the bread,' that is the bread of monarchy; 'Dip your piece of bread in the vinegar,' by this are the sufferings (the beatings of the Messiah) meant, as it says in Isaiah 53:5, 'He was wounded for our transgressions.'"[37]

Rabbi Huna (c. 350)[38] in the name of Rabbi Acha (c. 320)[39] said: "The sufferings are divided into three parts; one for the (that is, for all) generations and for the fathers, and one for the generation of religious persecution (at the time of Hadrian), and one for the king, the Messiah; that is what was written in Isaiah 53:5, 'he was pierced through for our sins, etc.'"[40]

Rabbi Berechiah (c. AD 350)[41] said, "God spoke to Israel: You said to me, 'We have become orphans without a father' [Lam. 5:3]. Also the redeemer, whom I will bring forth from you will not have a father, as it says (Zech. 6:12), 'Behold a man whose

---

For further discussion of the Talmud and the *amoraim*, see the discussion below in the section entitled "The Babylonian Talmud."

[37] Hermann L Strack und Paul Billerbeck, *Kommentar zum Neuen Testament aus Talmud and Midrasch*, IV teilen, fünfte unveränderte Auflage (München: C. H. Beck'sche Verlagsbuchhandlung, 1969 [=1926], I 27; cf. II 285.

[38] Rabbi Huna, i.e., Huna ben Avin ha-Kohen (mid-fourth century), was born in Babylon where he studied under Rabbi Joseph. He immigrated to the land of Israel where he became a community and academic leader. When he transmits, i.e., speaks in the name of a respected teacher, he frequently does so in the name of Aḥa. Cf. Shmuel Safrai, "Huna ben Avin ha-Kohen," *EncJud*, 8:1075.

[39] Rabbi Acha, i.e., Aḥa bar Ḥanina, was a teacher in Palestine. He was from Lydda but lived in Galilee. In Tiberias he studied under Rabbi Assi, from whom he received the tradition of Rabbi Johanan. Despite his Palestinian origin, his teachings are found mostly in the Babylonian Talmud and not the Jerusalem Talmud. See Zvi Kaplan, "Aḥa bar Ḥanina," *EncJud*, 2:440.

[40] Str.-B., II 287.

[41] Rabbi Berechiah, a Palestinian *amora*, is sometimes referred to as Rabbi Berechiah ha-Kohen. He was a student of Rabbi Ḥelbo, whose aggadic sayings as well as those of other scholars, he reported (Zvi Kaplan, "Berechiah," *EncJud*, 4:595). For further discussion of the *aggadah*, see the discussion below in the section entitled "The Babylonian Talmud."

name is Branch, for from his place he will branch out'; and so
Isaiah 53:2 says, 'he grew up before him like a tender shoot.'"[42]

THE BABYLONIAN TALMUD[43]

The word "Talmud" (תַּלְמוּד) means "study" or "learning" and is used in
a variety of senses: (1) the opinions and teachings which disciples acquire
from their predecessors to expound and explain them to others; (2) the
whole body of one's learning; and (3) a teaching (technical phrase
Talmud lomar) derived from the exegesis of a biblical text. The word is
most commonly used as a central text of Judaism in which the Jewish
teachers comment upon and discuss the Mishnah.[44] The Talmud has
two parts: the Mishnah (the written compendium of the Jewish oral law
(c. AD 200) and the Gemara, the comments and discussions of the
amoraim[45] upon the sayings of the *tannaim*,[46] which took place in the
Jewish academies in Babylonia (modern Iraq) between c. AD 200 and AD
500[47] There is a passage in the Talmud in which Isaiah 53 is interpreted
messianically.

---

[42] Str.-B., I 49–50.

[43] The following quotation from the Talmud is taken from *The Babylonian Talmud*, 18
vols., ed. I. Epstein (London: Soncino, 1978 [Quincentenary Edition]).

[44] Bathja Bayer "Talmud," *EncJud*, 15:750–55; Elieser Beck, "Talmud, Babylonian,"
EncJud, 15:755–768.

[45] The *amoraim* (Aramaic אֲמוֹרָאִים, sg. אֲמוֹרָא, "sayer," "spokesmen") were the rabbis of
the post-mishnaic period, whose activities were centered on the interpretation of the
Mishnah. The discussions of the *amoraim* constitute the bulk of the Talmud. See Shmuel
Safrai, "Amora," *EncJud* 2:863–65; idem., "Amoraim," *EncJud* 2:865–875.

[46] The *tannaim* (Aramaic תַּנָּאִים, sg. תַּנָּא, "to hand down orally," "to teach") were the
sages who taught from the time of Hillel to the time of the compilation of the Mishnah,
i.e., the first and second centuries AD. "Thus the tannaitic period covers a period from
about 20 to about 200 AD, the approximate date of the final redaction of the Mishnah by
Judah ha-Nasi." The term refers either to a teacher mentioned in the Mishnah or who
were from Mishnaic times. See Daniel Sperber, "Tanna, Tannaim," *EncJud* 15:798–803
(esp. 798).

[47] The most important academies were in Nehardea, Sura, Pumbedita, Maḥoza, Naresh,
and Mata Meḥasya (Beck, "Talmud, Babylonian," 755).

SANHEDRIN 98B[48]

"Rab said, 'The world was created only on David's account.' Samuel said: 'On Moses' account.' R. Joḥanan said, 'For the sake of the Messiah. 'What is his [the Messiah's] name?'—The School of R. Shila said: 'His name is Shiloh, for it is written, *until Shiloh come* [Gen. 49:10].'[49] The School of R. Yannai said, 'His name is Yinnon, for it is written, *His name shall endure for ever: e'er the sun was, his name is Yinnon* [Ps. 72:17].'[50] The school of R. Ḥaninah maintained, 'His name is Ḥaninah, as it is written, *Where I will not give you Ḥaninah* [Jer. 16:13].'[51] Others say, 'His name is Menaḥem the son of Hezekiah, for it is written, *Because Menaḥem ["the comforter"], that would relieve my soul, is far* [Lam. 1:16].'[52] The Rabbis said, 'His name is "the leper scholar,"[53] as it is written, *"Surely he hath borne our griefs*

---

[48] *The Babylonian Talmud, Seder Nezikin*, 4 vols., vol. 3: *Sanhedrin* 98b, trans. H. Freedman, 667.

[49] As the editor (H. Freedman) notes, "Each school evinced intense admiration of its teacher in naming the Messiah after him by a play on words" (p. 667).

[50] The MT of Psalm 72:17 has יָנִין (yānîn). This is the 3d pers. msc. sg. hiphil jussive of נִין. This may be rendered "increase" or "sprout forth," thus, "let his name have increase." The MT also has as a marginal reading the word יִנּוֹן (yinnôn). This is the 3d pers. msc. sg. niphal jussive. This may be rendered "may his name be propagated or spread." This is an interesting feature of the Hebrew Bible called Kethiv (כְּתִים, "it is written") and Qere ("to be read"). When the Jewish scholars known as the Masoretes or Massoretes (from the post-biblical root, *msr*, "to hand down") during the period of 600 to 1000 added diacritical notations (vowels) to the Hebrew text, they added additional observations about the text in the margins. For example, they corrected recognized errors in the margins. They left the uncorrected word in the text (kethiv), and placed what they believed to be the correct reading in the margin (qere). The students of the school of R. Yannai took the qere reading as a proper name, Yinnon. See BDB, s.v. "נוּן, נִין," 630; J. Weingreen, *A Practical Grammar for Classical Hebrew*, 2d ed. (London: Oxford University Press, 1959), 22–23; IBHS, § 1.5.4d (21–22).

[51] In this text, which reads "I will show you no favor," the word "favor" renders the Hebrew חֲנִינָה (ḥănînāh), which a student of the school of R. Ḥaninah took as a proper name.

[52] The word "comforter" in Lamentations 1:16 is a rendering of the Hebrew מְנַחֵם (mᵉnaḥēm).

[53] Raimundus Martinus preserved a "much better reading" according to Jewish scholar Peter Schäfer. His manuscript read, "Those from the house of Rabbi say, 'The sick (*hulya*)' is his name, as it is written, *Surely he has borne our infirmities* (*holayenu/holyenu*) [Isa. 53:4].'" Schäfer writes, "Here the name of the Messiah and the proof text fit perfectly well—as does the reading, 'those from the house of Rabbi say,' which makes

and carried our sorrows: yet we did esteem him a leper, smitten of
God and afflicted [Isaiah 53:4]."'"

There are two other passages in the Talmud which, although they do
not quote or allude to Isaiah 53, speak of the Messiah as one who suffers
and identifies with the poor and diseased.

SANHEDRIN 93B[54]

"The Messiah—as it is written, 'And the spirit of the Lord shall
rest upon him, the spirit of wisdom and understanding, the
spirit of counsel and might, the spirit of knowledge of the fear of
the Lord. And shall make him of quick understanding (*wa-
hariho*) in the fear of the Lord' [Isa. 11:2-3]. R. Alexandri said,
'This teaches that he loaded him with good deeds and suffering
[as with millstones].'"

SANHEDRIN 98A[55]

"R. Joshua ben [son of] Levi (3d cent. AD) met Elijah standing
by the entrance of R. Simeon b. Yohu's tomb. He asked him,
'Have I a portion in the world to come?' He replied. 'If this
Messiah desires it.' R. Joshua ben Levi said, 'I saw two, but

---

more sense than 'the leper from the house of Rabbi.' It is with good reason that Abraham
Epstein has suggested that the version in *Pugio Fidei* is indeed the original version of our
midrash in the Bavli [Babylonian Talmud], which was cleansed by the Bavli's censor,
who sought to reserve the Messiah's vicarious suffering for Christianity alone." See: Peter
Schäfer, *The Jewish Jesus: How Judaism and Christianity Shaped Each Other* (Princeton:
Princeton University Press, 2012), 253; Abraham Epstein, *Mi-qadmaniyot ha-jehudim:
Mehqarim u-reshimot* (Jerusalem: Mosad ha-Rav Kook, 1956–57), 100–103 (Hebrew);
also: Michael Fishbane, "Midrash and Messianism: Some Theologies of Suffering and
Salvation," in *Toward the Millennium: Messianic Expectation from the Bible to Waco*, eds.
Peter Schäfer and Mark Cohen (Leiden: Brill, 1998), 57–71 (esp. 59). Fishbane writes,
"The verbal play between the name Hulya ('The Afflicted One') and the word *holayenu*
(MT חֲלָיֵנוּ "sicknesses") is just right, and I am therefore inclined to suspect that Martini's
citation preserves an authentic Jewish teaching of a suffering messiah, excised from the
Talmudic tradition through internal or other censorship." Cf. Raimundus Martinus,
Pugio Fidei Raymundi Martini Ordinis Praedicatorum Adversus Mauros et Judaeos [*The
Dagger of Faith by Raymond Martini, the Order of Preachers, Against Moors and Jews*]
(Leipzig: Friderici Lanckisi, 1687; reprint Farnborough: Gregg, 1967), 862. For more on
Raymond Martini, see discussion below on Sifra Leviticus.

54 *The Babylonian Talmud, Sanhedrin* 93b, (626–27).

55 *The Babylonian Talmud, Sanhedrin* 98a, (664).

heard the voice of a third.'[56] He then asked him, 'When will the Messiah come?'—'Go and ask him himself,' was his reply. 'Where is he sitting?'—'At the entrance.' 'And by what sign may I recognize him?'— 'He is sitting among the poor lepers: all of them untie [them] all at once, and rebandage them together, whereas he unties and rebandages each separately [before treating the next], thinking, 'Should I be wanted, [it being time for my appearance as the Messiah] I must not be delayed [though having to bandage a number of sores].' So he went to him and greeted him, 'Peace upon thee, Master and Teacher.' 'Peace upon thee, O son of Levi,' he replied. 'When wilt thou come Master?' asked he. 'Today,' was his answer. On his returning to Elijah, the latter enquired, 'What did he say to thee?'—'Peace upon thee, O son of Levi,' he answered. Thereupon he [Elijah] observed, 'He thereby assured thee and thy father of [a portion in] the world to come.' 'He spoke falsely to me,' he rejoined, 'stating that he would come today, but he has not.' He [Elijah] answered him, 'This is what he said to thee, "Today if ye will hear his voice."'

MIDRASHIM

In rabbinic literature the word "Midrash" (Hebrew מִדְרָשׁ, pl. מִדְרָשִׁים)[57] retained the meaning "study, inquiry," but its main use was in the meaning "scriptural interpretation." The word could refer to the procedure of interpretation as well as the product of that interpretation. It was also used of a collection of such interpretations (pl. *midrāšîm*). Midrash began in oral form in the period of the Second Temple in two

---

[56] "[Joshua son of Levi} saw only himself and Elijah there, but heard a third voice—that of the Shekinah" (H. Freedman, trans., *Sanhedrin* 98a (664, n. 6).

[57] The word מִדְרָשׁ occurs twice in the Hebrew Bible (2 Chron. 13:22; 24:27), and in both cases it is rendered by one English word, although the versions do not agree on the word. They offer "treatise" (Darby, NASB), "story" (KJV, ESV), "annals" (NKJV), "writings" (HCSB), "annotations" (NIV). NET, REB, and TEV differ by having a different English word for each verse. NET has "writings" in 2 Chronicles 13:22 and "scroll" in 24:27. REB has "discourse" in 13:22 and "annals" in 24:27. TEV has "history" in 13:22 and "commentary" in 24:27. BDB (s.v. "מִדְרָשׁ," 205) has "study, exposition." The noun is derived from the verb דָּרַשׁ, for which BDB (s.v. "דָּרַשׁ," 205) offers a variety of definitions depending on the context (e.g., seek, inquire, seek with application, study," etc.).

kinds, *aggadah* and *halakhah*. *Aggadah* or *haggadah* (Heb. אַגָּדָה, הַגָּדָה, "narrative") was the creation of Palestinian Jewry living in trying times and was an attempt to derive guidance from the Torah, to educate the people and to strengthen their faith. It took the form of homilies on the sacred text that used "narratives, legends, doctrines, admonitions to ethical conduct and good behavior, words of encouragement and comfort, and expressions of hope for future redemption."[58] *Midreshei Halakhah* (מִדְרְשֵׁי הֲלָכָה, "Midrashim of the *halakhah*")[59] are rabbinic expositions on the legal portions of Scripture (the Pentateuch). They were homilies taking the Mosaic legislation of the past and applying it to the circumstances of contemporary life. "The Midrash was gathered, edited, and placed in written form between the years AD 400 and AD 1550.

Biblical scholars today use the term *Midrash* as a name for a *literary genre*. Unlike the rabbis who used the term for the activity of study and interpretation or for a type of exegesis, modern scholars use the term to designate a specific corpus or body of literature. "The Midrash, then, was the traditional literature that arranged the rabbinic material in biblical sequence around specific texts. It was that literature which was so structured that it started with a biblical text and then set down in connection with the text edifying thoughts or legislation which the rabbis had drawn out of that text."[60]

SIFRA

The Sifra (Aram. סִפְרָא; corresponding to Heb. סֵפֶר, "a book") is a halakhic Midrash on the book of Leviticus compiled around the end of the second century AD by R. Ḥiyya[61] or at the end of the fourth century

---

[58] Moshe David Herr et al, "Aggadah," *EncJud* 2:354–364.

[59] The noun הֲלָכָה is derived from the verb הָלַךְ, meaning "to go, come, or walk" (BDB, s.v. "הָלַךְ," 229). The noun speaks of "the act of going or coming." When used of rabbinic teaching it is used in the sense "way of acting," "habit," "usage," "custom," and especially "guidance" and "the norm of practice" (Joseph Jacobs, "Halakah," *JE* 6:163).

[60] Addison S. Wright, "The Literary Genre Midrash," *CBQ* 28 (1966): 105–138, 417–457 (esp. 119). Biblical scholars generally divide the history of the Midrash into four periods: The Early Period (400–640), the Middle Period (640–1000), the Late Period (1000–1200), the Period of Yalkutim (anthologies [1200–1550]). See Moshe David Herr, "Midrash," *EncJud* 11:1507–1514 (esp. 1511–1512).

[61] Rabbi Ḥiyya (also called *Rabbah*, "the Great") was born in Babylonia, but he emigrated to the land of Israel. Cf. Zvi Kaplan, "Hiyya," *EncJud* 8:793–796.

AD by an unknown redactor. It is a collection of various interpretations of Leviticus arranged by its editor as a running commentary, chapter by chapter and verse by verse.[62] According to the Talmud, the editor was of the school of R. Akiba.[63]

Sifra Leviticus 12.10 (on Lev. 5:17)

According to Raymundus Martini[64] the text in S. Lv. reads:

> R. Yosé the Galilean said, "Come forth and learn the righteousness of the King Messiah and the reward of the just from the first man who received but one commandment, a prohibition, and transgressed it: consider how many deaths were inflicted upon himself, upon his own generations, and upon those that followed them, till the end of all generations. Which attribute is the greater, the attribute of goodness, or the attribute of vengeance?" He answered, "The attribute of goodness is the greater, and the attribute of vengeance is the less; how much more then, will the King Messiah, who endures affliction and pains for the transgressors (as it is written, 'He was wounded for our transgressions' [Isa. 53:5]) justify all generations! And this is

---

[62] Moshe David Herr, "Sifra," *EncJud* 14:1517–19.

[63] *Sanhedrin* 86a (566–67).

[64] The quotation from Sifra Leviticus is a matter of much disagreement because of the version found in Raymond Martini (1220–1285), a Spanish Dominican friar, evangelist, and polemicist (Esther Sulman, "Martini, Raymond," *EncJud* 11:1065–66; see above footnote on the *Babylonian Talmud, Sanhedrin* 98b). He was the author of *Pugio Fidei* (The Dagger of Faith), which was published around 1280, was lost for some time, and was found and republished in Paris in 1651 and then Leipzig in 1687. He studied Hebrew and other languages and trained a group of friars to evangelize Muslims and Jews. *Pugio Fidei* would be viewed as an apologetics text by Christians but as an anti-Jewish polemic by Jews. Well read in rabbinical literature, Martini sought to prove from that literature that Jesus was the Jewish Messiah and that he had abrogated the Jewish law. It has been argued by Christians that Martini's reading is the true one but was excised by Jews because of its messianic interpretation of Isaiah 53. But it has been argued by Jews that Martini arbitrarily grouped sentences out of their original context to give them a Christological meaning. Jeremias (παῖς θεοῦ, 5:696.), says that Martini "usually proves to be trustworthy," but cautiously concluded that his reading here is "probably secondary." E. B. Pusey, on the other hand, strongly defended the readings of Martini, acknowledging that the manuscripts he used have long since perished. See Pusey's "Introduction to the English Translations," in Driver and Neubauer, *The Fifty-Third Chapter of Isaiah According to the Jewish Interpreters*, 2:xxix–xxxv.

what is meant when it is said, 'And the Lord made the iniquity of us all meet upon him [Isa. 53:6].'"[65]

According to the generally received text, however, Sifra Lv. reads:

> R. Jose said, "If thou art minded to know how great is the reward of the righteous in the world to come, go and learn from the first man, upon whom was laid only one negative commandment, and he transgressed it; see how many deaths were inflicted upon him and upon his generations, and upon the generations of his generations to the end of his generations, and which attribute is greater, the attribute of goodness or the attribute of vengeance?" He saith, "the attribute of goodness. If the attribute of vengeance be the less, see how many deaths were inflicted upon him and on his generations, and on the generations of his generations unto the end of all generations. He who turneth from the unclean (פִּגּוּל, *pigûl*, "offence thing," Lev. 7:18, NASB) and from that which remaineth over [of the sacrifice] (הַנּוֹתָר, "what is left over," Lev. 7:16, 17, NASB), and humbleth himself on the day of atonement, how much more does he merit for himself and for his generations, and for the generations of his generations until the end of all generations!"[66]

---

[65] Raymond Martini, *Pugio Fidei*, 674. The translation used here is that Driver and Neubauer, *The Fifty-Third Chapter of Isaiah According to the Jewish Interpreters*, 2:10–11.

[66] The translation used here is that Driver and Neubauer, *The Fifty-Third Chapter of Isaiah According to the Jewish Interpreters*, 2:lxxv. E. B. Pusey defended Martini's reading over the received text. He wrote, "Admitting fully the right of the Jews to adapt their texts for their own private use and to erase the mention of 'the merits of the Messiah' when they no longer believed them, the omission seems to me to have spoiled the argument. As it stands in Martini, the contrast is clear, between the one sin of one hitherto sinless [Adam] and the merit of the Sinless Sufferer. But since every righteous man has committed many more sins than Adam, there is no contrast between his one disobedience and their observance of a few commands. To me it seems inconceivable, that a mind which could conceive so grand a contrast as that between God's attributes of justice and mercy could have sunk to so poor a contrast, and have imagined (contrary to fact) that two or three ritual observations could have been meritorious for all generations, whereas Ezekiel declares, that the father's observance of the moral law would not avail to the son who habitually broke it. The passage, as it stands in the printed text, seems to me to indicate an omission, such as Martini's text supplies, 'the merit of the Messias' being a known phrase. See "Introduction to the English Translations," in Driver and Neubauer, 2:lxxv.

TANHUMA MIDRASH (ON NUMBERS 1:2, 4)[67]

According to Raymundus Martini, the text reads:

> "R. Nahman says, 'The word "man" in the passage, "Every man
> a head of the house of his fathers" (Num. 1:4), refers to the
> Messiah the son of David, as it is written, "Behold the *man*
> whose name is Zemah" (the branch; where Yonathan interprets,
> "Behold the *man* Messiah (Zech. 6:12);" and so it is said, "A
> *man* of pains and known to sickness."'"[68]

MIDRASH RABBAH[69]

> "The fifth interpretation [of Ruth 2:14] makes it refer to the
> Messiah. 'Come hither:' approach to royal state. 'And eat of the
> bread' refers to the bread of royalty; 'And dip thy morsel in the
> vinegar' refers to his sufferings, as it is said, 'But he was
> wounded because of our transgressions (Isa. 53:5). 'And she sat
> beside the reapers,' for he will be deprived of his sovereignty for
> a time, as it is said, 'For I will gather all nations against
> Jerusalem to battle; and the city shall be taken (Zech. 14:2).
> 'And they reached her parched corn,' means that he will be

---

[67] Tanḥuma Bar Abba (2d half of the 4th cent.) was a Palestinian *amora* and a prolific *haggadist.* He was distinguished for his defense of Jews and Judaism against non-Jews. There is a story that "in one of Tanḥuma's conversations with non-Jews the emperor suggested that Jews and non-Jews become one nation. To this Tanḥuma replied, 'But we who are circumcised cannot possibly become like you.' The emperor answered, 'You have spoken well. Nevertheless, whoever gets the better of the emperor in debate must be thrown into the *vivarium*' ('arena of wild beasts'), Tanḥuma was thrown in, but came out safely. A heretic who was present maintained that this was because the animals were not hungry, whereupon he was thrown in and was eaten" (Moshe David Herr, "Tanhuma Bar Abba," in *EncJud*, 15:793–96 [esp. 793], citing *The Babylonian Talmud, Sanhedrin* 39a, trans. Jacob Shachter, 249)

[68] Martini, *Pugio Fidei*, 664. The translation used here is that Driver and Neubauer, *The Fifty-Third Chapter of Isaiah According to the Jewish Interpreters*, 2:11.

[69] *Midrash Rabbah* (רַבָּה, "great"), i.e., "Midrash of the Great Commentaries" refers to a collection of the whole of the aggadic midrashim published in Venice in 1545. This collection included all of the commentaries on the Pentateuch (Genesis Rabbah, Exodus Rabbah, Leviticus Rabbah, Numbers Rabbah, Deuteronomy Rabbah) as well as commentaries on the Five Rolls (Songs Rabbah, Ruth Rabbah, Esther Rabbah, Lamentations Rabbah, Ecclesiastes Rabbah).

restored to his throne, as it is said, 'And he shall smite the land with the rod of his mouth' (Isa. 11:4)."[70]

YALKUT SHIMONI

The Yalkut (Hebrew יַלְקוּט, *yalqûṭ*)[71] of Shimoni is a comprehensive midrashic anthology covering the whole Bible.[72] The "aim of the compiler was to assimilate the bulk of rabbinical sayings at his disposal, following the order of the verses of the Bible. It contains more than 10,000 statements of *aggadah* and *halakhah*, covering all the books of the Bible, most of its chapters, and including commentaries on a substantial part of individual verses."[73]

Yalkut 2.620[74]

The passage reads:

"נְסַכְתִּי (Ps. 2:6).[75] According to another view this means, 'I have *woven* him,' cf. מַסֶּכֶת (Jud. 16:14),[76] i.e., 'I have drawn him out

---

[70] *Ruth Rabbah* 5.6, trans. L. Rabinowitz, in *Midrash Rabbah*, ed. H. Freedman, 3d ed. (London: Soncino, 1983), 8:64. Also see Driver and Neubauer, *The Fifty-Third Chapter of Isaiah According to the Jewish Interpreters*, 2:9. For a modern analysis of *Ruth Rabbah* by a distinguished Jewish scholar, see Jacob Neusner, *The Mother of the Messiah in Judaism: The Book of Ruth* (Valley Forge, PA: Trinity Press International, 1993), esp. 89–96.

[71] The word יַלְקוּט is from the verb לָקַט, which means "pick, gather up, or glean." Hence, a יַלְקוּט is a collection, anthology or compilation. In the OT the word is used of a receptacle or pouch (1 Sam. 17:40, NASB). Cf. BDB, s.v. "לָקַט," 544–45.

[72] The author or compiler of the Yalkut was probably Simeon ha-Darshan ("Simeon the preacher"), referred to by M. Prinz as "Rabbenu Simeon, chief of the preachers of Frankfort." He lived in the thirteenth century. Cf. Jacob Elbaum, "Yalkut Shimoni," in *EncJud* 16:707–709 (esp. 707).

[73] Elbaum, "Yalkut Shimoni," 707.

[74] The translation used here is that Driver and Neubauer, *The Fifty-Third Chapter of Isaiah According to the Jewish Interpreters*, 2:10. I have added some punctuation.

[75] The verb נָסַכְתִּי (1st pers. sg. qal perf. of נָסַךְ) is taken from the line, "I have installed my king upon Zion" (NASB). The verb is translated "installed" in NASB, and "woven" in Yalkut. The verb means "to pour out," but its meaning in Psalm 2:6 is widely disputed. For example, it has been understood as "poured out" in the sense of anointing ("I have anointed my king") or "poured out" in the sense of casting metal or setting firmly in place ("I have installed my king"). See Franz Delitzsch, *Biblical Commentary on the Psalms*, trans. Francis Bolton (Edinburgh: T. & T. Clark, 1871), 1:94. BDB (s.v. "נָסַךְ," 651) has, "to set, install." The rabbinical reading "to weave" is possible (cf. Isa. 25:7, where NASB has "spread") but very unlikely in this context.

of the chastisements.' R. Hunâ, on the authority of R. Aḥâ says, 'The chastisements are divided into three parts: one for David and the fathers, one for our own generation, and one for the King Messiah; and this is that which is written, "He was wounded for our transgressions."'"

It is not for the present writer to comment on the rabbinical exegesis here. I only point out that the text applies Isaiah 53:5 to the Messiah.

LATER WRITINGS

THE JEWISH LITURGY

The following hymn "by the famous hymn writer, Eleazar ben Qualir, who, according to the Jewish historian Leopold Zunz, lived in the ninth century AD is taken from the Service for the Day of Atonement, translated by David Levi.[77] In it are gathered up the teachings of the Synagogue about a suffering Messiah."[78] I have noted in brackets allusions to 53:5-6.

> Before he created anything,
>> God established His dwelling place and ינון (Yinnon).[79]

> The lofty armoury (His house) He established from the
>> beginning,
>> Before any people or language existed.

---

[76] The feminine noun מַסֶּכֶת is related to the verb נָסַךְ and is translated "web" in Judges 16:14 (NASB). See BDB, s.v. "מַסֶּכֶת," 651; *HALOT*, s.v. "מַסֶּכֶת," 1:606. In Yalkut the noun is interpreted as "chastisements."

[77] David Levi, trans., מחזור מכל השנה כמנהג פולין: *The Festival Prayers, According to the Ritual of the German and Polish Jews,* vol. 3: מוסף ליום כפור: *Additional Service for the Day of Atonement* (London: Abrahams & Son, 1872), 33.

[78] Baron, *The Servant of Jehovah,* 156–57. The translation of the hymn given here combines elements of the translations of Baron and Levi (33).

[79] According to the Talmud, Yinnon is one of Messiah's names. See: *The Babylonian Talmud, Seder Neziḳin,* 4 vols., vol. 3: *Sanhedrin* 98b (12:667). The Talmud bases this on Psalm 72:17, which it renders, "His name shall endure forever: e'er the sun was, his name is Yinnon."

It was His pleasure that His Shekhina (divine presence) should
    dwell there,
To guide those gone astray into the path of rectitude.

Though their sins were red like scarlet [cf. Isa. 1:18],
    They were preceded by his words, 'Wash you, cleanse
        yourselves' [cf. Isa. 1:16],

If His anger was kindled against His people,
    Yet the Holy One poured not out all His wrath.

We are ever threatened by destruction because of our evil deeds,
    And God does not draw nigh us—He, our only refuge.

Our righteous anointed [Messiah our righteousness] [80] has
    departed from us,
We are horror-stricken, and have none to justify us.

He has borne the yoke of our iniquities, and our transgression,
    And is wounded because of our transgression [Isa. 53:5-6].

He bears our sins on his shoulder,
    that he may find pardon for our iniquities [Isa. 53:6].

By his stripes we shall be healed—[Isa. 53:5]
    O Eternal One, it is time that you should create him anew!

O bring Him up from the terrestrial sphere,
    Raise Him up from the land of Seir, [81]

---

[80] In his notes Levi interprets the reference to "our righteous anointed" to King Josiah. As McCaul observed, however, the context favors a reference to the Messiah (cf. A. McCaul, *The Doctrine and Interpretation of the Fifty-Third Chapter of Isaiah* (London: London Society's House, 1888), 25). He notes: (1) This is a known title of Messiah. (2) The hymn commences and concludes with a reference to Messiah. Levi acknowledged that Yinnon was a reference to Messiah. (3) Levi also confessed that the words, "O Eternal One, it is time that you should create him anew" is a reference to the Messiah.

[81] "Seir stands here for Edom, and by Edom the Talmud means Rome, where…the Messiah now lives in deep humiliation and suffering" (Baron, *The Servant of Jehovah*, 157, n. 1; cf. *Babylonian Talmud, Sanhedrin* 98a [12:664, n. 7]).

To announce salvation to us from Mount Lebanon,[82]
Once again through the hand of Yinnon.

Alexander McCaul, professor of Hebrew and Rabbinical Literature
at King's College, London, drew attention to another remarkable
passage, this one in Levi's translation of the festival prayers for the feast
of Passover.[83] The Hebrew text reads:

בְּרָה דּוֹדִי עַד שֶׁיָּפוּחַ קֵץ מַחֲזֶה חִישׁ וְנָסוּ הַצְּלָלִים
מִזֶּה יָרוּם וְנִשָּׂא וְנָבַהּ נִבְזֶה יַשְׂכִּיל וְיוֹכִיחַ וְגוֹיִם רַבִּים
יַזֶּה חֲשׂוֹף זְרוֹעֶךָ קְרָא כָזֶה קוֹל דּוֹדִי הִנֵּה זֶה

Levi translated as follows, "Accelerate our redemption, my beloved,
before the end of the vision; hasten and cause the shadows to flee away;
he that will be high and greatly exalted; though now despised; he will
cause them to understand, he will also reprove and cast away many
nations; uncover thine arm and we will cry aloud thus, it is the voice of
my beloved. Lo! He cometh."

McCaul, unhappy with Levi's translation, added "a more literal
version"[84]:

> "Fly, my beloved, until the end of the vision speak. Hasten that
> the shadows may flee away. Let Him be *exalted,* and *extolled,* and
> *high,* that is now *despised.* Let Him *deal prudently,* and reprove,
> and *sprinkle many nations.* [Uncover thy arm and we will cry
> aloud, 'It is the voice of my beloved. Lo! He cometh!']"

McCaul argued that this Passover prayer contains clear allusions to
Isaiah 52–53 and Messiah.[85] He pointed out to his Jewish readers that

---

[82] "Lebanon stands here for the Mount of the Temple, from which Messiah is to
proclaim to Israel that the time of salvation has come" (Baron, *The Servant of Jehovah,*
157, n. 2).

[83] David Levi, מחזור מכל השנה כמנהג פולין: *The Festival Prayers, According to the Ritual
of the German and Polish Jews,* vol. 5: מחזור של פסח: *Service for the Feast of Passover*
(London: H. Abrahams, 1859), 55; cf. A. McCaul, *The Doctrine and Interpretation of the
Fifty-Third Chapter of Isaiah* (London: London Society's House, 1888), 22–23.

[84] McCaul, *The Doctrine and Interpretation of the Fifty-Third Chapter of Isaiah,* 22–23.

[85] According to McCaul (*The Doctrine and Interpretation of the Fifty-Third Chapter of
Isaiah,* 23), Levi's second edition (*Service for the Feast of Passover,* 72), to which I do not

his argument was not based on his translation but on the Hebrew words in the text. He drew attention to four expressions in three verses which are clearly quoted: (1) The words יָרוּם וְנִשָּׂא וְגָבַהּ [yārûm wᵉnissā' wᵉgābah], translated here, "Let Him be exalted, and extolled, and high," are taken from Isaiah 52:13, where it is rendered, "He will be high and lifted up and greatly exalted" [NASB]. The Hebrew words are exactly the same in both places. (2) The word יַשְׂכִּיל [yaśkîl], rendered by McCaul, "deal prudently," is also taken from Isaiah 52:13, where it is rendered "will prosper" [NASB]. Again, the argument rests on the Hebrew words, and in both the Passover prayer and Isaiah the word is the same. (3) The words וְגוֹיִם רַבִּים יַזֶּה [wᵉgôyim rabbîm yazzeh], rendered "and sprinkle many nations," is taken from Isaiah 52:15, where it is rendered, "He will sprinkle many nations" [NASB]. Again, the same Hebrew words are used in both places.[86] (4) The word נִבְזֶה [nibzeh], rendered "despised," is taken from Isaiah 53:3, where it is translated "he was despised" [NASB]. McCaul wrote, "The Jews, from the hour of their dispersion to this very day, do in their non-controversial writings, and their solemn and public prayers to a heart-searching God, apply this prophecy to the Messiah."[87]

BOOK OF ZOHAR

The book of Zohar (זֹהַר [zōhar] "Splendor," "Radiance")[88] is the foundational work in the literature of Jewish mystical thought known as the Kabbalah.[89] It is written in Aramaic the day-to-day language of Israel

---

have access, contains a note stating that the words refer to "the true Messiah." I have Levi's edition of 1859 before me, which does not have these words.

[86] It should be noted that there is a slight variation from the Isaiah text in the Passover prayer. The word order in Isaiah changes the placement of יַזֶּה, putting it at the beginning of the phrase (יַזֶּה גּוֹיִם רַבִּים). In addition, Isaiah lacks the connective waw before גּוֹיִם, which explains why the prophet has the daghesh ג while the prayer does not.

[87] McCaul, *The Doctrine and Interpretation of the Fifty-Third Chapter of Isaiah*, 23.

[88] For a full introduction to *The Book of Zohar*, see Gershom Scholem, "Zohar," in *EncJud* 16 (1972): 1194–1215

[89] For a full introduction to Kabbalah, see Gershom Scholem, "Kabbalah," in *EncJud* 10 (1972): 490–654. The Hebrew word Kabbalah (קַבָּלָה, "received [doctrine]") originally referred to the Hagiographa ("the Writings") and the Prophets as distinct from, and in contrast to, the Pentateuch. It was also used of "oral traditions handed down either from teacher to disciple, or as part of a family tradition" (Editor's note on "Kabbalah," in *EncJud* 10: 654; also see Scholem, "Kabbalah," 494). Today the term is most commonly used "for the esoteric teachings of Judaism and especially for Jewish mysticism, particularly the form which it assumed in the Middle Ages from the twelfth century

in the Second Temple period (539 BC–AD 70). The Zohar first appeared in Spain in the thirteenth century, where it was published by Moses de Leon. He claimed to have compiled the Zohar from texts and fragments that came to him from the East. De Leon ascribed the work to Shimon bar Yochai, a rabbi who lived in the second century during the Roman persecution.[90] The following sections, interpret Isaiah 53 in a messianic fashion:

Section וַיַּקְהֵל (wayaqhēl, or Vayak'hel)[91]

> "Happy is the portion of the just in this world and in that which is to come! The souls which are in the Garden of Eden below go to and fro every new moon and Sabbath, in order to ascend to the place that is called the Walls of Jerusalem…. After that they journey on and contemplate all those that are possessed of pains and sicknesses and those that are martyrs for the unity of their Lord, and then return and announce it to the Messiah. And as they tell him of the misery of Israel in their captivity, and of those wicked ones among them who are not attentive to know their Lord, he lifts up his voice and weeps for their wickedness: and so it is written, 'He was wounded for our transgressions, he was crushed for our iniquities' [Isa. 53:5]. Then these souls return and abide in their own place. There is in the garden of Eden a palace called the Palace of the sons of sickness: this palace

onward. In its wider sense it signifies all the successive esoteric movements in Judaism that evolved from the end of the period of the Second Temple and became active factors in the history of Israel" (Scholem, "Kabbalah," 490).

[90] Orthodox Jews accept this dating of the work, but many modern scholars follow Gershom Scholem, who ascribed the work to Moses de Leon himself. See Scholem, "Zohar," *EncJud* 16:1193–1215 (esp. 1210, 1214–15). An Orthodox Jewish response was offered in Hebrew by R'Mehachem Mendel Kasher in the periodical *Sinai* (1958). Kasher's arguments are summarized by Eli Clark in an online article, "Authenticity of Sefer Ha Zohar" «http://www.avakesh.com/2007/05/in_honor_of_lag.html» Accessed 6/6/15. Kasher's Hebrew article may be accessed at «http://www.daat. ac.il/data/kitveyet /sinay/hazohar-2.htm». E. B. Pusey defended the early date of the Zohar, but his colleagues (Driver and Neubauer) defended the late date. See Driver and Neubauer, "Preface," *The Fifty-Third Chapter of Isaiah According to the Jewish Interpreters*, 2:v.

[91] This (וַיַּקְהֵל) is the first word ("and he [Moses] assembled") in the *parashah* (פָּרָשָׁה, *pārāšāh*, "portion," i.e., "section") corresponding to the twenty-second weekly Torah portion in the annual Jewish cycle of Torah reading and the tenth in the book of Exodus (Exodus 35:1–38:20).

the Messiah then enters, and summons every sickness, every pain, and every chastisement of Israel; they all come and rest upon him. And were it not that he had thus lightened them off Israel and taken them upon himself, there had been no man able to bear Israel's chastisements for transgression of the law: and this is that which is written, 'Surely our sicknesses he hath carried.'"[92]

Section פִּינְחָס (Pîn⁽ḥās, or Pinchas [Heb. for Phinehas])[93]

"The children of the world are members one of another. When the Holy One desires to give healing to the world, he smites one just man amongst them, and for his sake heals all the rest. Whence do we learn this? From the saying, 'He was wounded for our transgressions, bruised for our iniquities' [Isa. 53:5], לנו ובהבורתו נרפא ['and by his injury we are healed'], i.e., by the letting of blood—as when a man bleeds his arm—there was healing for us—for all the members of the body. In general a just person is only smitten in order to procure healing and atonement for a whole generation: and this is the mystery of the saying, 'There is a just man and it goes ill with him, [a wicked man and it goes well with him'].[94]

---

[92] "Section Vayak'hel," in *The Zohar by Rav Shimon bar Yochai*, rev. ed., edited and compiled by Rabbi Michael Berg (New York: The Kabbalah Center, 2003), § 333–336 (12:338–40). The translation used here is that of Neubauer and Driver, *The Fifty-Third Chapter of Isaiah According to the Jewish Interpreters*, 2:14–15.

[93] This (פִּינְחָס), a name (Phinehas), is the sixth word and the first distinctive word in the *parashah* (i.e., section) corresponding to the forty-first weekly Torah portion in the annual Jewish cycle of Torah reading and the eighth in the book of Numbers (Num. 25:10–30:1).

[94] "Section *Pinchas*," in *The Zohar by Rav Shimon bar Yochai*, § 110 (20:90). The translation used here is that of Neubauer and Driver, *The Fifty-Third Chapter of Isaiah According to the Jewish Interpreters*, 2:15. According to Neubauer and Driver, the concluding quotation in this section is an allusion to *The Babylonian Talmud, Seder Zerai'im: Berakoth* 7a, trans. Maurice Simon, 33.

MIDRASH KONEN[95]

"The fifth mansion in Paradise is built of onyx and jasper, and set stones, and silver and gold, and fine gold, surrounded by rivers of balsam: before the entrance flows the Gihon; a pavilion (?) is there of 'all trees of frankincense' [Song of Sol. 4:14], with sweet odors, and beds of gold and silver, and richly-variegated garments: there dwell Messiah son of David, and Elijah, and Messiah son of Ephraim; there also is the 'litter of the wood of Lebanon' [Song 3:9], like the tabernacle which Moses made in the wilderness; all the furniture thereof and 'the pillars thereof of silver, the bottom of gold, the seat of purple,' and within it, Messiah son of David who loveth Jerusalem. Elijah takes him by his head, lays him down in his bosom, holds him, and says, 'Bear thou the sufferings and wounds wherewith the Almighty doth chastise thee for Israel's sin;' and so it is written, 'He was wounded for our transgressions, bruised for our iniquities' [Isa. 53:5], until the time when the end should come."[96]

'ASÉRETH MÊMROTH[97]

"The Messiah, in order to atone for them both [Adam and David], will make his soul a trespass-offering, as it is written next to this, in the Parasha, 'Behold my servant: אָשָׁם ['āšām (Isa. 52:13; 53:10)], i.e., cabbalistically, 'Menaḥem son of

---

[95] Midrash Konen (c. AD 1100) is a mystical/esoteric Midrash on creation which contains many non-biblical elements. It may be found in Adolph Jellinek, *Bet haMidrash*, 6 vols., 2d ed. (Jerusalem: Bamberger and Wahrmann, 1938), 2:23–39. Jellinek's work is "a collection of minor Midrashim in the original Hebrew or Aramaic, with introductions" (cf. Raphael Patai, *The Messiah Texts* [New York: Avon, 1979], 114–15; 351).

[96] The translation used here is that Driver and Neubauer, *The Fifty-Third Chapter of Isaiah According to the Jewish Interpreters*, 2:394.

[97] 'Aséreth Mêmroth is a kabbalistic work written in the seventeenth century by Menaham Azariah who concluded "from the fact that the Messiah makes his soul an *'āšām* ("guilt offering," Isa. 53:10) that he must be Menahem ben 'Ammiel—one of the many names of Messiah ben Joseph. The ground for this astonishing assumption is that the numerical values of the consonants in *'āšām* and *Menaham ben 'Ammiel* are the same, namely, 341!" (North, *The Suffering Servant in Deutero-Isaiah*, 16). For the gematria behind these calculations see Driver and Neubauer, *The Fifty-Third Chapter of Isaiah According to the Jewish Interpreters*, 2:394, footnote.

Ammiel.' And what is written after it. 'He shall see his seed, shall have long days, and the pleasure of the Lord shall prosper in his hand'" [Isa. 53:10][98]

P'SIQTHA

"The Holy One brought forth the soul of the Messiah, and said to him Art thou willing to be created and to redeem my sons after 6000 years? He replied, I am. God replied, If so, thou must take upon thyself chastisements in order to wipe away their iniquity, as it is written, 'Surely our sicknesses he hath carried' [Isa. 53:4]. The Messiah answered, I will take them upon me gladly."[99]

PESIKTA RABBATI

"[At the time of the Messiah's Creation], the Holy One, blessed be He, will tell him in detail what will befall him: There are souls that have been put away with thee under My throne, and it is their sins which will bend thee down under a yoke of iron and make thee like a calf whose eyes grow dim with suffering, and will choke thy spirit as with a yoke; because of the sins of those souls thy tongue will cleave to the roof of thy mouth. Art thou willing to endure such things? ... The Messiah will say: Master of the universe, with joy in my soul and gladness in my heart I take this suffering upon myself ..."[100]

---

[98] The translation used here is that Driver and Neubauer, *The Fifty-Third Chapter of Isaiah According to the Jewish Interpreters*, 2:394–95.

[99] This quotation is given in Driver and Neubauer, *The Fifth-Third Chapter of Isaiah According to the Jewish Interpreters*, 2:iv, 10. They attribute the quotation to the Latin translation of Antonius Hulsius (1615–1685) in his work *Theologia Judaica* (Breda, the Netherlands: Subbingius, 1653), 328. His reading was taken from אַבְקַת רוֹכֵל ('Avqat Rokēl ["the perfumer's powders," Song of Songs 3:6]). Hulsius asserts on his cover page that he has restored the true Scriptural readings that have been glossed by rabbinical writers. 'Avqat Rokēl or Avkat Rokhel is attributed to Machir ben Isaac Sar Hasid (see *Avkat Rokhel* אבקת רוכל, trans. R. Isaac Jacob Puppenheim, ed., R. Isaac Jacob ben Saul Abraham of Minden [2d printing, Amsterdam: Kosman Gompert, 1697]). For a synopsis of the publishing history and content of *Avkat Rokhel*, see Marvin J. Heller, *The Seventeenth Century Hebrew Book: An Abridged Thesaurus*, 2 vols. (Leiden: Brill, 2011), 2:1311. As Fishbane notes, this quotation is a striking alternate version to a reading found in *Pesikta Rabbati* (6th or 7th century A.D.). Michael Fishbane, "Midrash and Messianism: Some Theologies of Suffering and Salvation," in *Toward the Millennium*, eds., Peter Schäfer and Mark Cohen (Leiden: Brill, 1998), 69.

[100] Piska 36.1 in *Pesikta Rabbati: Discourses for Feasts, Fasts, and Special Sabbaths*, trans. William G. Braude, YJS (New Haven: Yale, 1968), 2:678–79 [for dating, cf, 1:26]. The Scripture index of this work does not contain a single citation from Isaiah 52:13–53:12.

APPENDIX 2

HEALING AND THE ATONEMENT IN ISAIAH 53

Matthew quotes Isaiah 53:4 in reference to Jesus' ministry of casting out demons and healing diseases. "When evening came, they brought to Him many who were demon-possessed; and He cast out the spirits with a word, and healed all who were ill. This was to fulfill what was spoken through Isaiah the prophet: 'HE HIMSELF TOOK OUR INFIRMITIES AND CARRIED AWAY OUR DISEASES'" (Matt 8:16-17). The meaning of Isaiah 53:4 and its relationship to Matthew 8:17 is one of the major interpretive problems of Isaiah 53. There have been at least five interpretations held by commentators,

VIEW # 1: THE SERVANT WAS MADE LEPROUS

According to the first view, Isaiah 53:4 suggests that the Servant actually bore the physical diseases of others. In support of this eccentric view, the word "stricken" (נָגַע, *nāga'*) in v. 4b has been translated as "made leprous."[1] There is no evidence in the New Testament that Jesus suffered from leprosy or any other disease.

VIEW # 2: THE SERVANT BORE SICKNESS VICARIOUSLY

LEADERS OF THE MODERN HEALING MOVEMENT

Proponents of the second view say that Isaiah 53:4 uses the words "sicknesses" and "pains" literally, and the verbs "bore" and "carried" are to be understood in terms of a vicarious bearing of the sicknesses of others on the cross.[2] A. J. Gordon wrote:

---

[1] See the notes on Isa. 53:4 in the above exposition. As noted there, both the Talmud and the Latin Vulgate interpreted the word "stricken" (נָגַע) to mean that Messiah was a leper.

[2] It is noteworthy that Delitzsch, who had no connection to the modern healing movement, adopted the view that the Servant vicariously bore our diseases. "But in the case before us, where it is not the sins, but 'our diseases'...and 'our pains' that are the

"The yoke of his cross by which he lifted our iniquities took hold also of our diseases; so that it is in some sense true that as God 'made him to be sin for us who knew no sin,' so he made him to be sick for us who knew no sickness. He who entered into mysterious sympathy with our pain which is the fruit of sin, also put himself underneath our pain which is the penalty of sin. In other words the passage seems to teach that Christ endured vicariously our diseases as well as our iniquities."[3]

A. B. Simpson, founder of the Christian and Missionary Alliance, also affirmed this view:

"Therefore, as he has borne our sins, Jesus Christ has also borne away and carried off our sicknesses; yes, and even our pains, so that abiding in him, we may be fully delivered from both sickness and pain. Thus 'by his stripes we are healed.' Blessed and glorious gospel! Blessed and glorious Burden-Bearer!"[4]

T. J. McCrossan agreed: "The clear teaching therefore is that Christ bore our sicknesses in the very same way that he bore our sins."[5] E. Howard Cobb added that there are only two reasons for unhealed sickness—a lack of faith and disobedience.[6]

---

object, this mediatorial sense remains essentially the same. The meaning is not merely that the Servant of God entered into the fellowship of our sufferings, but that He took upon Himself the sufferings which we had to bear and deserved to bear, and therefore not only took them away (as Matt. 8:17 might make it appear), but bore them in His own person, that He might deliver us from them. But when one person takes upon himself suffering which another would have had to bear, and therefore not only endures it with him, but in his stead, this is called *substitution* or representation" (Franz Delitzsch, *Biblical Commentary on the Prophecies of Isaiah*, trans. James Martin [Edinburgh: T. & T. Clark, 1877; reprint ed., Grand Rapids: Eerdmans, 1965], 2:316).

[3] A. J. Gordon, *The Ministry of Healing, or, Miracles of Cure in All Ages*, 3d ed. (New York: Revell, 1882), 16–17.

[4] A. B. Simpson, *The Gospel of Healing*, rev. ed. (New York: Christian Alliance Publishing Co., 1915), 17.

[5] T. J. McCrossan, *Bodily Healing and the Atonement* (Seattle, WA: T. J. McCrossan, 1930), 18.

[6] E. Howard Cobb, *Christ Healing* (London: Marshall, Morgan, and Scott, 1952), 20–21, 98–102.

Simpson explained the steps to healing as follows:

(1) First, be fully persuaded of the teaching of the Word about healing.

(2) Second, be fully assured of the willingness of God to answer the prayer of faith.

(3) Third, be sure that you are right with God. Confess your sins and make restitution as much as you are able.

(4) Fourth, "commit your body to Him and claim His promise of healing in the name of Jesus by simple faith. Do not merely ask for it, but humbly and firmly claim it as His covenant pledge, as your inheritance, as a purchased redemption right, as something already fully offered you in the gospel, and waiting only your acceptance to make good your possession." From that moment on the person seeking healing should reject all doubting and abandon all remedies and medical treatment. "God has become the Physician, and He will not give His glory to another."

(5) Fifth, act in faith and ignore all symptoms of the illness.

(6) Sixth, be prepared for trials.

(7) Seventh, use your regained health in service to God.[7]

LEADERS OF THE "WORD OF FAITH" MOVEMENT

A similar understanding of Isaiah 53:4 and healing is actively promoted by the Word of Faith movement. Gloria Copeland wrote, "Jesus bore your sicknesses and carried your diseases at the same time and in the same manner that he bore your sins. You are just as free from sickness and disease as you are free from sin. You should be as quick to refuse sickness and disease in your body as you are to refuse sin."[8] Kenneth Hagin, the father of the modern "faith" movement, says that God "made him sick with your diseases that you might be perfectly well in Christ."[9]

---

[7] Simpson, *The Gospel of Healing*, 75–97.

[8] Gloria Copeland, *And Jesus Healed Them All* (Ft. Worth: Kenneth Copeland Ministries, 1984): 4. The underlying theology is the same. (*Healing Belongs to Us* [Tulsa: Faith Library, 1969], 16.)

[9] Kenneth E. Hagin, *Healing Belongs to Us* (Tulsa: Faith Library, 1969), 16. For an incisive evaluation of the Word of Faith/"Health and Wealth Gospel," cf. D. R. McConnell, *A Different Gospel*, rev. ed. (Peabody, MA: Hendrickson, 1995). Also see

Proponents of this view argue that it is always God's will to heal. Hagin wrote, "I am fully convinced—I would die saying it so—that it is the plan of Our Father God, in His great love and in His great mercy, that no believer should ever be sick; that every believer should live his full lifespan down here on this earth; and that every believer should finally just fall asleep in Jesus."[10] F. F. Bosworth wrote, "It is impossible to have real faith for healing as long as there is the slightest doubt as to its being God's will."[11] Gloria Copeland declares, "You must know that it is God's will to heal you. Until this fact is settled in your mind and spirit, you cannot approach healing without being double minded and wavering."[12] She insists, "Believing in healing is not enough. You must *know* that it is God's will for *you* to be healed."[13] Colin Urquhart adds one must erase the word "if" from one's thinking. The words, "if it be Thy will" is "destructive of true faith."[14] Copeland agrees. "'If it be Thy will' is unbelief when praying for healing."[15]

CRITIQUE

A complete evaluation of Word of Faith teaching is beyond the scope of this article.[16] However, a few observations are in order.

David W. Jones and Russell S. Woodbridge, *Health, Wealth, and Happiness: Has the Prosperity Gospel Overshadowed the Gospel of Christ?* (Grand Rapids: Kregel, 2011).

[10] Kenneth E. Hagin, *Seven Things You Should Know About Divine Healing* (Tulsa: Faith Library, 1983), 21.

[11] F. F. Bosworth, *Christ the Healer: Sermons on Divine Healing* (River Forest, IL: F. F. Bosworth, 1924; reprint ed., Whitefish, MT: Kessinger, 2010), 84.

[12] Gloria Copeland, *God's Will for Your Healing* (Ft. Worth: Kenneth Copeland Ministries, 1972), 3.

[13] Copeland, *God's Will for Your Healing*, 9.

[14] Colin Urquhart, *Receive Your Healing* (London: Hodder and Stoughton, 1986), 49.

[15] Gloria Copeland, *And Jesus Healed Them All* (Ft. Worth: Kenneth Copeland Ministries, 1984), 3. Copeland (11) goes so far as to tell her followers that they should not seek help from doctors and medicine when they are sick. See also Urquhart, *Receive Your Healing*, 18.

[16] A careful treatment which pays attention to the scriptural texts is C. Samuel Storms, *Healing and Holiness: A Biblical Response to the Faith-Healing Phenomenon* (Phillipsburg, NJ: Presbyterian and Reformed, 1990), 12–35 and passim. To be fair I should note that Storms now openly identifies with the charismatic movement. However, he has not changed his views, so far as I know, on the Word of Faith movement.

(1) First, a careful exegesis of Isaiah 53:4 and Matthew 8:17 indicates that Christ died a substitutionary death for our sins, not our diseases (see exposition above and notes below).

(2) Second, "the New Testament makes a clear distinction between the atonement wrought by the Lord Jesus with respect to sin, and the cosmic effects that spring forth from that atonement in relation to all else."[17] Sin causes a terrible breach between the individual and God which requires expiation (removal) and satisfaction (propitiation). Here one might cite B. B. Warfield, who said, "Atonement can be made only for fault [sin, transgression, iniquity, rebellion]" and should be directly applied only to sins.[18] Thus the atonement is a work of propitiation (Heb. 2:17; Rom. 3:25), a work of reconciliation (2 Cor. 5:18-21), and a work of justification (Rom. 3:23-26). All this was accomplished by the substitutionary work of Christ on the cross (Matt. 20:28; Rom. 8:3; 1 Cor. 15:3; 2 Cor. 5:21; Gal. 2:20; 3:13). Sickness and disease, on the other hand, exist on the natural and physical plane and are, of themselves, non-moral and non-spiritual.[19] Sickness does not cause a barrier between an individual and God.[20] "There is no guilt to disease or sickness. Having diabetes or a head cold is not sinful. The Bible tells us 'to confess our sins,' but nowhere does it say that we should pray 'forgive us our cancer.... If sickness is not a sin, how can it incur a penalty."[21]

(3) Third, it is erroneous to say that God wills complete health for all believers at all times. The NT provides a number of examples of sick believers that the Lord did not will to heal (Paul, 2 Cor. 12:7-10; Epaphroditus, Phil. 2:25-30; Timothy, 1 Tim 5:23; Trophimus, 2 Tim. 4:20).[22]

---

[17] L. F. W. Woodford, "Divine Healing and the Atonement—a Restatement," *Journal of the Transactions of the Victoria Institute* 88 (1956): 47–62 (esp. 52).

[18] Benjamin B. Warfield, *Counterfeit Miracles* (1918; reprint ed., London: Banner of Truth, 1972), 175–76.

[19] I do not mean to suggest that various sinful behaviors cannot cause illness.

[20] Woodford, "Divine Healing and the Atonement—a Restatement," 50–52.

[21] Storms, *Healing and Holiness*, 16–17.

[22] Cf. H. A. Ironside, "Divine Healing—Is It In the Atonement?" in *Divine Priorities and Other Messages* (New York: Revell, 1945), 96–104.

(4) Fourth, there is no explicit promise in Scripture that God wills perfect health for his people or that he is always willing to heal them.[23]

(5) Fifth, it is clear that the Lord often uses sickness and other trials to discipline his children (2 Cor. 12:7-10; Heb. 12:4-11).

(6) Finally, it is presumption and not faith to demand healing because one assumes he or she perfectly knows God's will. "When we exercise our faith in God we submissively and sincerely acquiesce to God and his will, whatever that will may be. Faith does not dictate what God's will is."[24]

VIEW # 3: THE SERVANT BORE SIN VICARIOUSLY AS A BASIS FOR HEALING

SICKNESS AND PAIN AS METAPHORS FOR SIN

According to the third view, Isaiah 53:4 uses the same kind of metaphorical or figurative language found in Isaiah 1:5-6, i.e., he uses "sicknesses" and "pains" to speak of sin. This may be identified as a metonymy of effect [sickness] for cause [sin].[25] The verbs "bore" and "carried" are understood in the sense of vicarious suffering, i.e., Christ took their sin and guilt upon himself and suffered the penalty as their substitute. Proponents generally say that on the cross Jesus bore the guilt of sin and its consequences, i.e., all the results of the curse of sin: disease, suffering, misery, and death. Their argument is that Matthew uses the Isaiah 53 citation in a gospel that makes several references to Jesus' "passion predictions." This makes it likely that Matthew 8:17 implies that Jesus' death is the basis for his healing of physical disease.[26]

---

[23] See Storms, *Healing and Holiness*, 28–35.

[24] Storms, *Healing and Holiness*, 31.

[25] E. W. Bullinger, *Figures of Speech Used in the Bible* (London: Eyre and Spottiswoode, 1898; reprint ed., Grand Rapids: Baker, 1968), 550–51.

[26] Douglas Moo, "Divine Healing in the Health and Wealth Gospel," *Trinity Journal*, New Series 9 (1988): 191–209 (esp. 204); D. A. Carson, "Matthew," in *The Expositor's Bible Commentary*, eds., Tremper Longman III and David E. Garland (Grand Rapids: Zondervan, 2000), 9:243–45.

THE PRESENCE OF THE KINGDOM

Many proponents of this view have been influenced by George E. Ladd's theology of the kingdom. In Ladd's view the kingdom of God has invaded the present age, but we await the full consummation of that kingdom in the future. The kingdom, Ladd asserted, is present "as a dynamic power," "as the divine activity," and "as the new age of salvation." Today we live "'between the times'; the old age goes on, but the powers of the new age have irrupted into the old age." [27] It is a commonplace among evangelical scholars to say that today the believer lives in an "already-not yet" tension of this "between the times" framework. Proponents of this third view fall into two broad categories. [28]

Subgroup A: Non-Charismatic Proponents
The first of the subgroups is made up of non-Charismatic evangelicals. While most agree that the kingdom was in some way inaugurated at Jesus' death and resurrection, they note that it has not come in its fullness. They argue that there is healing in the atonement in the sense that forgiveness of sin has future benefits, and the proof of this will be the resurrection of the body. The bodily aspects of Christ's atoning work await the transformation of our bodies into glorious bodies not subject to disease, decay, or death. In short, many of the great cosmic changes associated with the OT promise of the kingdom are "not yet" here. This is perhaps the most common view among evangelical commentators. [29] I

---

[27] George Eldon Ladd, *A Theology of the New Testament*, rev. ed., ed. Donald A. Hagner (Grand Rapids: Eerdmans, 1993), 66–67; idem., *The Presence of the Future* (Grand Rapids: Eerdmans, 1974), 149, 171, 195 and passim.

[28] Cf. the helpful survey of views on healing in W. Kelly Bokovay, "The Relationship of Physical Healing to the Atonement," *Didaskalia: The Journal of Providence Theological Seminary* 3 (Oct., 1991): 24–39 (esp. 24–25).

[29] E. W. Hengstenberg, *Christology of the Old Testament*, trans. Theodore Meyer and James Martin (Edinburgh: T. & T. Clark, 1854–58; reprint ed., Grand Rapids: Kregel, 1956), 2:283; Franz Delitzsch, *Biblical Commentary on the Prophecies of Isaiah*, trans. James Martin (Edinburgh: T. & T. Clark, 1877; reprint ed., Grand Rapids: Eerdmans, 1965), 2:316; Edward J. Young, The Book of Isaiah, NICOT (Grand Rapids: Eerdmans, 1972), 3:345; John N. Oswalt, *The Book of Isaiah, Chapters 40–66*, NICOT (Grand Rapids: Eerdmans, 1998), 387, n. 7; Robert D. Culver, *The Sufferings and the Glory of The Lord's Righteous Servant* (Moline, IL: Christian Service Foundation, 1958;), 66–67, footnote; F. Duane Lindsey, *The Servant Songs: A Study in Isaiah* (Chicago: Moody,

agree with proponents of this view that there will be a transformation of our bodies and a release from all diseases in the future resurrection (1 Cor. 15:52–54; Phil. 3:21; 1 John 3:2). I hesitate, however, to base this conviction on Isaiah 53:4. In that chapter the prophet was narrating the life of the Messiah, and at verse 4 he had reached the point where he was describing his earthly ministry. He noted that during that time of ministry the Messiah would heal people. Neither Isaiah nor Matthew connected this ministry to the atonement.

Subgroup B: Charismatic Evangelicals

The second subgroup is made up of Christians usually connected with some form of charismatic renewal. Those in the "third wave" of the charismatic renewal base much of their teaching about healing on the kingdom theology of Ladd. Their focus is on an "inaugurated eschatology," i.e., they emphasize the "already" aspect of the kingdom, and they put much more in that category (e.g., gift of tongues, miraculous gifts of prophecy and healing) than do proponents of Subgroup A.[30]

CRITIQUE

Three observations are in order. First, the main objection to either of these variations of view # 3 is that Matthew 8:17 clearly states that Isaiah 53:4 was fulfilled during Jesus' earthly ministry when he healed people. Second, this third view is inconsistent with Matthew's method of quoting the Old Testament.

> "Matthew's method of quotation from the Old Testament Scriptures is of importance. On no less than eleven occasions (RV) he uses the phrase, 'That it might be fulfilled,' and on every occasion he draws upon the Scriptures quoted in order to relate their fulfillment *to the actual events there and then recorded*, as, e.g., the Virgin birth (1:22), the time spent in Egypt (2:15), the mourning of the women of Bethlehem (2:17) and so on. In

1985), 119–20; Douglas Moo, "Divine Healing in the Health and Wealth Gospel," *Trinity Journal*, New Series 9 (1988): 191–209.
[30] See John Wimber and Kevin Springer, *Power Evangelism* (San Francisco: Harper and Row, 1986), 2–14; idem., *Power Healing* (San Francisco: Harper, 1987), 36–37.

this passage (8:17) Matthew was not referring to our Lord's coming passion when he drew upon this quotation, but he was referring to the actual events he was then describing."[31]

Third, Isaiah 53:4 is a prophecy of Jesus Christ. This prophecy is quoted only once in the New Testament, and that is in Matthew 8:17. It is striking, in light of the use of these texts by those who argue for healing in the atonement, that the one NT text which quotes Isaiah 53:4 relates it to Jesus' earthly ministry of healing and not to his atoning work on the cross. Might one suggest that Matthew 8:17 is the Holy Spirit's inspired commentary and explanation of Isaiah 53:4?

VIEW # 4: THE SERVANT EXPERIENCED SICKNESS AND SORROW HIMSELF AND WAS ABLE TO SYMPATHIZE WITH THE SUFFERINGS OF OTHERS

Proponents of the fourth view say that Isaiah 53:4 and Matthew 8:17 both refer to actual physical illnesses and diseases and not to sins. They do not, however, use the terms "to bear" or "to carry" in a vicarious way. Rather, they are referring to the Servant's sympathetic bearing of the troubles of life. The thought is not (as in Matt. 8:17) that Jesus took away sickness and pain by healing others; rather, in becoming a man he experienced sickness and pain in his own person. "Jesus 'took our infirmities and bore our diseases' by becoming incarnate rather than by offering atonement. By coming to earth, he entered into the very conditions that we find here, including sorrow, sickness, and suffering. Experiencing sickness and sorrow himself, and sympathizing as he did...with human suffering, he was moved to alleviate the miseries of this life."[32]

---

[31] Woodford, "Divine Healing and the Atonement—a Restatement," 58. Italics added.

[32] Millard J. Erickson, *Christian Theology*, 3d ed. (Grand Rapids: Baker, 2013), 763–68 (esp. 767); also see Arno Clemens Gaebelein, *The Healing Question* (New York: "Our Hope," 1925), 74.

VIEW # 5: DURING HIS EARTHLY MINISTRY THE SERVANT HEALED SICK PEOPLE

Finally, there is the view that Isaiah 53:4 and Matthew 8:17 both refer to actual physical illnesses and diseases and not sins.[33] This is important for the present discussion because the LXX spiritualizes Isaiah to read that the Servant carried away "our sins" (τὰς ἁμαρτίας ἡμῶν). The Hebrew text, however, says that he carried away our "sicknesses" (חֳלָיֵנוּ, ḥŏlāyēnû) and "sorrows" (מַכְאֹבֵינוּ, mak'ōbênû). Matthew ignores the Septuagint and gives his own literal translation of the Hebrew. He wrote, "He himself took our debilitating illnesses [ἀσθενείας, astheneias] and carried away our diseases [νόσους, nosous]." Also of interest is Matthew's choice of verbs. Because they might indicate that Jesus became sick, Matthew replaces the Septuagint's φέρει (pherei, "carries") with ἔλαβεν (elaben, "took away") and added (ἐβάστασεν, ebastasen] "carried away"). This choice of verbs in Matthew, Gundry argues, indicates his recognition that Jesus' actions were not vicarious. Matthew recognized "that Jesus' vicarious physical suffering and death were yet to come. For now, Jesus heals with a lordly 'word.'"[34]

---

[33] Proponents of the fifth view agree with proponents of view # 4 in three important particulars. They agree that Isaiah 53:4 and Matthew 8:17 both refer to actual physical illnesses and diseases and not to sins, and they agree that the terms "to bear" and "to carry" are not used in a vicarious way. Furthermore, they agree that the "healings" described in both verses took place before the cross. The difference is that proponents of view 5 stress the Servant's removal of the sicknesses and pains of others by physically healing them during his earthly ministry. While they affirm the Servant's sympathy and empathy with men in their sorrows and griefs [Isa. 53:3], they assert that this is not the point in Isaiah 53:4 and Matthew 8:17. The point in these texts is actual healing. During his public ministry Jesus took away or removed the diseases and illnesses of people by healing them. The cross came later.

[34] Robert H. Gundry, *Matthew: A Commentary on His Handbook for a Mixed Church Under Persecution* (Grand Rapids: Eerdmans, 1994), 150.

SUMMARY

These observations lead to the question, "Was it Matthew's intention to teach that physical healing is in some way 'in the atonement'?" The following observations suggest a negative answer:[35]

(1) First, Matthew's citation of Isaiah 53:4 "is made in the context of Jesus' healing those who were *physically* sick."[36] There is no suggestion that Matthew connects Isaiah 53:4 to Christ's redemptive work.

(2) Second, the events recorded in Matthew 8 took place many months before Jesus' death to make atonement for sin. Matthew does not connect these miracles to the cross but to Jesus' messianic power to heal (cf. Mark 5:30; Acts 2:22; 10:38).[37] Whatever Matthew may have believed about other verses in Isaiah 53, it is clear that he understood verse 4 to have been fulfilled in Jesus' ministry in Galilee rather than upon the cross.[38] Petts writes, "There is certainly no hint of a *double entendre* here, and the suggestion that Matthew is not only recording and interpreting events in Galilee but also pointing us forward to the passion[39] is almost certainly a case of the wish being father to the thought."[40]

---

[35] In the following discussion the writer is following David Petts, "Healing and the Atonement" (Ph.D. thesis, University of Nottingham, 1993), 122–28.

[36] Petts, "Healing and the Atonement," 125.

[37] John Wilkinson, "Physical Healing and the Atonement," *EvQ* 63 (April, 1991): 149–67 (esp. 159). Wilkinson adds (160), "The uniform presentation of the gospels is that his healing was due to his power. This is why his healing miracles are called mighty works (*dunameis*) or simply works (*erga*). They demonstrated his power, and because this also indicated who he was, they were also called signs (*sēmeia*). Our conclusion must be that the writers of the gospels do not connect the healing activity of Jesus with the atonement accomplished by his death, but with his power which was demonstrated in his life." Alan Hugh M'Neile adds, "The passage [Isa. 53:4], *as Matthew employs it*, has no bearing on the doctrine of the Atonement" (*The Gospel According to St. Matthew* [1915; reprint ed., London: Macmillan, 1961], 108).

[38] See, for example, D. A. Carson's labored attempt to prove this very thing ("Matthew," in *The Expositor's Bible Commentary*, 9:243–45).

[39] Petts, "Healing and the Atonement," 127.

[40] Petts, "Healing and the Atonement," 127.

To sum up, the evidence given here suggests that view #5 is the correct view.

APPENDIX 3

POPULAR OBJECTIONS TO THE DOCTRINE

OF SUBSTITUTION

THE INNOCENT CANNOT SUFFER FOR THE WICKED[1]

In modern theology there are those who oppose the doctrine of substitution, and they offer a number of reasons. The first objection is that this idea of the atonement makes the innocent suffer for the wicked. Apart from the biblical question about the atonement, we may say that the innocent often suffer for the transgressions of others.[2] For example, a father babysits his little child to give his wife some time with friends. He leaves the baby alone in the house while he walks to the corner convenience store. Carelessly he has left a cigarette burning on the couch, and the couch catches fire while he is out. Soon the house is in flames, and the baby dies.

Turning to the biblical question, objectors to the doctrine of substitution argue that the idea demeans the character of God. It demeans his justice, because he punishes an innocent man (Jesus) for the guilty. It demeans his love, because he acts like a stern and vindictive being who demands death to appease his wrath. It demeans his pardoning grace, because he demands payment before he will forgive.

Proponents of the doctrine of substitution have responded in the following way: The determining factor for the evangelical Christian is the teaching of Scripture. The apostle Peter wrote, "**Christ also died for sins once for all, the just for the unjust** (δίκαιος ὑπὲρ ἀδίκων, *dikaios hyper adikōn*), **so that He might bring us to God**" (1 Pet. 3:18). The idea that the innocent one has suffered for the guilty is plainly scriptural. Christ voluntarily took the place of sinners, so his act of substitution

---

[1] Louis Berkhof, *Systematic Theology*, 4th ed. (Grand Rapids: Eerdmans, 1949), 378, 382; Charles C. Ryrie, *Basic Theology*, 2d ed. (Chicago: Moody, 1999), 330.

[2] "Where is the propriety of saying that the innocent cannot justly suffer for the guilty, when we see that they actually do thus suffer continually, and everywhere since the world began?" (Charles Hodge, *Systematic Theology* [New York: Scribner, 1872; reprint ed., Grand Rapids: Eerdmans, 1975], 2:530).

involved no injustice on God's part. Far from demeaning or derogating the justice of God, this interpretation upholds it. God's justice demanded that sin be punished. Had he forgiven man without satisfying his holy demands, he would not have been righteous (cf. Rom. 3:26). If God had acted strictly according to justice only, he would have left sinners to perish in their sins. It is incorrect to say that the love and pardoning grace of God did not flow until satisfaction for sin was rendered. In point of fact, God sent his Son in love before payment for sins was rendered.

SUBSTITUTION IN PENAL MATTERS IS ILLEGAL[3]

It is generally admitted that in the case of a pecuniary debt, payment by a substitute is permissible. For example, if a student owed $7,000 to the college and could not pay, it would be quite legal for his parent, teacher, or friend to pay the debt for him. In such a case the person paying the bill takes upon himself the debt and becomes the substitute debtor.[4]

While it may be in order for someone to pay a pecuniary debt for another, this is not the case with a penal debt. For example, if a man committed murder and was convicted, the law would not allow another to serve his life sentence or be executed in his place.[5] The reason for this is that other parties are involved, and an injustice would be done to them by such a substitution.[6] In such a crime at least five parties are involved: the murderer, the victim, the victim's family, the supreme law making authorities (the President, the Congress, etc.), and the judge.

---

[3] Hodge, *Systematic Theology*, 2:530–31; Berkhof, *Systematic Theology*, 378.

[4] John M. Armour, *Atonement and Law* (Chicago: Bible Institute Colportage Association, 1885), 116.

[5] Turretin, who taught penal substitution, explained, "*In a pecuniary debt*, the payment of the debt by the very act frees the debtor (by whomsoever the payment is made) because the person who pays is not attended to here, but only what is paid. Hence the creditor (payment being received) is not said to have treated the debtor with indulgence and to have forgiven the debt because he has received just as much as was due to him. But *in a penal debt* the case is different because the obligation regards not only things but persons (i.e., not only what is paid, but also him who pays, so that the punishment may be borne by the transgressor)." See Francis Turretin, *Institutes of Elenctic Theology* 14.10.8, trans. George Musgrave Giger, ed., James T. Dennison, Jr. (Phillipsburg, NJ: P & R Publishing, 1994), 2:419 (italics mine).

[6] Cf. the discussion in Archibald Alexander Hodge, *The Atonement* (1867; reprint ed., Grand Rapids: Eerdmans, 1953), 199–200.

But suppose we have a case in which all of these involved parties are the same person? This is exactly the case with regard to sin against God.

- God is the supreme lawmaker.
- God is the victim, i.e., he is the One who has been sinned against.
- God is, as it were, the victim's family. The triune God (Father, Son, and Holy Spirit) has been sinned against.
- God is the guilty party, i.e., the sins of mankind are laid to the charge of God the Son, who becomes the sin bearer.
- God is the judge.

Berkhof argues that those who argue that penal substitution is illegal are raising an objection against the moral law of God.[7] In point of fact, Jesus Christ did die as his people's substitute. In short, God is "the fountain of all law," and whatever he does is right (and legal)![8] A. A. Hodge adds that this doctrine "transcends all natural analogies." In the end we can no more fully understand it than we can the doctrine of the Trinity or the hypostatic union of Christ.[9]

A. A. Hodge makes a further point. The doctrine of substitution rests on the doctrine of our union with Christ.[10] The Bible teaches that Adam and Christ were representative men, that each of them was in some way united to humanity. There was a union of the entire human race in the person of Adam. In Eden he stood probation for the whole race as its natural head and covenant representative. Adam sinned, and the penalty of that sin has fallen upon all those he represented, viz., the human race as a whole (Rom. 5:12, 18). The penalty included spiritual death, physical death, a curse upon the earth, the necessity of hard labor, and pain in childbirth. Each of these penalties has fallen upon all of Adam's descendants.

There is also a union of all believers in the person of Jesus Christ, **"the last Adam"** and the **"second man"** (1 Cor. 15:45, 47). Several figures are used in Scripture to portray this union:

---

[7] Berkhof, Systematic Theology, 378.

[8] A. A. Hodge, *The Atonement*, 199.

[9] A. A. Hodge, *The Atonement*, 203.

[10] See the discussions in A. A. Hodge, *The Atonement*, 203–207; Charles Hodge, *Systematic Theology*, 2:520–21; Berkhof, *Systematic Theology*, 379.

- The foundation stone ("corner stone") and the building stones (1 Pet. 2:4-6).
- A vine and its branches (John 15:4, 5).
- A body and its parts (Rom. 12:4, 5; 1 Cor. 12:12, 27; Eph. 5:30, 32).
- A husband and his wife (Eph. 5:31, 32; Rom. 7:4; Rev. 19:7-9; 21:9).

Just as all those "in Adam" sinned representatively in their natural and covenant head, so all those "in Christ" are made righteous, i.e., justified or acquitted (Rom. 5:18-19). That union with Christ and the substitutionary atonement are linked is obvious from the following texts: **"He Himself bore our sins in His body on the cross"** (1 Pet. 2:24). He became **"sin** [i.e., sin bearer] **on our behalf"** and we have been made **"the righteousness of God in Him"** (2 Cor. 5:21). **"In Him we have redemption through His blood"** (Eph. 1:7). We have been **"baptized into His death...buried with Him...[and] we shall also be [united with Him] in the likeness of His resurrection"** (Rom. 6:3-5). God has **"raised us up with Him, and seated us with Him in the heavenly places in Christ Jesus"** (Eph. 2:6).

In summary we may say four things: First, Christ voluntarily assumed the legal responsibilities of his people. Second, his Father recognized and accepted his representative status. Third, Christ assumed a human nature in order to carry out his responsibilities as our representative and substitute. Fourth, the Father indicated his acceptance of his Son's substitutionary work by raising him from the dead (Rom. 4:25).

GOD THE FATHER IS GUILTY OF INJUSTICE IF HE PUNISHES THE SON[11]

This objection is a variation of the one we have just considered. Berkhof long ago observed, "It appears that all the objections are really variations on the same theme."[12] This view says that the Father was unjust to

---

[11] Berkhof, *Systematic Theology*, 379

[12] Berkhof, *Systematic Theology*, 379.

sacrifice his Son for the sins of mankind. Some contemporary feminist theologians have called the doctrine "cosmic child abuse."[13]

Proponents of substitution answer this objection as follows: First, believing Christians must not succumb to the attitude that is willing to make whatever havoc they please with Scripture. Scripture, not philosophy, ideology, intuition, or autonomous reason, is to have supreme authority in all questions upon which it touches. Second, it was not the Father alone but the triune God who as a whole agreed on the plan of redemption. There was a solemn agreement—some would say, a covenant—between the three persons of the Godhead (cf. John 17:3-5; Tit. 3:5-6). It is evident, in a passage like Ephesians 1, for example, that the three persons of the Trinity acted in consort for our redemption. The Father chose us in eternity past and predestined us to adoption as sons (vv. 4-5). It is through the sacrifice of the Son that we have redemption (v. 7). It is through the Holy Spirit that we are convicted of sin and sealed forever as God's people (vv. 13-14; cf. John 16:8-11).

Third, it is clear from the New Testament that the Son voluntarily undertook the work of bearing the penalty of our sin and satisfying the demands of a holy God. Fourth, the sacrificial work of Christ brought great glory to Him as our Mediator. "It meant for Him a numerous seed, loving worship, and a glorious kingdom" [Phil. 2:9-11; Heb. 2:9; Isa.

---

13 "Feminist and womanist theologians raise two general critiques: the atonement, they charge, encourages passive tolerance of abuse by glorifying suffering, and presents an image of cosmic child abuse whereby God the Father willingly sacrifices the Son" (Nancy J. Duff, "Atonement and the Christian Life: Reformed Doctrine from a Feminist Perspective," *Interpretation* 53 [Jan., 1999]: 21–33 [esp. 23]). Charles Hodge made an observation about liberal scholars of his time who reject this or that doctrine that is true today. They know what the Bible says; in fact they will often give a very competent exegesis of the biblical texts that bear on the subject. Nor are they ignorant of the history of doctrine. They will discuss with great accuracy what the Fathers, the Medieval writers, and the Reformers have said about a subject. Then something interesting happens to their discussion. Many will leave the Bible untouched and unrefuted and go on to present their contradictory theories—not on the basis of Scripture, but on the basis of their own reason and intuition. Intuitively and ideologically they are convinced that what the Bible says cannot be true. A loving God could not permit sin. A benevolent God would not allow his creatures to suffer. God could not possibly know the future free acts of men. A fair God would not deny a woman the right to abort a child or preach in a church. Certainly the Jewish writers of Scripture, who were familiar with sacrifice, could accept a notion like substitutionary atonement, but to the contemporary reader such an idea seems too violent and irrational. We must not forget what is at stake here. It is a question that is as old as the human race: "Indeed, has God said?" (*Systematic Theology*, 2:527–30).

53:10; Rev. 5:9-13; 11:15; 20:4-6].[14] Finally, all these objections act as boomerangs, for they return with vengeance on the heads of all those who...deny the necessity of an objective atonement.[15] The fact is that the Father *did send* his Son into the world, and Jesus *did die* as a sacrifice for our sins. If such a death was both unnecessary (see below) and illegal, and if the Father was unjust to sacrifice his Son, then we really do have a moral problem on our hands. The various objectors are all suggesting that the Father made his innocent Son die without cause. Such a God would be cruel indeed. The responses to these objections by evangelical theologians who embrace the authority of Scripture have been more than adequate.

SUBSTITUTIONARY ATONEMENT IS NOT TAUGHT IN THE GOSPELS

The doctrine of penal substitution was not taught by Jesus, say opponents of the doctrine; it is a novelty taught by Paul. They argue that it is what Jesus taught that counts, not what Paul taught.

In response, the following points can be made: First, this argument is an overt denial of the unity of Scripture. Contrary to the impression left by red-letter Bibles, the entire New Testament is the teaching of Christ through his Spirit.

Second, the argument is a commonplace in modern theology. Paul is regularly demeaned by exponents of various alternatives to orthodox, evangelical theology—whether they are feminists, opponents of substitution, proponents of biblical errancy, or deniers of God's sovereignty in salvation, etc. Third, it is true that substitution does not stand out as clearly in the Gospels as it does in the Epistles, but this is due to the fact "that the purpose of our Lord's personal ministry in his life and death was not so much the *full preaching* of the atonement, as the *full accomplishment* of the atonement in order [that the atonement might be preached]."[16]

Fourth, it is simply not true that the Gospels contain no mention of substitution. At the very beginning of his ministry, the Lord Jesus was

---

[14] Berkhof, *Systematic Theology*, 379.

[15] Berkhof, *Systematic Theology*, 379.

[16] Thomas J. Crawford, *The Doctrine of Holy Scripture Respecting the Atonement*, 4th ed. (Grand Rapids: Baker, 1954), 405.

pointed out as "the Lamb of God who takes away the sin of the world" (John 1:29). This title, connected as it is with the Passover (Ex. 12:1-13) and the "Suffering Servant" (Isa. 53:4-7), carries with it the connotation of substitution. Jesus himself used a related metaphor: "I am the good shepherd; the good shepherd lays down His life for (ὑπέρ, *hyper*) the sheep" (John 10:11).[17] In one of his great "I Am" statements he said, "I am the living bread that came down out of heaven; if anyone eats of this bread, he will live forever; and the bread also which I will give for (ὑπέρ, *hyper*) the life of the world is My flesh" (John 6:51). He also said, "The Son of Man did not come to be served, but to serve, and to give His life a ransom for (ἀντί, *anti*) many" (Mark 10:45; cf. Matt. 20:28). In the upper room he spoke of the greatness of his love, "Greater love has no one than this, that one lay down his life for (ὑπέρ, *hyper*) his friends" (John 15:13). At the Last Supper, anticipating his death, Jesus said of the cup, "This is My blood which is poured out for many for forgiveness of sins" (Matt. 26:28).

SUBSTITUTION IS UNNECESSARY[18]

Some opponents of the doctrine argue that substitution is unnecessary for one or more of the following reasons: (1) They deny that sin is guilt and therefore it does not call for atonement. (2) They argue that God is the universal Father of all who loves and forgives all men. (3) They assert that if mere human beings can forgive one another without demanding satisfaction, then surely God can do the same.

Defenders of the doctrine respond, "What was necessary was precisely what was done. The Son of God assumed our nature, took the place of sinners, bore the curse of the law in their stead, and therefore

---

[17] Cf. Murray J. Harris, "Prepositions and Theology in the Greek New Testament," in *NIDNTT*, 3:1171–1215. Harris demonstrates that the prepositions ἀντί [*anti*] and ὑπέρ [*hyper*] are used to indicate substitution in a number of texts (1179–80 on ἀντί, and 1196–97 on ὑπέρ). See also Murray J. Harris, *Prepositions and Theology in the Greek New Testament* (Grand Rapids: Zondervan, 2012), 52–53; on ἀντί in Mark 10:45 (= Matt. 20:28) and echoes of these texts in Isa. 52:13–53:12; 213–216; on ὑπέρ, especially in 2 Cor. 5:14 and Gal. 3:13.

[18] Hodge, *Systematic Theology*, 2:541–42; Berkhof, *Systematic Theology*, 382.

rendered it possible that God should be just and yet the justifier of the ungodly" [Rom. 3:26].[19]

Defenders of substitution make the following rejoinders: First, the Bible teaches that men are sinful, and therefore guilty (Matt. 6:12; Rom. 3:19, 23; 5:18; Eph. 2:3). Not only does the Bible assume the guilt of mankind, but the sense of guilt is universal and ineradicable. It is not irrational; it is grounded in our consciences and our natures as fallen creatures.

Second, the notion of the universal fatherhood of God and universal salvation because of his love is unbiblical. While God is a God of love (1 John 4:8), he is also a God of holiness (Lev. 11:44; Isa. 6:3; Hos. 11:9) and justice (Rom. 1:32; 2:6, 9; 6:23; 2 Thess. 1:8). Although all mankind may be called "his children" by creation (Acts 17:28), only those who have received Christ as Savior are his children by redemption (John 1:12-13).

Third, it is true that men as private individuals forgive without satisfaction, but this is not possible for a man acting in the capacity of a judge with laws to uphold. God is a father, true, but he is also a judge (Gen. 18:25; Ps. 9:8; Isa. 2:4; Acts 17:31).

---

[19] Hodge, *Systematic Theology*, 2:542. Franz Delitzsch, the noted Old Testament scholar, wrote, "If we keep in view the damnable nature of human guilt, and do not fritter away by over-subtle interpretations the three great verities in relation to God's plan of salvation testified to in Scripture,—(1) that God made Him who knew no sin to be sin for us, i.e., imputed our sin to Jesus Christ [2 Cor. 5:21]; (2) that Christ, the sinless One, taking the burden of our guilt, became a curse for us, i.e., endured the lightning of God's wrath which should have fallen upon us [Gal. 3:10, 13]; or, as the Scripture also says, that God executed the judgment upon sin in the person of His Son, who took upon Himself our flesh and blood, and offered Himself up for us as a sin-offering or atonement for our sins [Heb. 10:5-10]; (3) that, in order that we may be able to stand before God, His righteousness is by faith so imputed to us, even as He allowed our sins to be imputed to Him in order to His making atonement for them [Rom. 4:5],—it is evident, so long as these three antecedent propositions are maintained, that Christ must be allowed to have suffered and died as our representative and in our stead, in order that we might not have to suffer that to which we were liable, and that instead of our dying we should have life in the life to which He attained through His vicarious death [John 3:16; Rom. 3:24-25; Eph. 2:1-6; 1 John 4:9-10]" (*Commentary on the Epistle to the Hebrews*, trans. Thomas L. Kingsbury [Edinburgh: T. & T. Clark, 1871; reprint ed., Minneapolis: Klock and Klock, 1978], 2:441–42).

SUBSTITUTION UNDERMINES THE LAW[20]

It is also claimed by opponents of substitution that it undermines the commandments of God and offers no incentive to personal holiness. This very objection was raised by Paul's opponents in the first century. The apostle preached the free grace of God, **"Where sin increased, grace abounded all the more"** (Rom. 5:20). Paul's opponents charged that his doctrine would lead people to sin all the more. Paul denied the charge: **"What shall we say then? Are we to continue in sin so that grace may continue? May it never be! How shall we who died to sin still live in it?"** (Rom. 6:1-2). He then went on to explain to the Romans their union with Christ in his death, burial, and resurrection. As regenerate people they could no longer live the way they once lived because they were no longer the people they once were (Rom. 6:1-14). They had been acquitted of their guilt, united to Christ, born from above, indwelt by the Holy Spirit, and empowered by God to live a different kind of life (Phil. 2:12-13).

When a person comes to see himself as a sinner under the judgment of God; when he (or she) really comes to see that Jesus Christ died in his place; when the cross of Christ becomes a window to show him the wickedness and cost of sin (**"My God, My God, why have You forsaken Me?"** Matt. 27:46); when he sees that Jesus has borne the wrath of God in his place, and that he is free from the penalty of sin—he does not become lax, he becomes thankful. This doctrine produces a desire to live in accordance with God's Word.

> "Bearing shame and scoffing rude,
>   In my place condemned He stood;
> Sealed my pardon with His blood;
>   Hallelujah! What a Savior!"

---

[20] Berkhof, *Systematic Theology*, 383.

APPENDIX 4

CHRISTIAN HYMNODY AND THE DOCTRINE OF SUBSTITUTION[1]

As Charles Hodge noted, the truth of substitution is reflected in the spiritual experience of Christians. Other theories of the atonement do not conform to the doctrine held by Christians of all stripes throughout church history. The theory that the work of Christ was basically didactic, i.e., he came to be a teacher; the theory that it was to provide an example to follow; the theory that its purpose was to produce a moral influence on the minds—these and other theories fail for two reasons: First, they do not account for the intimate, personal relationship shared by Christ and the believer which is found throughout the New Testament. Second, these theories make no provision for the expiation of sin or for stilling the pain of a guilty conscience.

The true doctrine of the atonement, which centers in penal substitution, finds expression in the great hymns of every orthodox body of Christians. In recent years, Stuart Townend has written:[2]

> How deep the Father's love for us,
>   How vast beyond all measure;
> That He would give His only Son
>   To make a wretch His treasure.
> How great the pain of searing loss,
>   The Father turns His face away,
> As wounds which mar the chosen One
>   Bring many sons to glory.

[1] Charles Hodge, *Systematic Theology*, (New York: Scribner, 1872; reprint ed., Grand Rapids: Eerdmans, 1975), 2:523–27

[2] Stuart Townend, "How Deep the Father's Love for Us," copyright © 1995, Thankyou Music (PRS) (adm. worldwide at CapitolCMGPublishing.com). International Copyright Secured. All rights reserved. Used by permission.

Behold the Man upon a cross,
    My sin upon His shoulders,
Ashamed, I hear my mocking voice
    Call out among the scoffers.
It was my sin that held Him there
    Until it was accomplished;
His dying breath has brought me life,
    I know that it is finished.

I will not boast in anything,
    No gifts, no pow'rs, no wisdom,
But I will boast in Jesus Christ,
    His death and resurrection.
Why should I gain from His reward?
    I cannot give an answer,
But this I know with all my heart:
    His wounds have paid my ransom.

Another contemporary hymn expresses the doctrine of penal substitution. It is the powerful "In Christ Alone" (Stanzas 2 and 3) by Keith Getty and Stuart Townend:

In Christ alone, who took on flesh,
    Fullness of God in helpless babe!
This gift of love and righteousness,
    Scorned by the ones He came to save.
Till on that cross, as Jesus died,
    The wrath of God was satisfied;
For ev'ry sin on Him was laid—
    Here in the death of Christ I live.

There in the ground His body lay,
    Light of the world by darkness slain;
Then bursting forth in glorious day,
    Up from the grave He rose again!
And as He stands in victory,
    Sin's curse has lost its grip on me;

For I am His and He is mine—
Bought with the precious blood of Christ.[3]

The same sentiments are reflected in this meditation upon Isaiah 53 by Frank Allaben (1867–1927):[4]

Who Thy love, O God, can measure—
Love that crush'd for us its Treasure,
Him in whom was all Thy pleasure,
Christ, Thy Son of Love?

Couldst Thou bruise Him, there forsaken
On the cross His love had taken,
'Gainst Thy Son Thy sword awaken,
'Gainst Thy Son of love?

Couldst Thou crush Him, Man of Sorrow,—
Pierce His soul with wrath's fierce arrow,
Melt that heart, rend joints and marrow—
Doom Thy Son of love?

Cross that outraged Love Paternal!
Cross of agonies supernal!
Cross of grief of the Eternal!
Cross of boundless love!

The same author also wrote the following hymn, which uses the typology of the burnt offering in Leviticus 1 to describe the substitutionary death of Christ:[5]

---

[3] Keith Getty and Stuart Townend, "In Christ Alone," Copyright © 2002 Thankyou Music (PRS) (adm. worldwide at CapitolCMGPublishing.com). International Copyright Secured. All rights reserved. Used by permission. The second verse expresses the doctrine of penal substitution well. In speaking of substitution one must use three words: "substitution," "penal," and "satisfaction." Christ died in our place (as our substitute), bearing the wrath of God against sin (a penalty), and by this act God was satisfied. An intricate part of the doctrine is the work of propitiation. Propitiation speaks of the diverting of God's wrath to a substitute and thereby satisfying his righteous demands (cf. Rom. 3:23–26).

[4] F. Allaben, "Who Thy Love, O God, Can Measure?" in *Hymns of Grace and Truth*, 2d ed. (Neptune, NJ: Loizeaux, 1904), 156–57 (Hymn # 197).

I have been at the altar and witnessed the Lamb
    Burnt wholly to ashes for me;
And watched its sweet savor ascending on high,
    Accepted, O Father, by Thee.

And lo, while I gazed at the glorious sight,
    A voice from above reached mine ears:
"By this thine iniquity's taken away,
    And no trace of it on thee appears.

An end of thy sin has been made for thee here
    By Him who its penalty bore;
With blood it is blotted eternally out,
    And I will not remember it more."

O Lord, I believe it with wonder and joy;
    Confirm, Thou, this precious belief;
While daily I learn that I am, in myself,
    Of sinners the vilest and chief.

Hodge himself reflected upon two hymns, one by an Arminian (Charles Wesley) and the other by a Calvinist (Augustus M. Toplady). He cites a number of lines from each and asserts that it is impossible to interpret them in any other way than as hymns about substitution. Wesley wrote, "Jesus, Lover of My Soul,"[6] in which we find the following expressions:

"Jesus, lover of my soul,
    Let me to Thy bosom fly."

Why, asks Hodge, should sinners fly to him if he is only a teacher or moral reformer?

"Hide me, O my Savior hide."

[5] F. Allaben, "I Have Been at the Altar," *The Believers Hymn Book* (London: Pickering & Inglis, n.d.), Hymn # 88.

[6] Charles Wesley, "Jesus, Lover of My Soul," in *The Hymnal for Worship and Celebration*, ed. Tom Fettke (Waco: Word, 1986), Hymn # 466.

"Hide from what?" asks Hodge. It can only be from the retributive justice of God, an attribute of God which modern writers tend to deny.

Toplady wrote, "Rock of Ages,"[7] in which are the following lines:

"Let the water and the blood,
     From Thy wounded side that flowed;
Be of sin the double cure;
     Cleanse me from its guilt and power."

Hodge asks, "How can such language be used by those who deny the necessity of expiation; who hold that guilt need not be washed away, that all that is necessary is that we should be made morally good? No one can say,—

'Nothing in my hand I bring,
Simply to Thy cross I cling,'

who does not believe that Christ 'bore our sins in His own body on the tree' (1 Pet. 2:24)."[8]

Toplady also wrote these lines,

From whence this fear and unbelief,
If God, my Father put to grief
     His spotless Son for me?
Can He, the righteous Judge of men,
Condemn me for that debt of sin
     Which, Lord, was charged to Thee?

Complete atonement Thou hast made,
And to the utmost farthing paid
     What e'er Thy people owed;

---

[7] Augustus M. Toplady, "Rock of Ages," in *The Hymnal for Worship and Celebration*, Hymn # 204.

[8] Hodge, *Systematic Theology*, 2:527.

How, then, can wrath on me take place,
If sheltered in God's righteousness,
   And sprinkled by Thy blood?

If Thou hast my discharge procured,
And freely in my place endured
   The whole of wrath divine;
Payment God will not twice demand,
First at my bleeding surety's hand
   And then again at mine.

Turn, then, my soul, unto thy rest;
The merits of thy great High Priest
   Have bought thy liberty;
Trust in His efficacious blood,
Nor fear thy banishment from God,
   Since Jesus died for thee.[9]

Other hymns, reflecting the doctrine of penal substitution contain these memorable verses:

Horatius Bonar, "I Lay My Sins on Jesus" (Stanza 1)

I lay my sins on Jesus,
   The spotless Lamb of God;
He bears them all, and frees us
   From the accursed load.
I bring my guilt to Jesus,
   To wash my crimson stains
White in His blood most precious,
   Till not a spot remains.[10]

---

[9] Augustus M. Toplady, "From Whence This Fear and Unbelief?" in *The Believer's Hymn Book,* Hymn # 51. In the fourth stanza I have included the line, "have bought thy liberty," which I have seen in other editions of the hymn. *The Believer' Hymn Book* has, "speak peace and liberty."

[10] Horatius Bonar, "I Lay My Sins on Jesus," in *The Hymnal for Worship and Celebration,* ed. Tom Fettke (Waco, TX: Word, 1986), Hymn # 340.

American Folk Hymn, "What Wondrous Love Is This" (Stanza 1)

> What wondrous love is this,
>   O my soul, O my soul!
> What wondrous love is this,
>   O my soul!
> What wondrous love is this
>   That caused the Lord of bliss
> To bear the dreadful curse
>   For my soul, for my soul
> To bear the dreadful curse
>   for my soul.[11]

Horatio Spafford, "It Is Well with My Soul" (Stanza 3)

> My sin—O the bliss of this glorious thought
>   My sin—not in part, but the whole—
> Is nailed to the cross and I bear it no more,
>   Praise the Lord, praise the Lord, O my soul![12]

Paul Gerhardt, "O Sacred Head, Now Wounded" (Stanzas 1 and 2)

> O sacred Head, now wounded
>   With grief and shame weighed down;
> Now scornfully surrounded
>   With thorns, Thine only crown:
> How pale Thou art with anguish,
>   With sore abuse and scorn,
> How does that visage languish,
>   Which once was bright as morn!
>
> What Thou, my Lord, hast suffered
>   Was all for sinners' gain;

---

[11] "What Wondrous Love is This," in *The Hymnal for Worship and Celebration*, Hymn # 177.

[12] Horatio G. Spafford, "It Is Well with My Soul," in *The Hymnal for Worship and Celebration*, Hymn # 493.

Mine, mine was the transgressions,
    But Thine the deadly pain.
Lo, here I fall, my Savior;
    'Tis I deserve Thy place;
Look on me with Thy favor,
    Assist me with Thy grace.[13]

Elizabeth Clephane, "Beneath the Cross of Jesus" (Stanza 2)

Upon that cross of Jesus
    Mine eye at times can see
The very dying form of One
    Who suffered there for me;
And from my smitten heart with tears
    Two wonders I confess—
The wonder of redeeming love
    And my unworthiness.[14]

Isaac Watts, "At the Cross" (Stanzas 1–2)

Alas! And did my Savior bleed?
    And did my Sovereign die?
Would He devote that sacred head
    For sinners such as I?

Was it for crimes that I have done
    He groaned upon the tree?
Amazing pity! Grace unknown!
    And love beyond degree!

Well might the sun in darkness hide
    And shut His glories in,

---

[13] Paul Gerhardt, "O Sacred Head, Now Wounded" (based on a Medieval Latin poem ascribed to Bernard of Clairvaux, trans. James W Alexander), in *The Hymnal for Worship and Celebration*, Hymn 178.

[14] Elizabeth C. Clephane, "Beneath the Cross of Jesus," in in *The Hymnal for Worship and Celebration*, Hymn # 183.

When Christ, the mighty Maker died
For man the creature's sin.[15]

Charles Wesley, "Arise, My Soul, Arise" (Stanzas 1–3)

Arise, my soul arise,
    Shake off thy guilty fears,
The bleeding Sacrifice
    In my behalf appears.
Before the throne my Surety stands,
    My name is written on His hands.

He ever lives above
    For me to intercede,
His all-redeeming love,
    His precious blood to plead.
His blood atoned for all our race,
    And sprinkles now the throne of grace.

Five bleeding wounds He bears,
    Received on Calvary,
They pour effectual prayers;
    They strongly plead for me.
"Forgive him, O forgive," they cry,
    "Nor let that ransomed sinner die."[16]

Charles Wesley, "And Can It Be?" (stanza 1)

And can it be that I should gain
    An int'rest in the Savior's blood?
Died He for me, who caused His pain?
    For me, who Him to death pursued?
Amazing love! How can it be
    That Thou, my God shouldst die for me?[17]

---

[15] Isaac Watts, "At the Cross," in in *The Hymnal for Worship and Celebration*, Hymn # 188.

[16] Charles Wesley, "Arise, My Soul, Arise," in *The Hymnal for Worship and Celebration*, Hymn # 199.

William Cowper, "There is a Fountain" (stanzas 1–4)

There is a fountain filled with blood
    Drawn from Immanuel's veins,
And sinners plunged beneath that flood
    Lose all their guilty stains.

The dying thief rejoiced to see
    That fountain in his day,
And there may I, though vile as he,
    Wash all my sins away.

Dear dying Lamb, Thy precious blood
    Shall never lose its power,
Till all the ransomed Church of God
    Be saved, to sin no more.

E'er since by faith I saw the stream
    Thy flowing wounds supply,
Redeeming love has been my theme
    And shall be till I die.[18]

In the old Inter-Varsity hymnbook, entitled simply *Hymns*, there are three hymns which beautifully express the doctrine of penal substitution. The allusions to Isaiah 53 are clear.

Annie Cousin, "O Christ, What Burdens Bowed Thy head!"

O Christ, what burdens bow'd Thy head:
    Our load was laid on Thee;
Thou stoodest in the sinners' stead,
    Did'st bear all ill for me.
A victim led, Thy blood was shed!
    Now there's no load for me.

[17] Charles Wesley, "And Can It Be?" in *The Hymnal for Worship and Celebration*, Hymn # 203.

[18] William Cowper, "There is a Fountain," in *The Hymnal for Worship and Celebration*, Hymn # 196.

Death and the curse were in our cup:
    O Christ 'twas full for Thee!
But Thou hast drain'd the last dark drop,
    'Tis empty now for me.
That bitter cup, love drank it up,
    Now blessing's draught for me.

Jehovah lifted up His rod:
    O Christ it fell on Thee!
Thou wast sore stricken of Thy God;
    There's not one stroke for me.
Thy tears, Thy blood, beneath it flowed;
    Thy bruising healeth me.

The tempest's awful voice was heard;
    O Christ it broke on Thee!
Thy open bosom was my ward,
    It braved the storm for me.
Thy form was scarred, Thy visage marr'd,
    Now cloudless peace for me.

Jehovah bade His sword awake:
    O Christ, it woke 'gainst Thee:
Thy blood the flaming blade must slake,
    Thy heart its sheath must be.
All for my sake, my peace to make:
    Now sleeps that sword for me.

For me, Lord Jesus, Thou hast died,
    And I have died in Thee:
Thou'rt risen—my bands are all untied;
    And now Thou liv'st in me;
When purified, made white, and tried,
    Thy glory then for me.[19]

---

[19] Annie R. Cousin, "O Christ, what burdens bowed Thy head!" *Hymns: The Hymnal of Inter-Varsity Christian Fellowship*, rev. ed., ed. Paul Beckwith (Chicago: Inter-Varsity Press, 1950), Hymn # 126.

Philip B. Bliss, "Man of Sorrows"

"Man of Sorrows," what a name
        For the Son of God who came
Ruined sinners to reclaim!
        Hallelujah! what a Savior!

Bearing shame and scoffing rude,
        In my place condemned He stood;
Sealed my pardon with His blood:
        Hallelujah! what a Savior!

Guilty, vile and helpless we;
        Spotless Lamb of God was He:
"Full atonement!" can it be?
        Hallelujah! what a Savior!

Lifted up was He to die,
        "It is finished," was His cry;
Now in heav'n exalted high:
        Hallelujah! what a Savior!

When He comes, our glorious King,
        All His ransomed home to bring,
Then anew this song we'll sing:
        Hallelujah! what a Savior![20]

Cecil F. Alexander, "There is a Green Hill Far Away" (stanzas 1 and 2)

There is a green hill far away,
        Outside a city wall,
Where the dear Lord was crucified
        Who died to save us all.

---

[20] Philip B. Bliss, "'Man of Sorrows' What a Name," *Hymns: The Hymnal of Inter-Varsity Christian Fellowship*, Hymn # 61.

We may not know, we cannot tell
    What pains He had to bear;
But we believe it was for us
    He hung and suffered there.[21]

Finally, here is another of Frank Allaben's hymns, one that speaks of the holiness of Christ's life, the sufferings of the cross, and the worshipful response of his people:

Life, life, of love pour'd out
    Fragrant and holy
Life, 'mid rude thorns of earth,
    Stainless and sweet!
Life, whence God's face of love
    Glorious but lowly,
Shines forth to bow us,
    Lord, low at Thy feet!

Grief, grief of love that drew
    hate's ev'ry arrow!
Grief that Thy suff'ring heart
    only could meet!
Grief, whence Thy face of love,
    Shining in sorrow,
Draws us, adoring,
    Lord, low at Thy feet!

Death, death of stricken love,
    Wrath's sea exploring!
Death, Life's mysterious death—
    Deep meeting deep!

---

21 Cecil F. Alexander, "There is a Green Hill Far Away," in *Hymns: The Hymnal of Inter-Varsity Christian Fellowship*, Hymn # 157.

Death, whence Thy bursting heart
    Fills ours—outpouring
All, all in worship,
    Lord, low at Thy feet![22]

---

[22] F. Allaben, "Life, Life of Love Poured Out," *Hymns of Worship and Remembrance*, (Dubuque, IA: Emmaus International, 1960), Hymn # 159.

APPENDIX 5

A COMPOSER, A DISGRACED ACTRESS, A DEBTOR'S PRISON, AND ISAIAH 53[1]

THE COMPOSER

Divine providence was surely at work in the life of George Frideric Handel (1685–1759) in the summer of 1741. For several years he had had a number of failures in opera and oratorio, and fashionable London had tired of his music.[2] In June or early July, his friend Charles Jennens, the well-educated owner of a large estate in Leicestershire and a subscriber to all of Handel's works, gave the composer the libretto (word-book) of a new work, *Messiah*. It consisted of carefully selected texts from the Psalms, Prophets, and Gospels (the King James Version, with very slight editorial modifications) that tell the story of Christ. However, the libretto was not a dramatic play or opera with narrative and explanatory dialogue. Jennens believed that the Old Testament, as well as the New Testament, spoke of Jesus Christ, and he assumed his hearers would supply the context (in the life of Christ) to the lyrics. The work fell into three parts: the prophecy of salvation, the redemptive

---

[1] These reflections were prompted by an invitation from my friend and colleague, David Glock, to come to his home for dessert and the screening of a new docudrama which explored the backstory of George Frideric Handel's renowned choral work, *Messiah*. Written by Mitch Davis and broadcast on BYUtv, it was a superb production. My mind was filled with Isaiah 53 at the time, and two events dramatized by Davis illustrated for me aspects of Isaiah's message.

[2] The story of Handel and his *Messiah* has been told by many authors. In addition to Mitch Davis's production of "Handel's *Messiah*," I have consulted Julian Herbage, *Messiah* (New York: Chanticleer Press, 1948), 9–22; Robert Manson Myers, *Handel's Messiah: A Touchstone of Taste* (New York: Macmillan, 1948), 88–103; Newman Flower, *George Frideric Handel: His Personality and His Times* (New York: Scribner's, 1948), 286–95; Paul Henry Lang, *George Frideric Handel* (New York: Norton, 1966), 332–56; Christopher Hogwood, *Handel* (New York: Thames and Hudson, 1984), 167–77; Jens Peter Larsen, *Handel's Messiah*, rev. ed. (New York: Norton, 1989), 96–185; Richard Luckett, *Handel's Messiah: A Celebration* (New York: Harcourt Brace & Co., 1992), 69–137.

sacrifice (including Christ's resurrection and ascension), and the promise of bodily resurrection and redemption from Adam's fall (including the victory over death and sin and the glorification of Messiah).[3]

About six weeks after receiving Jennens' work, Handel set to work composing the musical score (Aug. 22, 1741). Many legends (Handel was in a trance; he was unconscious of the world around him; he left his meals untouched; he had a vision of heaven, etc.) surround his work. Perhaps the most often repeated, and the most probable, is the report of his servant that when Handel completed Part II with the "Hallelujah Chorus," he found the composer at the table with tears streaming down his face. Legend has Handel exclaiming, "I did think I did see all heaven before me, and the great God Himself." One thing is certain: he composed the entire work in twenty-four days. Quite apart from the legends, this was an incredible feat of musical composition.[4]

Late in the summer, Handel received an invitation from William Cavendish, Lord Lieutenant of Ireland, to visit Dublin and perform some of his oratorios for the pleasure of that nation. In light of the situation in London, this was a welcome invitation. In September and October he exchanged letters with three charitable institutions in Ireland (Mercer's Hospital, the Charitable Infirmary, and the Charitable Musical Society for the Relief of Imprisoned Debtors). Handel agreed to contribute a portion of his profits to Dublin charities and to perform a special oratorio solely "for the benefit and enlargement of poor and distressed prisoners for debt in the several [jails] in the city of Dublin."[5]

Between December 23, 1741 and April 3, 1742, Handel presented two series of concerts, each consisting of six performances. To his delight, Dublin received his works with much acclaim. On March 27, 1742 it was announced that Handel would present his new "Grand Oratorio, called *Messiah*" at the "New Musick Hall in Fishamble Street." Advertisements requested that ladies come without hoops in their skirts and gentlemen come without their swords in order to accommodate as large an audience as possible. The first performance took place at noon

---

[3] Luckett, *Handel's Messiah*, 69–75; Lang, *George Frideric Handel*, 342; Hogwood, *Handel*, 168.

[4] For a defense of the legends, see Flower, *George Frideric Handel*, 289; for a more skeptical view, see Lang, *George Frideric Handel*, 336–37.

[5] Myers, *Handel's Messiah*, 88–89.

on Tuesday, April 13, 1742. The music hall was packed with seven hundred in attendance.

THE ACTRESS

Handel had a small but "very respectable orchestra" to work with. The male chorus was made up of fourteen men and six boys from the choirs of Dublin's two cathedrals. Of the soloists the principal performers were the Italian soprano, Signora Christina Maria Avolio, and the London actress, Mrs. Susannah Cibber. The Dublin press agreed that the Italian soprano was "an excellent singer," but "it was Mrs. Cibber who won the tears of the audience."[6] Her mezzo-soprano voice had a very limited range, but she brought to the concert the skills of an accomplished tragic actress. *Messiah* (part II) contains a number of lines from Isaiah 53 (vv. 3, 4-6, 8),[7] and Handel composed the "He was despised" aria expressly to suit the range and pathos of her voice.

Susannah Cibber was in Dublin at this time to escape London.[8] Her husband, Theophilus Cibber, was a theater manager and actor who showed little ability in both spheres. Personally, he was careless with money, he drank to excess, and he frequented prostitutes. He married Susannah because of her box office potential, but was not successful in finding her suitable roles. One of his creditors was a young country gentleman named William Sloper. To alleviate his debt to Sloper, Cibber arranged for his wife to spend time socially with him. A love affair began, and Cibber was complaisant until his wife eloped with her lover. Cibber tried unsuccessfully to kidnap his wife, pursued her with a lawsuit, and then sued Sloper for "assaulting, ravishing, and carnally knowing" his wife. The trial, with lurid details supplied by a spy, delighted the London press and its readers.[9] Mrs. Cibber and Sloper retreated to the country for three years until she came out of hiding in 1741 to act in a play in Dublin.[10]

---

[6] Myers, *Handel's Messiah*, 99.

[7] George Frideric Handel, *Messiah*, An Oratorio, ed. Friedrich Chrysander, Kalmus Classic Edition (Berlin, 1902; reprint ed., Miami, FL: Belwin, n.d.), xv–xvi, 122–151.

[8] See Luckett, *Handel's Messiah*, 110–11, 128–30; Lang, *George Frideric Handel*, 335–36.

[9] Luckett, *Handel's Messiah*, 111; cf. Lang, *George Frideric Handel*, 336.

[10] "Mrs. Cibber…was in Dublin at the time, living down the scandal of the lawsuits brought against her by her profligate husband" (Herbage, *Messiah*, 18).

At this point, Handel renewed his acquaintance with the charming actress and invited her to take part in his oratorio. Her performance was well received. Her singing of the "He was despised" aria has become the stuff of legend. "From the depths of her tragic (and notorious) life she sang this famous aria with such tender grief" that the audience was spellbound. Sitting in one of the box seats was Patrick Delany, Chancellor of St. Patrick's Cathedral. He was so enthralled by the beauty of her voice, her emotional intensity, and, perhaps, the implications of the lyrics for a woman living in shame and disgrace, that he rose to his feet and exclaimed, "Woman, for this be all thy sins forgiven thee." Delany certainly overstepped his bounds by making such a pronouncement,[11] but he did understand the implications of Isaiah's prophecy for Susannah Cibber—and for that matter, all sinners.

THE DEBTORS

The proceeds from ticket sales amounted to about £400. The money was divided equally among the three charities, each receiving £127.[12] Especially noteworthy is the outcome at the debtors' prisons. One hundred and forty-two people were released as a result of the funds raised.[13] Myers wrote, "By an appropriate coincidence Handel's supreme tribute to Him who came to break the bonds and set the prisoners free

---

[11] Hogwood (*Handel*, 176) wrote that Delany spoke "somewhat presumptuously for a divine." Myers (*Handel's Messiah*, 100) said that Delany "forgot himself (and his Bible)." Herbage remarked that Delany's pronouncement was "an involuntary compliment to her artistry, though an unfortunate reference to her private life" (*Messiah*, 21). Luckett wrote that Delany's exclamation "fits all we know of this impulsive and generous man" (*Handel's Messiah*, 130).

[12] The announcement in the *Dublin Journal* (March 27, 1742) read, "For Relief of the Prisoners in the several Gaols, and for the Support of Mercer's Hospital in Stephen's Street, and of the Charitable Infirmary on the Inns Quay" (Hogwood, *Handel*, 175).

[13] "George Frideric Handel," *Christian History.net* (Aug. 8, 2008). Accessed Feb. 3, 2015. These amounts do not seem large by today's standards. However, the "purchasing power calculator" on «MeasuringWorth.com» provided these interesting amounts (accessed Aug. 12, 2015). The purchasing power of £400 (1742) would be worth £50,790.00 [$79,232.40] today [actually 2014, the latest calculations available]. The same site suggests that the economic power could be as high as £6,786,000.00 [$10,586,160.00]. Today [2014] the purchasing power of £127 (1742) would be £17,710.00 [$27,627.60], and the economic power would be £2,155,000.00 [$3,361,800.00]. The "purchasing power" figures alone indicate that the first performance of Handel's *Messiah* raised a significant amount of money.

literally proclaimed deliverance to the [captives] at its first performance. 'There was,' wrote the Reverend John Mainwaring, 'a peculiar propriety in this design from the subject of the Oratorio itself.'"[14]

As noted above in our discussion of the restitution offering (Isa. 53:10; see chapter 5), Jesus covered the guilt of his people, guilt in the sense of a debt owed to God. He satisfied the demands of the justice of God. In fact, he paid a penalty plus 20 percent, i.e., his sacrifice outweighed the guilt of sinners. **"Where sin increased, grace abounded all the more"** (Rom. 5:20). In a passive sense he met the demands of justice against the sinner as a rebel under the sentence of death. In an active sense his death was the supreme act of obedience to the will of God whereby he discharged to the uttermost penny the debt we owed. In the words of Ellis J. Crum's hymn,

> He paid a debt He did not owe;
> I owed a debt I could not pay;
> I needed someone to wash my sins away.
> And now, I sing a brand new song, "Amazing Grace."
> Christ Jesus paid a debt that I could never pay.

> O such great pain my Lord endured
> When He my sinful soul secured
> I should have died there but Jesus took my place
> So now I sing a brand new song
> "Amazing Grace"
> Christ Jesus paid a debt that I could never pay.[15]

---

[14] Myers, *Handel's Messiah*, 102.

[15] Ellis J. Crum, "He paid a Debt He Did Not Owe," © 1977 Ellis J. Crum, Publisher (Admin. By Sacred Selections R. E. Winsett LLC). All rights reserved. Used by permission.

Subject Index

AUTHOR INDEX

SCRIPTURE INDEX

Genesis

2:7	122n30
4:13	81
5:24	100n37
15:2	125
18:25	202
22	118
22:8	97n30
22:65	118
24:14	12n51
26:24	12n51
30:1	125
31:36	71
38:9	122n29
39:6	48
49:10	167
49n24	40n21
50:7	152n172
50:17	152n172

Exodus

1:9	136n93
2:13	105n64
4:10	12n51
7:1	136n93
11:1	104
12:1-13	201
12:46	110
14:3	12n51
20:2-3	11n51, 79
20:5	12n51
21:1-2	91
21:5-6	91
22:9	71
23:1	105n64
30:10	152n172
32:32	152n172
34:9	152n172
35:1–38:20	179n91

Leviticus

1	207
1:4	89
1:11	207
4:3	123
4:4	89
4:6	27
4:13	123
4:22	123
4:27	123
5:1	142
5:17	142
5:14–19	123
5:14	124
5:15	124n38
6:1–7	123
6:2-4	124n39
6:4	124n39
6:5-7	124n39
7:7	152n172
7:16-18	172
10:17	142, 143
11:44	202
12:9–10, 13–14	67n33, 67n33,
104	
16:7	73n62
16:14, 19	27
16:21	89
16:30	152n172
17:11	122n30
17:14	122n30
17:16	142
19:4	80
19:31	80
20:6	80
20:18–19	140n114
20:19-20	142
24:15	142
26:32	24

	136n93
52:14	**21–25,**
	48n50,
	136n93,
	150
52:15	13–14n56,
	26–32
	43n27,
	112n82,
	126, 133,
	136n93,
	150, 151,
	152, 161,
	178
53	14n56,
	16, 17,
	35–153
	112n82,
	150, 151,
	160
53:1-3	**35–57**
53:1	13n56,
	38–44,
	112n82,
	161,
	163n28
53:1-2	160
53:1–6	22
53:1-9	11, 98,
	151
53:2	**44–51,**
	105n63,
	112n82
53:2-3	161
53:2–9	9n45
53:3	8n40,
	43n27,
	51–56,
	112n82,
	132n80,
	171n64,
	178, 221
53:3–6	175

53:4–5	112n82
53:4-6	6, **59–90**
	143, 221
53:4-7	201
53:4-9	150
53:4	13n56, 24,
	54, **61–67,**
	112n82,
	135n89,
	142n130,
	167n53,
	168, 183,
	185, 187,
	188, 190,
	191, 192
	193
53:5	8n40,
	68–77,
	112n82,
	134, 160,
	162,
	164n33,
	165, 171,
	173, 175,
	176, 179,
	180, 181
53:5-6	112n82,
	176
53:6–7	112n82
53:6	**77–87,**
	87n117,
	142n130,
	148, 172,
	176
53:7-9	**91–114**
53:7–8	13n56,
	112n82
53:7	**93–98,**
	111, 112,
	160–161,
	163n28,
	164
53:8–9	112n82
53:8	6, 8n40,

23:9	95
23:33	14n56, 112n82
23:34	112n82, 144n144, 145n144
23:41	111
23:46	69
24:17-21	64
24:26	33
24:27	xi, 112n82
24:27, 46	14n56, 112n82

John

1:7	153
1:12	153
1:12-13	202
1:29	14n56, 97, 112n82, 201
3:16	87, 153, 202n19
5:18	65
6:51	201
7:45	95
7:48–49	53
8:46	113
10:11	201
10:18	140
11:38-44	41
11:45–53	99n36
11:48	145n144
12:7	145n144
12:37-38	41–42
12:38	13n56, 112n82
13:8	28
15:4, 5	198
15:13	201
16:7-11	119
16:8-11	199
17:3-5	199

17:4-5	119
17:20	145n144
18:20-21	99
18:33-38	94
18:38	100
19:1	94, 114
19:1-3	94
19:5	18
19:6	111
19:9	95
19:11	95
19:18	114
19:31	110n77
19:32–34	110
19:36–37	110
19:38	107, 110

Acts

2:22	192
2:23	65, 110, 118n8, 119, 148
2:27	113
2:33	28
2:38	153
2:44	153
3:13	14n56, 112n82
3:14	113
4:30	113
7:52	113
8:26-39	14
8:32-33	13n56, 112n82
10:36	75n71
10:38	192
10:43	14n56, 112n82
16:31	153
17:28	202
17:31	202
20:21	153
23:3	95

26:23	162	9:1-5	39
		10:16	13n56, 39, 112n82
Romans		11:5	44
1:28–32	60	11:26	61
1:32	202	12:4, 5	198
2:6	202	15:21	13n56, 112n82
2:9	202	53:4	187
2:9-19	143		
3:10–18	80	**1 Corinthians**	
3:19	87, 202	2:2	116
3:23	60, 80, 143, 202	2:8	91
3:23-26	187, 207n3	2:8-9	116
3:24-25	202n19	2:9	14n56, 112n82
3:25	187	5:7	14n56, 97n30, 110n78, 112n82
3:26	135, 153, 196, 202	12:12	198
4:5	153, 202n19	12:27	198
4:25	14n56, 112n82, 198	15:3	14n56, 112n82, 187
5:1	75n71, 153	15:45	197
5:8–9	75n71	15:47	197
5:12	78n82, 197	15:52–54	190
5:18	197, 202	**2 Corinthians**	
5:18-19	198	5:18-21	187
5:19	14n56, 112n82, 134n83	5:21	60, 82, 85, 112, 187, 198, 202n19
5:20	125, 203, 223	12:7-10	187
6:1-2	203		
6:1-14	203	**Galatians**	
6:3-5	198	2:20	187
6:23	60, 202	3:10	85, 202n19
7:4	198	3:10-13	60
8:3	187	3:13	83, 187, 202n19
8:34	145n144, 187		

1:19	112
2:4-6	198
2:21-23	113
2:22	13n56, 111, 112n82, 113
2:23	14n56, 112n82
2:24	14n56, 63n19, 112n82, 198, 209
2:25	14n56, 112n82
3:18	113, 195

1 John

2:1	145n144
2:1-2	113
3:2	190
3:3	113
3:5	14n56, 112n82, 113
4:8	202
4:9-10	202n19

Revelation

1:18	126
5:5-6	137n96
5:6	14n56, 112n82
5:9	28
5:9-13	200
5:12	112n82
11:15	200
12	14n56, 112n82
13:8	14n56, 112n82
14:5	14n56, 112n82
19:7-9	198
19:14	137n100, 139
19:16	138
20:4-6	200
21:9	198

INDEX OF OTHER ANCIENT TEXTS

THE AUTHOR

David MacLeod was born in Nova Scotia, Canada, and raised in Massachusetts. He is a graduate of Worcester State University (B.S.Ed) and Dallas Theological Seminary (Th.M., Ph.D.). In the past he taught at Western Bible College (now Colorado Christian University) and Dallas Seminary. Since 1983 he has taught at Emmaus Bible College in Dubuque, Iowa, where for several years he served as Dean for Biblical Studies. He is presently Professor Emeritus of Bible and Theology.